GERMANY: BEYOND THE STABLE STATE

BOOKS OF RELATED INTEREST

Church and State in Contemporary Europe: The Chimera of Neutrality
edited by John T.S. Madeley and Zsolt Enyedi

The Enlarged European Union: Diversity and Adaptation
edited by Peter Mair and Jan Zielonka

The Swiss Labyrinth: Institutions, Outcomes and Redesign
edited by Jan-Erik Lane

Europeanised Politics? European Integration and National Political Systems
edited by Klaus H. Goetz and Simon Hix

Recasting European Welfare States
edited by Maurizio Ferrera and Martin Rhodes

The Changing French Political System
edited by Robert Elgie

Compounded Representation in West European Federations
edited by Joanne B. Brzinski, Thomas D. Lancaster and Christian Tuschhoff

Politics and Policy in Democratic Spain: No Longer Different?
edited by Paul Heywood

Britain in the Nineties: The Politics of Paradox
edited by Hugh Berrington

Crisis and Transition in Italian Politics
edited by Martin Bull and Martin Rhodes

Southern European Welfare States: Between Crisis and Reform
edited by Martin Rhodes

The Euro-Mediterranean Partnership: Political and Economic Perspectives
edited by Richard Gillespie

The State in Western Europe: Retreat or Redefinition?
edited by Wolfgang C. Müller and Vincent Wright

The Regions and the European Community
edited by Robert Leonardi

The Regional Dimension of the European Union
edited by Charlie Jeffery

National Parliaments and the European Union
edited by Philip Norton (new in paperback)

GERMANY
Beyond the Stable State

Editors

HERBERT KITSCHELT
WOLFGANG STREECK

FRANK CASS
LONDON • PORTLAND, OR

First published in 2004 in Great Britain by
FRANK CASS AND COMPANY LIMITED
Crown House, 47 Chase Side, Southgate,
London N14 BP, England

and in the United States of America by
FRANK CASS
c/o ISBS, 920 NE 58th Avenue, Suite 300,
Portland, OR 97213 3786, USA

Website: www.frankcass.com

British Library Cataloguing in Publication Data

Germany : beyond the stable state
1. Capitalism – Germany 2. Industrial relations – Germany
3. Germany – Economic conditions – 1990– 4. Germany – Social
conditions – 1990– 5. Germany – Politics and government –
1990–
I. Kitschelt, Herbert II. Streeck, Wolfgang
330.9'43

ISBN 0 7146 5588 0 (hb)   *22.596372*
ISBN 0 7146 8473 2 (pb)

Library of Congress Cataloging-in-Publication Data

Germany: beyond the stable state / editors Herbert Kitschelt,
Wolfgang Streeck.
    p. cm.
Includes bibliographical references and index.
    ISBN 0-7146-5588-0 (hb) – ISBN 0-7146-8473-2 (pb)
    1. Germany–Politics and governments–1990–. 2. Germany
–Economic conditions–1990–. 3. European Union–Germany
I. Kitschelt, Herbert.
II. Streeck, Wolfgang, 1946– III. Title.
    JN3971.A91G4635 2003
    320.943–dc22   2003015389

This group of studies first appeared in a Special Issue of
West European Politics (ISSN 0140-2382), Vol.26, No.4 (October 2003),
[Germany: Beyond the Stable State].

Printed in Great Britain by MPG Books Ltd., Bodmin, Cornwall

Contents

From Stability to Stagnation: Germany at the Beginning of the Twenty-First Century

HERBERT KITSCHELT and
WOLFGANG STREECK

Among political and economic elites as well as in public opinion a sense of malaise has spread across Germany since the mid-1990s, after the initial enthusiasm about German unification, the end of the Cold War and the acceleration of European integration. In the early 1980s West Germany was widely celebrated, and indeed celebrated itself, as an island of economic prosperity, social peace and political stability in an increasingly turbulent world. Reflecting the opinion of the time, *West European Politics* published a Special Issue in 1981 under the title of *Germany: Perspectives on a Stable State*. During the 1970s and early 1980s, when the United States was in a deep crisis of economic performance and public confidence, the German industrial strategy of 'diversified quality production' became an admired model world-wide, echoing Helmut Schmidt's proclamation of *Modell Deutschland* in his first election campaign of 1976 when he prided himself on his government's achievement of apparently unshakeable tripartite consensus with business and labour.

Two decades later, German political and social institutions and the policies they support still look very much like the 1980s. But now suspicions are rampant, inside Germany as much as outside, that political and institutional stability may no longer be an asset. Dramatically declining economic performance has raised the question whether Germany can cope with the economic, demographic and cultural challenges of a new century. Indeed as the contributions to this volume show, a case can be made that the same institutions that once provided for economic prosperity and social cohesion today impede adjustment and stand in the way of a sustainable response to new problems. Germany (and this in fact is the argument we will develop in this introduction) appears to be stuck in a 'high equilibrium trap' – a situation in which the institutional and cultural legacies of a successful past shape the actors' interpretations of self-interest and of feasible strategies, as well as the choices available to them, in such a way as to prevent them from doing what they would otherwise have to do in order to improve economic outcomes.

Until the September 2002 federal election, German political elites and mass publics had not yet reached the point where the symptoms of the crisis had become sufficiently painful to make the cost of profound change appear lower than the losses incurred by continued muddling through. Just as in Japan, citizens have been losing confidence in the political elites, but they do not see better alternatives. In both countries, the odd spectacle unfolds of governing parties becoming unpopular without a viable opposition emerging (Japan) or an existing opposition being able to benefit (Germany).[1] Given Germany's painfully slow, incremental process of political and economic change, for some time there is likely to be a growing gap between rapid problem accumulation and slow problem-solving in existing political and economic institutions.

The task of this volume is not to speculate about the duration of the crisis, let alone the nature of its outcomes, but to contribute to the analysis of its origins and current dynamics. This introduction sets out the theme by briefly going over the nature and origins of the 'German system'. We then provide some empirical evidence for that system's diminishing economic performance in the subsequent decade and discuss some of the institutional factors that have stood in the way of a successful defence against decline. Following this, we investigate why there is little hope for the German political system to overcome its present immobility, making continued social and economic decline the most likely scenario for the future. Finally, we address, in a general way, what a German recovery would require and what political configurations might conceivably bring about real change.

VIRTU AND FORTUNA: WHAT MADE THE GERMAN SYSTEM WORK?

The post-war German political economy, as it came into its own in the early 1980s, consisted of a unique configuration of institutional mechanisms to co-ordinate capital, labour and public authority. Many elements of this configuration already existed in the early years of industrialisation, while others evolved only after World War II.[2] Together, the institutions that later seemed to compose a coherent 'German model' performed exceedingly well in the global political-economic context of the 'Golden Age' of post-war economic recovery and, particularly, increasing international trade, allowing West Germany superior economic performance in comparison to other advanced capitalist countries. They also supported a remarkably successful adjustment to the era of declining mass production in the 1970s and 1980s when Germany, just as Japan, managed to steer clear of the Fordist production model much faster than other countries, including especially the United States.[3]

This is not to say, however, that German institutions as they existed in the 1970s and 1980s were consciously designed to match the economic challenges of their time. From the 1960s to the late 1980s, their economic virtue was more discovered than planned. To paraphrase Machiavelli, it was to a large extent conditional on good fortune: on favourable external circumstances whose contingent requirements the German political economy happened to meet better than the institutions of other countries. If only for the heterogeneity of its origins, the German political-economic system could never, not even in its economic heyday, be explained as a product of self-interested actors designing institutional arrangements for purposes of economic and political efficiency. A functionalist logic that does not recognise historical contingency cannot explain the emergence of a web of institutions, even if it has beneficial consequences for almost all actors operating under it and contributing to its modification.

Nor can a functionalist logic be relied upon to provide a new institutional design when a formerly successful system experiences a crisis due to changing external conditions. The problem in such moments is not one of inventing another, better adjusted coherent system to be put in the place of the old one. Rather it is to develop and make use of a political capacity for practical experimentation and serendipitous innovation by which to discover new niches for a political economy's distinct capabilities in its evolving environment. Therefore, the reason we believe Germany to be in a severe crisis is not primarily that its economic institutions no longer match contingent conditions as well as in the past – this is not unusual and cannot really be avoided. It is because the very stability and incrementalism of its political system – once a distinctive German asset – now seems to stand in the way of a constructive response to the new and highly uncertain demands of a changed world.

The following is a stylised account of central aspects of the German system in its historical stable state, as it came under pressure in the 1990s. The German post-war political economy was organised by institutions that made for high continuity and smooth incremental change, in industry as well as in politics. Germany as a socioeconomic system used to be distinguished by modest cyclical swings over time and generally compressed distributions around high means. Outliers were rare, both at the low and at the high end. Risks were highly ensured, or could not be taken due to institutional constraints, or taking them was not worth it as rewards were never excessively high. Entrepreneurialism, political or otherwise, is not highly rewarded. There were ample opportunities for actors to prevent other actors from doing something unusual. In stable external conditions this regime supported strategic long-termism and protected actors from being surprised by activist politicians or overly ambitious competitors. The suspicion is that in more turbulent circumstances, what used to be a virtue of stability may have turned into the vice of stagnation.

The *organisation of capital* in the German system is accomplished by corporate hierarchies, inter-firm networks and interactions between firms and public agencies. Large and medium sized firms in Germany are predominantly privately held or in the hands of a few large stockholders exercising tight supervision over managerial agents. Chief executive officers are 'first among equals', who must negotiate fundamental decisions about company policy with the executive boards and the supervisory boards of their firms. Corporate leadership cadres have risen through the ranks of the firm and have typically gained their experience in engineering and production divisions. In its investment and growth strategies, the German firm relies mostly on internal resources or bank loans, leaving only a modest role for bond and stock equity markets. The latter are dominated not only by large stockholders, but also by universal banks which own significant shares of company stock and exercise proxy voting rights on behalf of small stockowners. This ownership structure has given rise to a web of interlocking company directorates enabling banks – often with large asset shares in several firms of the same industry – to play a crucial role in companies' choice of strategy or in their reorganisation.

Within each industry, German business is characterised by a balance of competition and co-operation. Firms compete in product markets but co-operate in the acquisition of inputs and in product and process innovation, particularly firms belonging to the crucial tier of medium sized, privately held engineering companies that account for a substantial share of German exports. Sectoral business associations, nationally tied together under the umbrella of the BDI (German Federation of Industry), provide for the sharing of valuable information among firms, facilitate co-operation and complementarity, and promote joint innovation and international trade strategies.

The *organisation of labour* is also multi-layered, ascending from the individual labour contract via participation in shopfloor decision-making and corporate governance to the levels of regional industrial sectors and national economic co-ordination. There is an extensive legal codification of labour contracts in Germany, watched by union specialists in labour law.

German labour law favours long-term, full-time employment contracts and severely limits the parties' ability to make fixed-term and part-time contracts, as well as the employer's ability to dismiss individual workers. For mass lay-offs, social plans have to be negotiated with employee representatives. The legal framework for workplace representation, the *Betriebsverfassungsgesetz*, supports elected works councils with rights to information, consultation, and participation in decision-making over working conditions. Works councils contribute to social peace and the smooth introduction of innovations by giving the shopfloor a voice in most aspects of everyday working life; they also militate towards the steady employment of a core workforce. A similar effect is caused by co-determination on company supervisory boards, where the number of labour representatives almost reached parity under legislation passed in 1976. Workforce representatives on major works councils and on the supervisory boards of large firms are almost always union members, which ties unions into decision-making at company level.

Wage bargaining in Germany proceeds within a regional and sectoral framework in which industry-wide labour unions and corresponding employer associations negotiate agreements that apply to all firms belonging to the association. Due to the wage leadership of the metal workers' union, this system approximates national peak-level bargaining because the first agreement in the annual bargaining campaign tends to be adopted by unions and employers in other sectors as well. Co-ordinated wage bargaining delivered industrial peace and relatively moderate, productivity-based real wage increases because the monopoly of labour representation made it all but impossible for radical minorities to disrupt bargaining and push for high nominal wages. At the same time, industry-wide co-ordinated wage settlements put pressure on the weakest firms to innovate or go out of business, allowing the strongest firms to accumulate excess profits for investment in their international competitiveness.

At the firm and sectoral level, an important element of the system of industrial relations are the institutions of vocational training, which bring together unions and employers in local chambers of commerce and trade serving as regulatory agencies. Because of the long-term nature of labour contracts, employers are willing to train entry-level apprentices who learn an occupation in firms while also attending public trade schools. This 'dual system' produces a skilled workforce attuned to the needs of industry and able to contribute to incremental innovation.

The *role of the state* and of public authority within Germany is one of *regulation, facilitation* and *delegation* by public agencies, rather than of direction. The sector of state-owned or subsidised companies is small and public anti-trust agencies keep a watchful eye on inter-firm competition. However, some regulations, such as the law on retail shop opening hours, limit the extent of competition, for example between small and large firms. Furthermore, there have been major exemptions from the principle of competition in the German economy. One important example is the banking sector, where the majority of business accrues to non-profit municipal and state-owned or co-operative savings institutions and banks. When borrowing funds, these public establishments have a competitive advantage vis-à-vis their private sector rivals because lenders see them as lesser credit risks. Other examples of restraints on competition include the health care sector, trucking and shipping, insurance and, of course, agriculture.

Before it was superseded by the European Central Bank, probably the most important market-conforming regulatory authority in the German system was the Bundesbank. Its sole mission was to protect the value of currency. Due to its autonomy from the elected government, the bank was able to stick to non-accommodating interest rate policies to make excessive wage settlements result in unemployment rather than inflation and to stand in the way of expansionary fiscal policies.

As to state *facilitation,* business development is promoted primarily through an infrastructure of public and semi-public research agencies (such as the *Fraunhofer Gesellschaft*), institutions of higher education (*Fachhochschulen* and universities), regional development agencies, as well as subsidised credit facilities for domestic business investments and international trade. *Delegation* of decision-making to the corporate sector takes place, for example, with respect to the specification and enforcement of industrial standards. Most importantly, according to the principle of autonomous wage bargaining (*Tarifautonomie*), business and labour negotiate wages without direct state intervention. And the German Federal Employment Office (Bundesanstalt für Arbeit), a huge bureaucratic organisation with 90,000 employees and field offices down to the local level, was until recently (see Streeck and Hassel, this volume) governed by a board consisting of representatives of employers, unions, and the different levels of the state.

Crucial for understanding the evolution of the German political economy from the 1950s to the 1980s, and its agonisingly slow revamping since then, is the post-war *party system.* Its centripetal logic replaced a centrifugal logic that in the inter-war period pitted anti-democrats of the Left and the Right against a feeble 'Weimar coalition' of democrats in the centre. The rupture of 1945 led in each of the former fascist countries – Italy, Japan, and Germany – to the creation of an inclusive non-socialist party trying to organise a cross-class electoral coalition, under the label of either Christian or Liberal Democracy. In Germany as a frontline state in the Cold War, post-war politics also involved a withering away and then the political repression of the radical Left. This created space for an ideologically inclusive labour unionism and the rise of a single hegemonic party of the Left, the SPD.

Another example for the decentralised organisation of the German polity is the *welfare state*. Many social services are delivered by private non-profit organisations aligned with associations or churches. Health care and pension systems involve self-governing bodies with client and provider representation, corresponding to central features of what Esping-Andersen[4] calls a conservative, Christian-democratic welfare state. It provides universal coverage for most citizens, but fragments the organisation of social insurance by sectors and occupational groups. Moreover, it fashions entitlements primarily in the form of transfers rather than benefits. These transfers are proportional to contributions levied as payroll taxes. The redistributive impact of a conservative welfare state is less than that of a social-democratic welfare state where better-off citizens contribute more through progressive general taxation but then obtain the same services as everybody else.

One main reason why the German state is unable to govern unilaterally is its decentralised organisation that makes for multiple institutional veto gates. Most operative administrative tasks are implemented by bureaucracies governed by the Länder or the localities. The entire federal German bureaucracy has fewer employees than a single US government department with its field offices. Furthermore, within the federal system, the Länder have rival or exclusive jurisdiction over a number of important policy areas, such as education.

Federalism also limits the national government's capacity to enact innovative policies. Because the Länder control the second chamber of the German legislature, the Bundesrat, and because most legislation is in areas where the Länder have rival jurisdiction, federal governments must seek the majority of state votes in the second chamber to be able to legislate. In periods of 'divided government', with a different partisan majority in Bundestag *and* Bundesrat, the passage of legislation is particularly cumbersome. Even with unified government, however, ambitious state governors belonging to a party represented in the national cabinet may act on interests different from those of their national leadership.

A final institution that deserves mentioning in this context is the German Federal Constitutional Court (Bundesverfassungsgericht). It exercises far-reaching powers to review the compliance of legislation with the constitution, even ahead of any case heard by a lower court ('abstract' review). Members of the federal parliament and state governors may submit new legislation to the Constitutional Court for review, and the court has handed down decisions that were at variance with those of veto players in other relevant political decision-making arenas.

Historical literature has traced the origins of the institutions of the German political economy and we have nothing new to add here. We would like to insist, however, on the heterogeneity of what in retrospect may appear as an institutional 'system'. Some central German institutions are relics of a pre-industrial past whereas others appeared by historical accident, especially by imposition of the US Allied High Command after World War II. The latter, for example, made it possible for a school of liberal economic institutionalists (*Ordoliberale*), inspired by F.A. von Hayek and politically represented by Ludwig Erhard, to become influential in the economic policy of the new Federal Republic.

Among the older institutions of the German political economy we find elements of corporate organisation (private firm ownership, large stockholders, universal banks, debt rather than equity financing) and industrial relations (industrial unionism and works councils) as well as the dual vocational training system. They go back to the time before industrialisation (vocational education growing out of the guild system); date from Germany's comparatively late industrialisation in the era of heavy industry and the beginnings of science-based industries (universal and investment banking, corporate governance, industrial self-regulation, public research institutes); came about under the post-1871 empire and Bismarckian authoritarianism (the basic institutions of the German insurance system); in the early twentieth century in the decades before World War I (industrial unionism, business associations and cartels); or just after World War I (works councils and, later, unemployment insurance).

Among recent post-World War II additions to the German system are the de-cartelisation of industry and the introduction of a strict competition regime, promoted by the Western allies in the belief that Germany's organised capitalism made National Socialism possible. Also, allied military governments imposed a 'balanced' federalism, dismembering what was left of Prussia and allocating broad powers to the Länder. They also insisted on an independent central bank and a strong constitutional court, provisions that were duly incorporated into the constitution of the Federal Republic. Co-determination at company level also had its origin in part in the British effort to politically neutralise the German coal and steel industry, after the American government had vetoed its nationalisation.

Finally, there are critical elements of the German system that have both ancient and modern roots. A case in point is Germany's party system, with its long-standing weakness of democratic liberalism. This originated when German unification in 1871 and Bismarck's coalition policies split the liberal movement in an anti-democratic national-liberal and a much smaller democratic left-liberal wing, the latter being destined to remain a marginal player between the vast blocs in the democratic camp of political Catholicism and Social Democracy. The relative strength of the German social democracy is old as well, of course, while the main innovation after 1945 was, as mentioned above, the Christian-Democratic Party with its cross-class appeal.

After 1949, Christian-Democratic politicians pursued a cross-class strategy primarily through a reorganisation and extension of the welfare state, particularly to the elderly and to small business, but also through improved benefits for core elements of the working class. The Christian-Democratic Party thus became the hegemonic party of the 1950s. Its success eventually compelled the SPD to give up its Marxist ideology to become a serious contender for political power, renouncing its objective to change property relations in favour of extending the democratic class compromise through the welfare state. Other major parties in post-war Germany thus contributed actively to the creation of the German welfare state, with the Social Democrats extending the menu of benefits beyond what christian democrats had initially envisaged. Both parties neutralised the small market-liberal opposition to welfare state expansion by co-opting it into the government or by marginalising it through a 'Grand Coalition' between 1966 and 1969.

THE GERMAN PERFORMANCE CRISIS OF THE 1990s

German success became notable in the 1970s and 1980s, when post-war reconstruction, the benefits of an under-valued currency and technological catching-up could no longer explain the country's superior economic performance and political stability. Particularly under the trying circumstances of the oil crises of the 1970s, the German political economy delivered lower inflation, lower unemployment and slightly better economic growth rates than were experienced by most other wealthy Western democracies. One explanation was that during this period exactly those industrial sectors expanded in global trade in which the German configuration of institutions had comparative advantages. These sectors included the chemical, electro-mechanical and machinery industries, in particular the production of durable consumer and investment goods requiring sophisticated engineering, including all sorts of transportation equipment (especially automobiles), power plants, chemical processing facilities, measurement and fine-mechanical equipment and machine tools.

In the sectors of German strength, precision engineering and quality production relying on highly skilled workers paid off in superior products amenable to improvement through incremental processes of organisational learning and technical innovation. Incremental learning is supported in Germany by an institutional fabric that relies on long-term labour contracts, peaceful labour relations and large or medium sized established firms embedded in co-operative networks with other firms in the same or complementary sectors. Moreover, internal recruitment of engineering-trained management and close relations to house banks made hostile takeovers and corporate break-ups almost impossible. Because German institutional arrangements lowered transaction costs in the interface between capital, labour and the state, German companies could produce goods at competitive prices controlling for quality, despite very high real wages and an appreciating currency.

However, if we place German economic performance in context, it appears the favourable conditions that made Germany excel in the 1970s and into the 1980s vanished in the subsequent decade. In order to compare, we look at the performance of four Anglo-Saxon countries with market-liberal institutions, such as stock market-based financial systems with corporate governance centralised around a single chief executive officer and a weak board, the absence of 'stakeholder' co-governance of corporations through worker participation, fragmented labour unions with limited capacity and willingness to engage in corporatist compacts, and the absence of firm-based vocational training resulting in a high share of low-skilled blue-collar workers and in reliance on general educational institutions for human capital acquisition. Next, we compare three countries with social-democratic or conservative-social democratic institutions and with co-operative corporate governance and industrial relations regimes. Two of them, Denmark and the Netherlands, are today widely discussed as new 'models' of superior economic and political performance.

Further, we include France and Italy, which are countries of almost the same size as Germany and endowed with mixed regimes of corporate governance, industrial relations, and economic state intervention. Like Germany, however, they have generous transfer-oriented conservative welfare states, promoted by conservative parties that governed for most of the post-war growth period with a cross-class, non-market-liberal appeal. Finally, we look at Japan. While Germany and Japan differ in their institutions of corporate governance, finance, industrial relations, and state–economy linkage, what unites them is the weakness of political liberalism in the electoral and legislative arena, workplace-based human capital formation, a bank-based financial system, and co-operative relations among businesses.

Table 1 shows GDP growth rates from 1990 to 2000 and growth per capita. The Anglo-Saxon market-liberal systems come out ahead of the Northern European social-democratic welfare states which, in turn, lead

TABLE 1

GROSS DOMESTIC PRODUCT AND PER CAPITA GROWTH 1990–2003

	1990–2000 Averages			2001 GDP growth, 2002 estimates and 2003 projections				Per capita growth
	GDP growth/a	Popula-tion growth/a	Per capita GDP growth/a	GDP growth 2001	GDP growth 2002 (est.)	GDP growth 2003 (proj.)	Per capita GDP growth 2001–3/a	1990–2010 (1990= 100)
Australia	4.1	1.2	2.9	2.8	3.5	3.2	1.9	161
Canada	2.9	1.0	1.9	1.5	3.5	3.1	1.7	43
UK	2.5	0.4	2.1	2.0	1.5	2.3	1.5	144
US	3.4	1.2	2.2	0.3	2.3	2.5	0.5	131
Denmark	2.4	0.4	2.0	1.0	1.5	1.7	1.0	135
Netherlands	2.9	0.6	2.3	1.3	0.1	0.9	0.2	128
Sweden	1.8	0.4	1.4	1.2	1.7	2.0	1.2	129
France	1.7	0.4	1.3	1.8	1.0	1.5	1.0	126
Germany	1.5	0.3	1.2	0.6	0.4	0.6	0.2	115
Italy	1.5	0.2	1.3	1.8	0.3	1.2	1.1	127
Japan	1.3	0.3	1.0	–0.3	–0.7	0.2	–0.4	106

Sources: GDP growth/a 1990–2000: World Bank, *World Development Report 2002* (Washington, DC: The World Bank, 2002), table 3, pp.236–7; Population growth/a 1990–2000: World Bank, *World Development Report 2002*, table 1, pp.232–3; GDP growth 2001, estimate 2002: OECD Economic Outlook, December 2002, statistical appendix; GDP growth 2003, projection: latest available forecasting average of economic research institutes, reported in *The Economist*, 15 Feb. 2003, p.97; Per capita GDP growth 2001–3: GDP growth figures, corrected by average population growth figures 1990–2000; Per capita growth 1990–2010: per capita GDP growth 1990–2000, plus projection of per capita growth 2001–3 for the entire period from 2001 to 2010.

France, Italy and Germany, the three large continental countries with co-operative or mixed market institutions. Japan trails everyone. But when comparing columns 1 and 3, note that the differences between countries and groups of countries shrink once population growth is taken into account. Germany grows less than the other countries except Japan, by up to one percentage point per year, although it is only marginally behind France, Italy and Sweden.

Germany's laggard position becomes more pronounced in the following decade. On a per capita base, economic growth in 2001–3 is barely perceptible (column 7).[5] It is less than half of the – low – per capita growth rate of other European countries (except the Netherlands), and especially far behind that of the market-liberal economies (with the exception of the United States). For an – inevitably shaky – projection, one may set each country's 1990 per capita income equal to 100 and use 1990–2000 historical growth rates and 2001–10 growth rates based on 2001–3 estimates. US per capita income would then move ahead of Germany's by 16 per cent in the short span of 20 years, and by a whopping 25 per cent ahead of Japan's (column 8). The best performers, by far, would be the other countries of the Anglo-Saxon group and Denmark. In other words, Germany has for some time belonged to a group of slow-moving countries, but must worry about trailing even that group and becoming more like Japan.

Next we examine German growth in relation to overall and sectoral employment for the most recent decade on which data are available, 1989–98 (Table 2). Economies can grow by adding more labour and by improving its use. As the table shows, Japan has been adding labour at an already very high level of employment for very low growth. It also has the largest industrial sector of all countries compared. In three de-industrialised or rapidly de-industrialising liberal market economies – Australia, Canada and the United Kingdom – high per capita growth combines with substantial labour savings and high employment, particularly in the private business sector and in consumption-related services. The United States, Denmark and, in particular, the Netherlands represent an intermediate combination of high growth with, mostly, rising labour input. While in the US higher labour input added to an already very high employment level, the employment increase in the Netherlands was the result of a successful effort to move away from 'welfare without work'.

Finally, Germany belongs to a category with low growth and declining employment, at low overall employment (except for Sweden, where employment is still high). For a welfare state this is the worst possible combination. The German disease is shared by other conservative welfare

TABLE 2

GROWTH AND EMPLOYMENT

	GDP growth per capita 1990–2000	Percentage of the 15–64-year-old population in employment					
		All employment		Industrial sector		Consumer-related services	
		Change 1989–98	1998	Change 1989–97	1997	Change 1989–97	1997
	(1)	(2)	(3)	(4)	(5)	(6)	(7)
Group I: high growth, strong labour savings							
Australia	2.9	−0.7	68.5	−3.0	15.1	1.8	35.4
Canada	1.9	−2.1	69.9	−2.4	15.7	−0.2	36.3
United Kingdom	2.1	−1.5	70.3	−4.5	18.6	1.7	35.2
Group II: high growth, weak labour savings							
Denmark	2.0	−0.3	75.8	−0.7	20.0	1.8	38.4
Netherlands	2.3	8.3	61.8	−0.7	15.0	4.1	34.9
United States	2.2	2.1	73.9	−1.5	17.6	3.1	41.7
Group III: low growth, strong labour savings							
France	1.3	−0.9	59.4	−2.6	14.7	2.2	29.5
Germany	1.2	−3.4	60.5	−2.0	23.1	1.3	28.1
Italy	1.3	−2.2	50.8	−1.2	16.1	−1.5	24.0
Sweden	1.4	−11.7	69.6	−6.2	17.9	−5.1	37.1
Group IV: low growth, weak labour savings							
Japan	1.0	2.9	74.8	0.4	24.9	3.3	34.7

Sources: Per capita GDP growth: see Table 1. Labour market participation data for all employment, business sector, industrial sector and consumer-related service sector: see F.W. Scharpf and V.A. Schmidt (eds.), *Welfare and Work in the Open Economy. From Vulnerability to Competitiveness* (Oxford: Oxford University Press 2000), Vol.1, data appendix, Tables A-5, A-7, A-9, and A-10.

states with co-operative or mixed market economies which, like Germany, have small consumer-oriented service sectors (column 9). Germany stands out for its very large industrial sector. In the decade from 1989 to 1998, this sector shrank considerably less than one would have predicted based on changes in the other countries except Japan.[6] Together with the high German export surplus, this testifies to the unbroken strength of German manufacturing. At the same time, like the other conservative welfare states, Germany appears to be stuck in a pattern where declining labour inputs in industry cannot be compensated by growing employment elsewhere. This is different in Sweden, which started from an extremely large consumer service sector in 1989 combined with an extremely high labour market participation rate, and shed employment in all sectors to restore competitiveness.

The employment problems of Germany and other continental European economies also relate to labour costs and competitiveness (Table 3). The first two columns show the total change of real unit labour costs in manufacturing for the last two decades of the twentieth century. They reveal that Germany suffered from rising labour costs in the 1980s, when labour costs elsewhere declined, followed by a significant reduction in the 1990s. Note that high growth performers in the 1990s had the greatest reduction in unit labour costs in the 1980s and 1990s taken together (column 3), such as the Netherlands, Canada, the United States and, based on a recent effort, also Sweden. Germany, it would seem, tried to restore its competitiveness in the 1990s mainly by shedding labour in its industrial core sector, where opportunities for economic and employment growth are limited.

Germany continues to enjoy overwhelming advantage in the export of conventional manufactured goods. Table 4 shows the percentage of world trade in different functional categories for 11 leading capitalist democracies in 2000. To make the data more easily comparable, we calculate the percentage of world trade per million inhabitants, multiplied by 100 to make figures more readable (column 1, in brackets). Germany performs extremely well overall. Its world market share is highest, however, in manufactured goods (column 3) while performance in the fastest growing segment of manufacturing, high technology products, is weaker (column 4). In the rapidly growing area of commercial services, German performance is weakest (column 5). In comparison, Britain, the United States and France, among the larger countries, generally have higher world market shares in the cutting-edge sectors of high technology and business services than in manufacturing. Japan is stronger than Germany in high technology markets but weak in business services.

Table 5 focuses only on the largest five economies. It presents the expected world market share in all goods and services taking into account population size[7] (row 1.1) and the difference to the actual share for each country (row 1.2) to provide a rough measure of relative competitiveness. Germany performs better than any other G-5 country in overall exports as well as manufacturing exports (row 1.3), but ranks only fourth in high technology and in commercial and business services (rows 1.4 and 1.5).

Moreover, the second part of Table 5 shows that since 1990 Germany has experienced the weakest overall growth in all exports as well as in its strong manufacturing sector (row 2.2). We take this to indicate that without diversification Germany's manufacturing base may melt away in coming decades. There is not one area where Germany's export growth equals or

TABLE 3

CHANGE IN LABOUR PRODUCTIVITY 1980–98

Percentage change in real unit labour cost

	1980–89	1990–98	1980–98
Australia	–6.9	–0.5	–7.4
Canada	–7.3	–7.4	–14.7
United Kingdom	–4.7	–3.2	–7.9
United States	–10.0	–3.2	–13.2
Denmark	–1.2	–4.7	–5.9
Netherlands	–14.4	–7.0	–21.4
Sweden	–4.8	–9.0	–13.8
France	–8.6	–0.2	–8.8
Germany	+2.5	–6.8	–4.3
Italy	–2.4	–5.7	–8.1
Japan	–4.9	+2.4	–2.5

Sources: Real unit labour costs: F. Scharpf and V.A. Schmidt (eds.), *Welfare and Work in the Open Economy*, Vol.1 (Oxford: Oxford University Press 2000), Vol.1, data appendix, Table A-17.

TABLE 4

WORLD EXPORT MARKETS:

COUNTRY SHARES OF WORLD GOODS AND SERVICE EXPORTS

	All goods and service exports (% of world exports per million inhabitants* 100 in brackets)	Merchandise exports (% of world exports)	Manufactured goods export (% of world exports)	High technology exports (% of world exports)	Commercial service exports (% of world exports)
	(1)	(2)	(3)	(4)	(5)
World	$7,950 bn	$6,350 bn	$4.953 bn (78% merchandise exports)	$990.6 bn (20% man'd goods exports)	$1,455 bn (89% all service exports)
Australia	1.0 (5.5)	1.00	0.4	0.3	1.2
Canada	3.95 (12.7)	4.4	3.6	3.4	2.5
UK	5.1 (8.4)	4.4	4.6	7.4	7.9
US	13.5 (4.8)	12.3	13.1	22.3	18.7
Denmark	0.9 (18.9)	0.8	0.6	0.7	1.7
Netherlands	3.6 (22.5)	3.3	3.0	5.3	3.5
Sweden	1.4 (15.0)	1.4	1.5	1.6	1.4
France	5.1 (8.7)	4.7	4.9	5.9	5.6
Germany	8.0 (9.8)	8.7	9.5	8.5	5.5
Italy	3.7 (6.4)	3.7	4.2	1.9	3.8
Japan	6.9 (5.4)	7.6	9.1	12.7	4.6

Sources: Calculated from World Bank, *World Development Report 2002*, pp.238–9; merchandise exports 2000, *World Development Report 2003*, pp.240–41; high technology exports 2000 as percentage of manufacturing exports, manufacturing 2000 as percentage of merchandise exports and World Bank Development Indicators (online), all goods and services.

TABLE 5

RELATIVE TRADE COMPETITIVENESS: THE G-5 COUNTRIES

	UK	US	France	Japan	Germany
1. Relative export shares *(per cent world trade, per million inhabitants*100)*					
1.1. Goods and services (expected share, predicted by country size)	9.0	3.2	9.1	6.3	7.9
1.2. Goods and services (difference of actual minus expected share)	−0.6	+1.5	−0.4	−0.8	+1.9
1.3. Manufactured goods (difference of actual minus expected share)	−1.3	+1.4	−0.4	+0.8	+3.5
1.4. High technology (difference of expected/actual share)	+3.3	+4.6	+1.3	+3.7	+2.4
1.5. Commercial and business services (difference of expected/actual share)	+4.1	+3.3	+0.8	−2.6	−1.3
2. Export growth *(annual per cent rate, 1990–2000)*					
2.1. Goods and services (world annual growth rate: 6.5)	3.9	7.1	3.3	5.2	2.8
2.2. Manufactured goods (world annual growth rate: 5.2)	4.8	8.3	4.7	5.0	2.3
2.3. High technology goods (world annual growth rate: 8.5)	7.6	8.7	9.0	6.8	7.2
2.4. Commercial and business services (world annual growth rate: 6.8)	7.9	7.5	0.3	4.6	5.2
3. Export-import ratios 2000 *(exports as per cent of imports)*					
3.1. Goods and services	91.6	72.6	102.0	110.3	100.7
3.2. Manufactured goods	82.9	66.8	102.3	208.7	138.1
3.3. Commercial and business services	124.0	130.0	132.0	58.9	60.9
4. Change in export-import ratios 1990–2000 *(difference of 2000 minus 1990 ratios)*					
4.1. Goods and services	+3.0	−12.6	+2.3	+7.2	−10.3
4.2. Manufactured goods	−4.0	−8.4	+5.8	−56.7	−8.4
4.3. Commercial and business services	+4.0	−5.0	+6.3	+13.0	−4.5

Sources: All calculations from sources given in Tables 3 and 4. The regression of population on goods and services export share/million of inhabitants is 24.31–8.60 log population/ million (r = −0.75).

surpasses world averages. German weakness is least pronounced in the high technology area, where Germany ranks fourth, but not far behind the leaders. The United States tops world average growth rates in all four categories, while Britain and France lead in one of each of the two most dynamically growing areas. Only Japan, like Germany, remains below the world average in all respects.

German export–import ratios in the aggregate of goods and services as well as in manufactured goods, while still high or at least balanced (rows 3.1 and 3.2), have lately been declining (rows 4.1 and 4.2). Also, the country's laggard position in commercial and business services has worsened (rows 3.3 and 4.3), confirming the picture of eroding German competitiveness.

Japan's extraordinary export–import ratio in manufactured goods declined in the 1990s (row 4.2), but the country begins to make up for this by improving its balance of trade in business services, with growth in the 1990s (row 4.3) albeit still at a very low level (rows 3.3). The competitiveness of Anglo-American liberal market economies continues to decline for general manufactured goods, which are increasingly imported from Asia, but holds firm in commercial and business services (rows 3.3 and 4.3). France shows the most balanced development, although its growth in commercial services is minuscule (row 2.4), notwithstanding a high export surplus in this area (row 3.3). It is fair to conclude that, from a dynamic perspective, Germany exhibits the weakest competitiveness profile among the world's five largest economies over the course of the 1990s.

What are the distributive correlates of German economic development? We can examine this in terms of wages and household incomes, with the two not necessarily yielding the same cross-national pattern given varying rates of labour market participation over time and across countries. Column 1 of Table 6 presents the 90–10 ratios of wages for men in the mid-1990s,

TABLE 6

PATTERNS OF WAGE AND INCOME INEQUALITY

	90: 10 ratios of wage earners' income (men only) mid-1990s	90: 10 ratios of wage earners income (% change) 1980– mid-1990s	Household GINI coefficient, mid-90s	Household GINI coefficient (% change) 1980– mid-1990s	Ratio of highest decile income or consumption to lowest decile mid-1990s
	(1)	(2)	(3)	(4)	(5)
Australia	3.0	+10.1	31.7	+10.5	12.7
Canada	3.8	+8.4	28.6	0	8.5
UK	3.4	+28.7	34.6	+28.1	10.5
US	4.8	+32.7	37.5	+21.4	16.9
Denmark	no data	no data	24.0	–6.6	5.7
Netherlands	2.7	+16.4	31.0	+9.9	9.0
Sweden	2.4	+11.8	22.2	+12.1	5.4
France	3.3	–2.7	32.4	+9.1	9.0
Germany	2.9	–4.7	30.0	+22.4	7.2
Italy	2.4	+16.7	34.6	+12.0	6.2
Japan	2.8	+7.3	no data	no data	4.5

Sources: Wage 90/10 ratios and their change, GINI coefficients: J. Pontusson, 'Social Europe versus Liberal America. Inequality, Employment and Social Welfare in the Global Economy' (manuscript, Department of Political Science, Cornell University, December 2000) Tables 2.3 and 2.8; GINI 90/10 ratios: World Bank, *World Development Report 2002*, Table 2, pp.334–5.

that is, the multiple of income received by a wage earner in the 90th percentile compared to a wage earner in the 10th percentile. Column 2 presents the percentage change in the multiple since 1980.

The figures show that Germany is one of the more egalitarian countries. From 1980 to the mid-1990s, inequality actually declined whereas in most other countries it rose substantially. The increase was particularly pronounced among the already inegalitarian market-liberal economies, led by the United States. But there is also a distinct increase in Sweden, Italy and the Netherlands, though from a baseline of high equality. Together with figures presented earlier, this suggests that for Germany the tenacious defence of wage compression in the industrial sector has made it impossible to create many new jobs in this sector or elsewhere, due to national co-ordination of wage bargaining across regions and sectors.

Greater wage compression in Germany, however, does not directly translate into greater household income equality, as captured by the GINI coefficient (columns 3 to 5). Because of the shrinking manufacturing sector and shrinking employment as a percentage of the population, fewer people benefit from wage compression. By the mid-1990s, Germany had a more equal distribution of household income than Anglo-Saxon market-liberal economies, except Canada, France or Italy (column. 3). But over the preceding 15 years income inequality had risen almost about as fast as in Britain and the United States (column 4). Still, this left the position of high-income compared to low-income households considerably lower than in all the market-liberal economies as well as in France and the Netherlands (column 6).

The overall picture, then, is one of a German political economy that produces only slow innovation and adjustment. Growth trailed most other major economies in the 1990s and the gap has recently widened. Industrial employment has fallen slower than one might have expected, given its comparatively high level in the late 1980s; similarly, consumer-oriented service employment has grown more slowly than the relatively small size of the sector would have led one to believe. Slow structural change combines with a gradual decline of unit labour costs in manufacturing and, reflecting Germany's traditionally strong competitiveness in established industrial sectors, only a minor decline in manufacturing employment. The German economy encounters difficulties entering new and technologically advanced industries and the growing sector of business services. Slow political and economic change coincides with a pattern of continued wage compression in industry accompanied, however, by rising inequality of household incomes.

THE ETIOLOGY OF DECLINE: WHY GERMANY HAS RUN INTO TROUBLE

The decline of the German political economy has multiple causes that often reinforce each other. While the symptoms of decline can generally be related to external shocks – such as increased exposure to international competition, technology-induced changes in terms of trade and relative competitiveness, or changes in demography and consumer demand – it is the ways in which political and economic actors have responded to these challenges that account for Germany's relative economic weakness in the new century.

Foremost among the challenges facing the German political economy are technology- and demand-induced gradual changes in the growth potential of economic sectors since the 1970s. Conventional manufacturing, where Germany's institutions of corporate governance, long-term employment and co-operative, organised industrial relations provide a comparative advantage, are no longer growing fast. In high technology sectors and especially in business and commercial services Germany lags behind other leading post-industrial economies, particularly those equipped with decentralised, fluid industrial relations, more precarious employment, and equity-driven capital markets.[8] While Germany has made the best of its still strong manufacturing sectors, such as machine tools, heavy engineering, automobiles and aerospace, these account only for shrinking segments of the post-industrial economy.[9]

Throughout the period under observation, Germany has maintained high levels of gross capital formation exceeded only by the Japanese economy (Table 7). This was good enough to stay abreast of developments in the traditional areas of Germany's strength. But the German political economy did not mobilise the additional capital needed to innovate in new areas because of the institutional bottlenecks it has encountered. Differences in gross fixed capital formation from 1990 to 2001 (Table 7, columns 2–5) do not explain different growth rates. Japan, which had the highest levels of investment in the 1990s, also had very low economic growth. What matters for economic growth is whether and to what extent *additional* investment is allocated to new and at the margin to highly productive areas of economic activity, even though accelerating rates of new investment are slow to translate into higher overall investment. Indeed *growth rates* of capital investment (Table 7, column 1) and per capita economic growth in the 1990s (Table 1, column 3) are robustly correlated ($r = +.75$).

There is also only a weak direct link between economic performance, for example per capita GDP growth, and the inflow of foreign direct investment

TABLE 7

GROSS FIXED CAPITAL FORMATION 1990–2001

	Annual change rates of gross fixed capital formation 1990–99 (%)	Levels of gross fixed capital formation (% of GDP)				Net balance of FDI, average 1990–99, % total capital formation*
		1990	1999	2000	2001	
Australia	6.1	21	22	25	24	8.0 (–5.6)
Canada	2.6	21	20	20	20	9.2 (–2.3)
UK	1.8	19	16	18	18	15.9 (+7.7)
US	7.0	17	19	20	21	6.0 (+5.2)
Denmark	4.8	20	21	20	22	11.4 (–8.9)
Netherlands	1.5	22	20	22	22	19.0 (+4.4)
Sweden	–2.2	21	14	17	18	32.0 (+14.6)
France	–1.6	22	17	19	21	8.5 (+0.2)
Germany	0.5	23	21	22	23	2.6 (–4.2)
Italy	–1.0	21	18	20	20	1.8 (–6.7)
Japan	1.1	32	29	26	26	0.2 (-4.5)

Notes: * in brackets: difference between actual and expected net FDI after stripping out log country population size.

Sources: Columns 1–3 from World Bank, *World Development Report 2000–1*, Table 11, pp.294–5 and Table 13, pp.298–9; column 4 from World Bank, *World Development Report 2002*, Table 3, pp.236–7, column 5 from World Bank, *World Development Report 2003*, Table 3, pp.238–9, column 6 from World Development Indicators, online (complete data for more than 6 countries only for 1990–99). The regression of log population on net foreign direct investment as percentage of total capital formation that yields the size-corrected expected values for each country is; FDI net = 27.84–11.02 log population (r = –0.62).

(Table 7, column 6), whether country size is ignored or stripped out of the data (figures in brackets). What can be said, however, is that large and slow-growing economies with reasonably open capital markets in the 1980s and 1990s display low rates of net foreign direct investment (Germany, Italy, Japan and, to a lesser extent, France). With the partial exception of France, these are also the countries in which institutional conditions are unfavourable to high competitiveness in the most dynamic areas of the post-industrial economy.

Germany's anaemic growth in capital formation and its low capacity to attract capital from abroad in the 1990s, together with its weak per capita economic growth, demonstrate the indispensable role of new investments for economic growth. What prevented an acceleration of capital investment? German institutional arrangements offer at least five reasons why investment extending Germany's comparative economic advantage into new sectors has not sufficiently taken place. We will not venture into calibrating the relative importance of each factor, but confine ourselves to a list of the causal mechanisms we believe to be at work.

1. The organisation of German capital and labour markets has offered too little flexibility for those new investments in manufacturing or business services that do not thrive when venture capital is hard to get, banks prefer to deal with established firms, regulatory obstacles prevent easy access to equity capital markets, and industrial relations make it difficult to hire people on an experimental, temporary basis. In addition, regulatory requirements have often sufficiently intimidated prospective investors to make them locate innovative activities outside Germany.

2. German institutions negatively affect not only the employment, but also the formation of human capital. Mediated by two hegemonic political parties that depend on the organisational and voting power of employees and former pensioners, the German welfare state has a strong bias towards protecting existing occupational structures and entitlements (Leibfried and Obinger, this volume). In the 1980s and 1990s, this shifted resources away from upgrading the educational system, as reflected in the deterioration of the universities in the last quarter of the twentieth century due to steadily falling real expenditure per student. By 2000, Germany had too few university graduates, many of them with inferior or outdated skills (Mayer and Hillmert, this volume). While this has recently been recognised, new resources for human capital investment would in effect have to be taken from social programmes serving powerful social-protectionist interests, in a competitive political environment in which parties going against such interests have invariably been punished in federal elections (Kitschelt, this volume).

3. The low level of additional investment necessary for structural economic change is further related to defensive labour supply management. Germany, in Esping-Andersen's terms,[10] is a conservative Christian-democratic welfare state that favours full-time wage earners and has coped with unemployment by taking growing numbers of people willing and able to work out of the labour market (Streeck and Hassel, this volume). As the number of contributors to the social insurance system declined while expenditure increased, payroll taxes went up even though individual benefits have been cut back since the 1970s. Relief was also provided by a temporary decline in the dependent population, due to the retirement of the small age cohorts affected by the war and to labour market entry of the post-World War II baby boom generation.

Still, the surpluses generated in the thriving manufacturing sector in the 1980s were in large part siphoned off to pay for early retirement and unemployment benefit, subsidising the labour market regime of the industrial period at the expense of new investment.

4. Incremental corrections may have reversed the decline, and in the late 1980s some steps in this direction were under way. They were undone, however, by the historical accident of German unification. Adding to and reinforcing the unfavourable dispositions of the German system, unification made it more difficult for politicians and the government to face up to the needs for political-economic reform (Wiesenthal, this volume). Foreign policy imperatives required the immediate absorption of the GDR into a unified Federal Republic. The speed of the incorporation made it all but impossible to contemplate changes in the West German institutional framework. The faltering East German economy – suffering from over-industrialisation, under-investment in infrastructure, and a no more than rudimentary service sector – instantly created millions of new beneficiaries of the German welfare state entitled to unemployment compensation, early and regular retirement pensions, social assistance, and training and retraining measures that often led nowhere. As a result, investment in structural change was even more crowded out by social consumption than before, and shifting resources from consumption to investment in business and human capital became politically even more difficult. Unification caused costly delays in the necessary restructuring of the German pension, health care and education systems, which in turn made it only harder, if not entirely hopeless, to address the same issues more than a decade later, with many more stakeholders in the status quo. If the surplus that can be extracted from a society is limited, dedication of a large share of it to social consumption and to the subsidisation of traditional structures cements such structures as it deprives the society of the means to invest in innovation.

5. European integration and financial globalisation have put additional strains on economic sectors that in the past could live with the German welfare state because they were protected from international competition. Since the Maastricht Treaty of 1992, many regulatory and fiscal supports have fallen by the wayside or been challenged, in sectors such as telecommunications, the railways, aviation and trucking, as well as banking and insurance. Other pressures on domestic firms from European integration include new rules on competition, affecting for example municipal savings banks, co-operative banks and state banks,

and public procurement. Typically liberalisation resulted in significant employment losses causing, in turn, further increases in social welfare spending.

So far, we have focused on the interrelated complex of market and technological pressures for change that have built up since the 1970s and clashed with the institutional predispositions of the German political-economic model, and on the reinforcement of such predispositions by unification. In a more forward-looking analysis, two further problems must be added that have gained virulence over the last several years, the effect of European integration on the political capacities of the German state and the beginning demographic revolution.

During the negotiations surrounding the Maastricht Treaty, Germany successfully insisted on the Europe-wide adoption of at least one crucial element of the German political-economic model, a powerful independent central bank as a guardian of monetary stability. In Germany, under conditions of co-ordinated wage bargaining, a case can be made that the anticipation of restrictive monetary policies with growth-dampening effects made unions put up with moderate nominal wage increases,[11] or at least made them support measures to increase productivity, including reduction of workforces through early retirement, to catch up with wage increases. Extension of the German monetary regime to the Euro currency area through the European Central Bank, however, required a number of countries to put up with a strong independent central bank that lacked the strategic capacities necessary for co-ordinated wage setting. As a consequence of different wage bargaining regimes in various European countries, and more generally of divergent business cycles, the restrictive monetary policies of the European Central Bank may hurt member states whose economic and institutional conditions require or permit more accommodating policies. This has recently been the case with Germany. High real interest rates under conditions of wage moderation have stifled economic growth at a time when domestic conditions, including the burden of unification, would have called for monetary expansion.[12] In this respect as in others, as Jeffery and Paterson argue (this volume), institutions German policy-makers bargained for at the European level now have begun to haunt them by inflicting additional burdens of adjustment on their domestic economy.

The greatest challenge in the long run, however, may be the impending demographic revolution. It interacts in a variety of ways with current German political-economic institutions. Germany is about to face a 'greying' of its population without historical parallel (Minkenberg, this volume). The ratio between the recipients of social transfers and the contributors to social insurance funds will grow progressively worse until the middle of the twenty-first century, unless more immigrants settle in Germany and assimilate into its economic, political and cultural environment; domestic fertility rises closer to replacement levels; more women join the labour force, as in market-liberal and social-democratic, but not in conservative welfare states; and the terms of retirement (age to qualify for full pension; pension levels; the relationship between pay-as-you-go and funded pension entitlements) become less generous.

Increasing immigration raises a large number of questions, many of which are addressed in Minkenberg's contribution. The older generation of current welfare state beneficiaries has the least tolerance for cultural pluralism and will not benefit from immigration in future decades. Moreover, better acculturation of more immigrants, to enable them to make productive contributions, would require significant investment. Not least, accelerated immigration would have to begin at a time when domestic labour markets have not yet been emptied by the demographic shift and unemployment is high, generating suspicion that newly arriving immigrants will only take jobs away from Germans.

The three other possible responses to the demographic crisis conflict with the Christian-democratic conservative welfare state and the corresponding industrial relations regime. Increasing employment may require less generous unemployment benefits. It would also involve an expansion of sectors providing personal care services. Given the ageing of the population, there will be high demand for such services, but it will become effective only if ways are found to make them affordable. Above all, this would require lower non-wage labour costs. The greatest reservoir of people to be drawn into the labour market is certainly women, many of whom currently stay at home with or without children. Enabling them to seek employment would require more childcare facilities and all-day schooling. The cost of these would probably have to be covered in part by employees themselves through higher taxes, and in part by reducing existing benefits accruing to clients of the health care and pension systems. Both would run into opposition from the social protectionist currents that defend the German welfare state.

COPING WITH DECLINE: POLITICAL MECHANISMS GENERATING IMMOBILITY

Under favourable conditions of the sort we have spelled out above, the key characteristics of the German political process – divided authority and jurisdictions, multiple veto points and veto players, disposition towards compromise and political stability among all actors – constituted a virtue that kept system parameters in place and led the system back to equilibrium after minor perturbations. However, when exogenous conditions fundamentally changed, at first imperceptibly, but then at an accelerating pace in the 1990s and after, the incrementalism and stability of German political institutions became fetters of productive adjustment and of creative coping with new situations. It will have to be seen whether the deepening economic crisis of the new century, in interaction with the electoral incentives of politicians, may result in institutional change giving rise to new problem-solving capacities in Germany's political economy.

German institutions and practices that used to provide for stability under conditions of comparative advantage, yet cause immobility in response to changing conditions eroding such advantage, can be divided into five complexes that interact with one another.

Functional interest mobilisation and intermediation. This arena is primarily the organisation of business and labour at firm, sectoral and economy-wide levels. The prevailing coping mechanisms here have been sectoral agreements between employers and wage earners, represented by business associations and trade unions. The bargaining mode promoted equalisation of market conditions for all firms in a sector, and wage compression within and even across skill profiles among workers. As the articles by Streeck and Hassel, Berger and Höpner, and Wiesenthal indicate, a growing number of firms, if not entire sectors, find that these arrangements limit their ability to adjust to changing markets. This applies particularly to medium sized enterprises with less flexibility in the redeployment of human capital and fixed assets. As long as unemployment benefits were generous and early retirement guaranteed workers almost painless exit from the labour market by their mid-50s, unions fought any change in the collective bargaining regime tooth and nail. The East German labour market situation in the 1990s only strengthened their passive resistance. Since unification, the bargaining system has been fraying at the edges, with individual employers exiting and sectoral collective agreements hollowed out by supplementary firm-level agreements between managements and works councils. Recently, unions have included rules in sectoral agreements to enable firms, with the permission of the parties to the sectoral agreement, to deviate from the latter if their works councils agree, for example to preserve employment or make new investment possible.

Electoral competition and partisan policy-making in the interplay between legislative and executive authority. Germany's party system is based on two major cross-class parties with a record and reputation of support for the country's welfare state, facing very weak market-liberal competitor (Kitschelt, this volume). The result is a pattern of centripetal competition in which any major party pursuing painful economic reforms is punished by an electorate in which a social-protectionist majority prevailed all the way through the 1998 and 2002 federal elections. As a consequence, neither the major governing party nor the opposition party have dared touch the political-economic status quo, and when they have tried or promised to do so, they have lost the election. Recent elections, however, also show a gradual realignment in which social-protectionist voters begin to move out of the Christian-democratic and possibly even the Green partisan constituencies and are replaced by more liberal-minded voters. This might embolden the main opposition party to exhibit a more clearly contoured market-liberal policy profile.[13] Under conditions of a deepening economic performance crisis, this could win it a West German majority large enough to create a reform-oriented national majority, even if social-protectionist views still prevail in East Germany.

Extra-institutional social movement issue politics. As Rucht shows, political street protest as a way of mobilising dissent continues to be vibrant. But this has not prevented many social movement entrepreneurs, particularly at the municipal level, to enter into bargaining arrangements with the political establishments that draw them and their followers into the political status quo. Especially left-libertarian movements (women, ecologists, local reform and democracy movements) have benefited from an expansion of public sector services and from increasing jurisdiction of political decision-making in areas that earlier would have been under the control of regulatory technocrats or left to market allocation. This tendency towards a 'politicisation of production' through multi-partite bargaining is exactly what may stifle the adjustment of businesses to changing market conditions. In the process, a large proportion of social movement activities has changed its character from challenging the political-economic status quo to defending the accommodations found with established parties and interest groups. Movements that clearly have resisted integration, such as right-wing anti-foreigner and racist groups, add in their own way to the defence of the status quo by making it politically more difficult to devise an immigration policy consistent with Germany's demographic realities and economic requirements in subsequent decades.

Multi-level territorial division of jurisdictions. It is not only the specific alignment of interests in the functional, electoral-representative and direct democratic political arenas that slows down authoritative decisions in Germany. As Scharpf pointed out more than a quarter of a century ago, German co-operative federalism is a system of interdependent state and national-level decision-making that makes it all but impossible to redistribute resources and co-ordinates decisions around the smallest common denominator of all veto players.[14] The co-operative nature of German policy-making is reinforced by the construction of the second legislative chamber, the Bundesrat, which consists of the state governments rather than of directly elected state representatives. Partisan and regional differences among state governments and between state and national governments can and often do block federal legislation. German co-operative federalism contrasts with 'market preserving' federalism in which subnational units are left to compete with each other within common national parameters that preserve certain collective goods.[15] As Wiesenthal concludes (this volume), a deepening crisis may induce a move from co-operative to market preserving federalism, in which states are free to engage in trial-and-error experimentation to find new ways to remedy political-economic deficiencies.

Judicial review of authoritative decisions by the Constitutional Court, whose members are appointed in a complicated process that requires consensus among the major parties and yields something like proportional representation. The Constitutional Court, however, is not simply an extension of partisan power. It has operated as an independent veto player on a number of occasions and blocked reforms, even those passed with cross-partisan support. Also on economic matters such as taxation and social insurance, the court has been a formidable power to restrain political innovation emanating from the legislative and executive arenas.

In the 1990s and later, all of the five categories of institutional mechanisms were used to block political-economic reforms. Nevertheless, institutions are not exogenously given and may themselves become objects of bargaining and formal or informal revision. For example, a lasting economic crisis may cause voter defections at the margin from what

Kitschelt characterises as the social-protectionist coalition ruling German politics. As politicians perceive promising electoral prospects of more vigorously liberal positions on economic reform, policies and their outcomes are likely to change.[16] As in Scandinavia, the electoral lure of liberalisation may extend even to social-democratic parties and governments, provided their strategists see little risk of their voters defecting to new leftist social-protectionist alternatives.[17] Perhaps a lasting crisis of economic performance may also alter the operation of functional interest intermediation, direct democratic politics, and judicial review in the German system.

FROM STAGNATION TO REFORM?

Social science deals with unique historical events and with decisions contingent on uncertain expectations. Its capacity to make precise predictions is, therefore, woefully limited, especially predictions relevant to the short time horizons of normal politics. Uncertainty rules, not just for the observer but also for the actors themselves. Social science can, however, inform us on the broad parameters of social situations and structures and on the general constraints and opportunities they present to actors trying to achieve their objectives within them.

The German crisis of hyper-stability, or stagnation, due to ingrained over-commitment to old institutions and historical entitlements and to underinvestment in new capabilities, is so deep and has become acute in so many arenas at the same time that it can clearly not be resolved at one stroke, at one time, and in one place. Not only the pension system is in the doldrums today, and not just health care, labour market policy, or the finances of local communities. University reform is needed as much as reform of vocational training, and the German system of industrial relations has reached its limits in the same way as, say, German immigration policy. Finding simultaneous solutions to this multiplicity of interrelated crises must overcharge the capacities of any single actor or institution, however farsighted and powerful.

Emblematic of what may be the ultimate deficiency the past politics of the 'stable state' have conferred on the German system of today would seem to be a law, passed under the Red–Green government in its first period of office, that makes it illegal for the Länder to collect fees from university students. Afraid of appearing *unsozial* to a broad middle class that believes it benefits from free university education – while actually suffering from its declining quality – the CDU/CSU let the legislation pass the Bundesrat.

Cases like this, in which an experimental search for new solutions at the ground level is narrowly circumscribed or altogether outlawed in the name of equality and social protection, abound in the German system. It is here, we believe, that the character of the 'German disease' of the early twenty-first century becomes most visible.

How curable is this disease? We suggest that the worsening economic crisis at the end of 2002 may finally have generated public perceptions and electoral incentives that at least in the short run may allow for more than cosmetic economic and institutional reforms. In early 2003, the humiliating defeat of the SPD in the first state elections of the new federal term destroyed any hope for the Red–Green coalition again to cobble together, on a case-by-case basis, majorities in the Bundesrat for individual pieces of legislation. What is worse, the prospect of losing the May 2005 Land election in North Rhine-Westphalia (NRW), the main SPD stronghold since 1966, raised the spectre of a two-thirds CDU/CSU majority in the Bundesrat, which would give the opposition a veto on each and every one of the government's legislative proposals. Neither the government nor the SPD may ever recover from this. It is conceivable that a political crisis has finally arrived that is as deep as the economic crisis – and deep enough to persuade the SPD to adopt a policy of liberal reform, against its own traditionalist constituencies, so as to reach out to centrist voters afraid that otherwise decline will continue indefinitely.

This, at least, may have been the rationale behind Schröder's much advertised official statement of policy (*Regierungserklärung*) of 14 March 2003, in which he embraced almost all of the economic and social policy reform proposals of the opposition during the 2002 election campaign, and in a number of points even went beyond them. Although the unions and the SPD had done what they could to water down its content, the declaration announced a series of measures that, if passed, would cut severely into social benefits and entitlements, for example by further reducing employment protection and limiting unemployment benefit to 12 months for most workers. It brought to a close a period of several months when Schröder appeared to be slowly gathering strength for a major change of direction, as implied at the end of the contribution by Streeck and Hassel. Indeed, on 3 March 2003 Schröder called a final meeting of the ill-fated Bündnis für Arbeit, only to declare it ended once and for all and advise the assembled representatives of unions and business associations that from now on the government would be legislating the necessary reforms on its own.

Behind this was a stratagem that can be understood only in the context of the intricacies of German federalism. Having failed to make the 'social partners' generate consensus policies that might then have been enacted with bipartisan support, the only way such support was to be had after the state elections of early 2003 was with policies devised against rather than with the unions. These, in fact, were the main losers of the new turn of events, together with the traditionalists in the SPD parliamentary party. Schröder's first term showed that an SPD chancellor cannot govern against the unions and the opposition at the same time. Since the unions could no longer be counted upon to deliver tripartite consensus, they were now pushed aside in pursuit of nothing less than a *de facto* Grand Coalition.

Why should the CDU/CSU let a Red–Green government that is at its mercy govern at all, even if it was dutifully executing opposition policies? Here Schröder seemed to count on pressure from business, less from its associations than from the CEOs of Germany's large firms, with whom he was always comfortable socialising. But there were also good party-political reasons that might have seemed convincing enough to at least some of the rival camps inside the opposition. Allowing the SPD to introduce the necessary harsh measures would mean that after a change of government in 2006 the CDU/CSU would no longer have to do so – and there is doubt whether, given the centrist tradition of the Christian parties, they could ever carry them out. The risk was, of course, that a successful SPD might be re-elected. Indeed, from a party-strategic perspective there might be equally good reasons to stonewall the government, let the crisis get even worse, and then take over and clean up.

On which of the two strategies the opposition would place its bets, and for how long, was difficult to predict at the time since that issue was intertwined with factional fights for party leadership in the forthcoming NRW and federal elections. It also depended on exogenous factors, like the development of the world economy. Moreover, it was entirely conceivable that eventually the SPD parliamentary party would balk and refuse to endorse legislation which by no stretch of the imagination could be defended as social-democratic – even though by deserting the chancellor it would very likely cause its own decimation in the 2006 election. In any case, the sort of change needed in Germany will clearly require more than temporary partisan configurations to make specific new policies rational in terms of electoral vote-getting.

Liberalisation has a variety of meanings, not all of which may be wholesome. But if institutional reform makes the centre of a political or economic system release territorial and functional policy arenas from co-ordination and allow them to find specific solutions for their specific problems – rather than force them to wait for general solutions to be found together that are equally valid for and acceptable to all – then liberalisation is very likely the agenda to which both government and opposition must turn in coming years if they want to resolve the multiplicity of German crises. Decentralisation by necessity results in uneven change, which, in turn, may engender inequality. It may also lead to frictions between less homogenous actors and institutions, and perhaps to conflict and disorder. One way such conflict may be resolved is by competition, which may further increase inequality, at least until the losers learn to catch up with the winners. All in all, the outcome of competition is unpredictable, and so are the innovative ideas actors will come up with in their effort to survive.

A number of authors, foremost among them Peter Katzenstein, have described the ingrained incrementalism of the semi-sovereign political system of post-war Germany.[18] Many of the contributors to this volume show how German incrementalism turned from a virtue into a vice when external conditions began to change rapidly. But then incrementalism is a problem only as long as uniform system-wide solutions are sought, and as tight coupling of system elements and narrow functional complementarity are generally accepted values to be enforced by joint decision-making. Basically that problem may be bypassed by decentralisation, freeing local or lower-level actors from burdensome obligations to take into account the effects of their action on other units and on the system as a whole. It is interesting to note in this context that it was also Katzenstein[19] who observed that change in Germany, if it happened at all, would take place at the ground level of institutions that are hard to reform from the centre, and within which precisely for this reason actors may become quite inventive in changing their operation if not their structure. Liberalisation in the sense of decentralisation would build on this capacity by encouraging rather than constraining independent local adjustment – in the relationship, to name just two examples, between Bund and Länder as well as in the interaction between sectoral collective agreements and workplace-based Alliances for Employment.

Perhaps the reigning paradox of post-war German politics is that precisely because of the dispersed distribution of political capacities among a variety of actors which was the essence of German semi-sovereignty, actors have learned all too well to co-ordinate with one another to ensure social cohesion against the institutional odds. This would explain why in a fundamentally multi-polar polity like Germany, institutional spheres and political decisions seem nevertheless to be so tightly coupled. Looser coupling would allow for more creativity from below, where creativity from above cannot be had because of the many 'joint decision traps' (Scharpf) and, today, because of simple problem overload. Again, for the sort of liberalisation that would make this possible, there would have to be more tolerance of diversity and uncertainty and less of the German *Angst* over centrifugal change.

Ultimately, we believe, the co-operative centre of German politics has no choice but to let go. In the same way, this applies to the national organisations of Katzenstein's 'centralised society'. The *politics of exception* under the *de facto* Grand Coalition that seemed to be taking shape in early 2003 would necessarily have to be, if it were to make a difference, one of decentralisation, to markets and local institutions, returning risks and gains to individual and collective actors at the micro-level, thereby enlisting their initiative and inventiveness to end stagnation and decline. The crisis being as profound as it is now, there may be a real chance that those championing liberalisation may for once escape electoral punishment, even though initially the strong will benefit more than the weak, who will have to give up entitlements to resources that must be diverted from subsidised consumption to innovative investment if German prosperity and social peace are to last.

NOTES

1. Just consider opinion polls at the time of this writing. Within months of the 22 September 2002 federal election, popular support for the re-elected Red–Green coalition collapsed after its announcement of a painful fiscal consolidation programme. But almost two-thirds of the respondents in the December 2002 ZDF *Politbarometer* survey rated the work of the CDU/CSU opposition as 'rather bad'. Almost as many respondents (58%) believed that a CDU/CSU government would not do better than the incumbent coalition. The Mannheim Forschungsgruppe Wahlen also found that citizen satisfaction with the opposition declined together with satisfaction with the government in late autumn 2002. See Deutsche Presse Agentur, 'Politbarometer: Wähler mit Rot-Grün so unzufrieden wie nie', DPA report of Friday, 15 December, 15:35 hrs: de.news.yahoo.com/021213/3/349g9.html.
2. For a detailed review of the institutional configuration characterising 'Model Germany', see Peter Katzenstein's *Policy and Politics in West Germany. The Growth of a Semisovereign State* (Philadelphia: Temple University Press 1987), which is still the most incisive and comprehensive summary we know. For a later account see Wolfgang Streeck, 'German Capitalism: Does it Exist? Can it Survive?' *New Political Economy* 2/2 (1997), pp.237–56.
3. See W. Streeck, 'On the Institutional Conditions of Diversified Quality Production', in E. Matzner and W. Streeck (eds.), *Beyond Keynesianism: The Socio-Economics of Production and Employment* (London: Edward Elgar 1991), pp.21–61.
4. G. Esping-Andersen, *Three Worlds of Welfare Capitalism* (Princeton: Princeton University

Press 1990), and *Social Foundations of Postindustrial Economies* (Oxford: Oxford University Press 1999).

5. Estimates for 2003 are more even debatable than normally but all available alternative point in the same direction.

6. Using levels of industrial employment in 1989 as predictors of change rates of employment in the ensuing decade (1989–98) and leaving out Germany and Japan, Germany's workforce in the industrial sector should have declined by 5.5% of total employment and Japan's by 5.2%. Actually, in Germany it declined by only 2.0% whereas in Japan it increased by 0.4%.

7. Because large countries export less than small countries, we have taken out the effect of country size by regressing exports per million inhabitants on logarithmic population size for our 11 countries (r = -75).

8. For Germany's relative comparative advantage in different manufacturing sectors from 1961 to 1997, see H. Siebert and M. Stolpe, 'Germany', in B. Steil, D.G. Victor and R.R. Nelson (eds.), *Technological Innovation and Economic Performance* (Princeton, NJ: Princeton University Press 2002), pp.112–47, Table, p.120.

9. For the link between market and technological challenges and the institutional advantages of different varieties of capitalism, see S. Casper, M. Lehrer and D. Soskice, 'Can High-Technology Industries Prosper in Germany? Institutional Frameworks and the Evolution of the German Software and Biotechnology Industries', *Industry and Innovation* 6/1 (1999), pp.5–20; P.A. Hall and D. Soskice, 'An Introduction to Varieties of Capitalism', in P.A. Hall and D. Soskice (eds.), *Varieties of Capitalism. The Institutional Foundations of Comparative Advantage* (Oxford: Oxford University Press 2001), pp.21–7; H. Kitschelt, 'Industrial Governance, Innovation Strategies, and the Case of Japan', *International Organization* 45/4 (1991), pp.453–93; D. Soskice, 'German Technology Policy, Innovation, and National Institutional Frameworks', *Industry and Innovation* 4/1 (1997), pp.75–96; and W. Streeck, *Social Institutions and Economic Performance. Studies on Industrial Relations in Advanced European Capitalist Countries* (London: Sage 1992).

10. See Esping-Andersen, *Three Worlds of Welfare Capitalism*. For the current predicament of the conservative German welfare state, discussed in a comparative context, see F.W. Scharpf, 'Economic Changes, Vulnerabilities, and Institutional Capabilities', and A.C. Hemerijck and M. Schludi, 'Sequences of Policy Failures and Effective Policy Responses', both in F. Scharpf and V.A. Schmidt (eds), *Welfare and Work in the Open Economy*, Vol.1 (Oxford: Oxford University Press 2000), as well as E. Huber and J.D. Stephens, *Development and Crisis of the Welfare State* (Chicago: University of Chicago Press 2001), especially pp.144–68 and 223–40.

11. See T. Iversen, *Contested Economic Institutions* (Cambridge: Cambridge University Press 1999), and R.J. Franzese, *Explaining Macroeconomic Policies* (Cambridge: Cambridge University Press 2002).

12. P.A. Hall and R.J. Franzese, 'Mixed Signals: Central Bank Independence, Coordinated Wage Bargaining, and European Monetary Union', *International Organization* 52/3 (1999), pp.502–36.

13. A similar process started in Austria about two decades earlier, when a long period of exclusion from government forced the Austrian People's Party (ÖVP) to rethink its Catholic cross-class strategy and move toward a sharper market-liberal appeal. It took, however, more than another decade of coalition government with the Social Democrats, and losses to the populist and anti-statist Freedom Party, to position the ÖVP firmly outside the old inter-party consensus on Austria's mixed economy with its large state sector.

14. F.W. Scharpf, B. Reissert and F. Schnabel, *Politikverflechtung. Theorie und Empire des kooperativen Föderalismus in der BRD* (Kronberg, Taunus: Scriptor 1976). See also F.W. Scharpf, 'The Joint Decision Trap. Lessons from German Federalism and European Integration', *Public Administration* 66 (1988), pp.239–78.

15. B.R. Weingast, 'The Economic Role of Political Institutions: Market-Preserving Federalism and Economic Development', *Journal of Law, Economics and Organization* 11/1 (1995), pp.1–31.

16. For a fascinating empirical confirmation of the democratic logic of inter-temporal

accountability and responsiveness in the US case, see R.S. Erikson, M.B. MacKuen and J.A. Stimson, *The Macro Polity* (Cambridge: Cambridge University Press 2002), especially chapters 7 to 9.

17. H. Kitschelt, 'Partisan Competition and Welfare State Retrenchment: When Do Politicians Choose Unpopular Policies?' in P. Pierson (ed.), *The New Politics of the Welfare State* (Oxford: Oxford University Press 2001), pp.265–302.

18. See Katzenstein, *Policy and Politics in West Germany.*

19. In his edited volume *Industry and Politics in West Germany: Toward the Third Republic* (Cornell University Press 1989).

PART I

NATIONAL UNIFICATION AND EUROPEAN INTEGRATION

German Unification and 'Model Germany': An Adventure in Institutional Conservatism

HELMUT WIESENTHAL

At first glance, Germany appears to have benefited extraordinarily from the collapse of East European communism. With the accession of the German Democratic Republic (GDR) to the Federal Republic of Germany (FRG) on 3 October 1990, Germany was able to overcome one painful result of its defeat in World War II: its split into two opposing parts along the front line of the Cold War. Moreover, reunification seemed to promise that West Germany would reinforce its already strong position among the world's leading economies.

But a few years after unification it became apparent that the event hurt German economic performance more than it helped. From 1992 to 2002, Germany experienced growth rates below its annual increases in productivity, resulting in rising unemployment and the weakest economic performance overall among the European Union countries. While economic reform issues took centre-stage in the 1998 and 2002 German federal election campaigns, the Red–Green government achieved little tangible change. This was in large part due to the fact that the unification process had contributed both to the worsening of Germany's economic performance and to political stalemate over economic reform. Failure to adapt to new challenges does not protect the status quo. Rather, it is likely to make the situation more painful.

In the process of unification, the transfer of Western political-economic institutions to post-socialist Eastern Germany took place just at a time when 'model Germany' was beginning to lose its capacity to deliver favourable economic outcomes, even in the Western heartland. To make matters worse, West German institutions were imposed on a social and economic fabric that lacked the organisational prerequisites to benefit from them. As a consequence, the transfer of institutions to Eastern Germany accelerated the crisis of the German model in the unified country.

This article addresses two questions. First, how and why did the process of unification negatively affect the nation's ability to sustain the German model? Second, why have the problems and detrimental consequences of institutional transfer nevertheless made it harder rather than easier to reform key pillars of the model? This study will focus first on the macroeconomic dynamics of East Germany's incorporation into the West. The fact that these dynamics made it harder for Eastern Germany to create microeconomic institutions and mechanisms like those in West Germany that would be able to sustain economic growth is discussed in the second section. Finally, Eastern German public opinion is opposed to any macro- and microeconomic reforms that might get Germany out of its predicament. The conclusion speculates that this leaves few options open for serious reform.

THE MACROECONOMICS OF GERMAN UNIFICATION

West Germany never relied on a counter-cyclical Keynesian fiscal policy, and especially not on demand-side deficit spending during periods of economic recession. The terms of unification, however, forced German economic policy-making into precisely that pattern.

Four general conditions shaped – if not over-determined – a post-socialist pathway of political-economic reform in the territory of the former German Democratic Republic that was unlike any chosen by neighbouring post-socialist countries. First, in terms of *international security and power relations*, Western elites perceived a fleeting window of opportunity to seize upon Gorbachev's willingness to trade the GDR in for a new era of co-operation with the West. Asserting a 'primacy of politics' over mundane economic details, the Bonn government hurriedly closed a deal with the four World War II allied powers to make rapid unification possible. International security considerations caused the Kohl government to ignore the warnings by leading economists and opposition leaders that the costs of rapid unification would be very high. The speed of unification, in turn, left little room for social experiments and required that existing institutions be transferred to the new German Länder which had previously constituted the German Democratic Republic.

Second, initial uncertainties about East German support for the rapid absorption of the GDR into West Germany shaped the pathway of unification. In the autumn of 1989, neither the East German civil rights associations nor the small group of reformers within the Communist Party that would later refashion itself as the Party of Democratic Socialism

(PDS) welcomed a 'capitalist' system. Instead, they preferred a modernised democratic socialist East Germany in an economic and political confederation with West Germany. West German politicians were able to overcome popular East German reservations by embedding unification into the process of deepening European integration. They also offered economic benefits to East Germans that would allow them to rapidly approach the standard of living enjoyed by West Germans. In this process, the memory of West Germany's 'miracle economy' of the 1950s and 1960s served as a helpful myth, even though the preconditions – such as an undervalued currency or a rapidly expanding post-war world economy – were manifestly missing in the early 1990s. The Eastern elites' principled aversion to unification was rendered ineffectual after the unequivocal popular pro-unity vote in the last GDR legislative election on 18 March 1990.

Third, the rapid speed and external West German control of the unification process came about as a result of the weakness of East German civil society and of nascent post-communist politics after 40 years of intense repression – which, since the 1960s, had not allowed dissidents to organise themselves in ways comparable to Hungary, Poland or Slovenia. Although some 20 East German civil action groups and organisations had been founded in the autumn of 1989, they played only a minor role in identifying and representing the citizens' interests. As a consequence, the Bonn government was able to drive forward the process of unification as a transfer of West German institutions with virtually no serious opposition – especially after the March elections had awarded the East German affiliates of the major West German parties an overwhelming majority in both the legislative and executive branches of the GDR government. All aspects of reform – whether in the form of direct institutional adoption, as a consequence of extensive bargaining, or as market-driven change[1] – thus boiled down to the external governance of unification by the West German political and economic elite. However, this could only be made palatable to the East Germans by granting them comprehensive economic benefits and protection from the costs of economic and institutional transformation.

Fourth, Western electoral and political-economic interests drove the speed of the unification process. Only a high pace of unification would guarantee the governing Christian Democratic–Liberal coalition government the opportunity to time the all-German elections sufficiently early to take advantage of the initial popular enthusiasm and optimism before its costs and frictions could surface and lead to disenchantment.

Against the backdrop of these conditions, the implementation of pluralist democracy and a market economy in East Germany and the legal unification of the country occurred within the span of less than one year. Economic, monetary and social union (EMSU) took effect in July 1990. This secured the transfer of West Germany's entire array of legal, social and economic institutions and became the framework for all subsequent regulations – in particular, the Unification Treaty, which resulted in the GDR's formal accession to the Federal Republic of Germany.

Thus, from the very start, Eastern Germany benefited from a proven and complete institutional system that included a legal framework, a judicial system, administrative agencies and representational bodies. Neither the political institutions of the market economy, the demarcation of sub-national administrative jurisdictions and local self-government nor the political-economic frameworks of social insurance, industrial relations and economic interest representation had to be invented from scratch. In addition to the transfer of institutions, the new Länder had the extraordinary advantage of being able to draw on economic resources from the formerly West German and now all-German public budgets and social security funds.

In macroeconomic terms, the rapid integration of East Germany, with comprehensive economic protection, compensation and improvement of the population's living standards, combined an extreme economic shock therapy with far-reaching insulation of the population from its consequences – in other words, with an anti-shock policy. Currency reform and privatisation were the shock element in the package. With the EMSU, the East German Mark was made equivalent to the western Deutsche Mark on a parity basis. Wages and transfer incomes were also fixed in a one-to-one relationship. This amounted to an overnight appreciation of the local currency by about 400 per cent, rendering almost all East German economic activity instantly uncompetitive with western products and services. Productivity levels in the east were estimated at only about 30 per cent of western levels, and thus far too low to meet the new labour costs faced by East German production units.

Although the purchasing power of the East Germans had quadrupled as a consequence of currency reform, there was popular pressure for further improvements. With the December 1990 all-German election approaching, the federal government succumbed to the temptation to promise inter-regional wage equalisation within five years, thus promoting unrealistic popular aspirations. The federal government generated expectations that later yielded an endemic problem of widespread popular dissatisfaction with the material results of subsequent economic developments.

The costs of shock therapy combined with anti-shock guarantees began to surface in the rapid tailspin of the East German economy that occurred throughout the 1990s. Growing imports, financed by huge income transfers from the west, caused the collapse of production in the east as well as a dramatic rise in unemployment.[2] Meanwhile, the newly installed privatisation agency operated by West German restructuring experts – the Treuhandanstalt – rapidly dismantled the state-owned industrial conglomerates, gave them a legal corporate governance framework, and weaned them off soft credits in order to prepare them for privatisation. Many of these firms were forced to shrink dramatically or had to go out of business before or after privatisation. Even then, about half of the survivors had to be granted state subsidies for restructuring and new investments, at least in the early years. Overall, the gainfully employed labour force in Eastern Germany shrank from close to ten million in 1989 to barely six million within a couple of years. Employment in manufacturing nose-dived from close to 50 per cent of the total to under 20 per cent, thus undoing 50 years of industrialisation in less than three years.

The painful restructuring and shrinkage of the East German economy were followed by a giddy surge, with growth rates of up to eight per cent (from a low floor) in the 1992–95 period – mostly fuelled by a giant building boom aided by western public investments in infrastructure and residential renovation. But then, in the period between 1995 and 2000, the structural weakness of the new Länder economy asserted itself again, with sluggish growth rates of only about half of the already modest western levels. In 2001, the eastern economy shrank by 0.5 per cent. Even generous investment incentives had been unable to compensate for the comparative disadvantage inflicted on the eastern economy by EMSU. Because currency union had removed devaluation as an option to restore eastern competitiveness, East German firms could not cover the huge increase in wages and social contributions – which far exceeded productivity – through price increases or reductions in the cost of factor inputs.[3] At the macroeconomic level, this produced extraordinarily high unemployment and a need for ever-higher fiscal transfers from West Germany, resulting in very large budget deficits. At the microeconomic level, federal and state governments were compelled to engage in industrial policy. The macro and microeconomic policies adopted in response to the eastern crisis were inconsistent with the practices that had traditionally been pursued under the auspices of the German model.

Soon after unification, unemployment in the east grew to a level twice as high as that of West Germany – not taking into account the substantial share of the former East German labour force that was sent into early retirement, had withdrawn from the labour market, or took part in public retraining programmes. At almost 20 per cent from 1996 on (23 per cent including hidden unemployment), East German rates exceeded those of all Central European countries. This extreme unemployment – resulting both from the wave of de-industrialisation and from higher labour market participation among East German women – constitutes Eastern Germany's basic political-economic problem. On the one hand, the only proper way of improving the macroeconomic situation (technically speaking) is through lower wages, lower tax rates and more flexibility in the labour market and in state regulation. On the other hand, politicians in both the east and the west are experiencing strong pressure to call for the final closure of the remaining east–west income gap of 15 per cent. While Eastern German voters are demanding the full equalisation of all living conditions, economically sound policies lack sufficient public support. The much lamented consequences are the ongoing migration of skilled younger people[4] and more than one million unoccupied apartments in the east.

In order to compensate for the extensive layoffs in industry and agriculture, huge transfer payments were directed to the east. Popular pressure demands that they continue until the GDP per capita approaches the western level. Meanwhile, labour productivity has risen to 78 per cent of the West German level but, due to high unemployment, eastern domestic production per capita remains at only two-thirds of the western level. Transfers and new debts of between 75 and 100 billion euros per annum finance East Germany's high consumption. The 'borrowed' share of East Germany's prosperity thus amounts to one-third of the total of investment and consumption. Cumulative total net financial transfers from the west between 1990 and 2002 reached 800 billion euros.[5] Much of this was invested in subsidised employment – above all, in the still over-staffed public sector.

One striking indicator of over-staffing is the proportion of wage income to regional GDP. This amounts to 112 per cent of its western equivalent, even though the average eastern individual wage is only 77 per cent of the West German level.[6] The most conspicuous consequence of East Germany's sponsored prosperity is thus the escalation of public debt. As a percentage of total GDP, Germany's state debt rose from 41.5 per cent in 1991 to 61.5 per cent in 1997. Correspondingly, interest payments increased from 11.4 per cent of the budget in 1991 to 18.9 per cent in 1999.[7] In 2002 and 2003, the federal government was unable to confine the budget shortfall to the three per cent ceiling fixed in the EU Stability Pact. Since unification, German macroeconomic policy has developed a propensity towards persistent counter-cyclical deficit financing.

Is there no way out of this economic malaise? Now an integral part of Germany, the new Länder lack autonomous macroeconomic control. Because all the important variables are externally controlled, only regional wage levels remain available for intervention. Early on in the unification process, the suggestion that lower eastern wages would trigger migration to the west helped legitimise the high-wage policy of (western-controlled) trade unions and employers' associations, although the underlying presumption lacked empirical evidence.[8] Since then, because of electoral imperatives, parties and state governments have found it increasingly difficult to resist the pressure for inter-regional wage equalisation. Proposals to make wages match the low level of labour productivity definitely seem unfeasible.[9] In 2002, the re-elected Red–Green coalition government promised a step-by-step equalisation of wages in the public sector until 2007 – of course, at the expense of the number of available jobs.[10]

The Results of Unification – A Mixed Blessing

Comparing East Germany's present situation with the state of the late GDR, one can easily see that the eastern economy has made tremendous progress. Although the period of thoroughgoing restructuring at company level is over, the economy as a whole continues to be subject to favourable structural change due to high investments in infrastructure and human capital. The share of its competitive sectors in the GDP keeps growing at the expense of inefficient traditional sectors. Forces of employment growth now appear to counterbalance those of decline. The number of firms going out of business, on the one hand, appears to offset the number of new investments on the other. But while a competitive economy is emerging, its size is still too small given the volume of labour supply.

When we examine East Germany in comparative context, there is more reason for satisfaction. Life has improved in almost every aspect, and far more so than in such countries as Poland or the Czech Republic. But this improvement does not translate into subjective satisfaction, because the reference is West Germany, not other post-communist countries. Because of their quest for 'full compensation', when real average incomes amount to only 85 per cent of western levels, many East Germans feel they are being treated as second-class citizens.

Even extraordinary levels of financial compensation for the departure from a socialist economy did not protect the German federal government from eastern discontent. Exuberant early West German promises about east–west equalisation, together with eastern ideological-cultural residues of socialism and resentment against income differences, have combined to turn most political issues into matters of social justice that make inter-regional relations appear to be almost a class conflict between 'the rich' and 'the poor'. Although 'post-unification dissatisfaction'[11] manifests itself above all in injured self-esteem, its common denominator – as well as the only feasible remedy – appears to be monetary. This constitutes the political pole of a fundamental dilemma. Whereas the macroeconomic situation demands patience and self-restraint on the part of the East Germans, the political debate – in both the new and the old Länder – is subject to the logic of party competition with its strong incentive to trigger unrealistic expectations. All vote-seeking parties (including the liberal FDP) try to benefit from the resulting dissatisfaction with the achieved levels of distributive justice. Consequently, the governments of all five new Länder remain strong advocates of continuing the sponsored eastern prosperity achieved through resource transfer from West Germany for an indefinite period of time.

THE MICROECONOMICS OF UNIFICATION AND MODEL GERMANY

The operation of the West German model relied on labour market institutions facilitating sectoral and national wage-bargaining concertation, led by large companies, but compatible with the needs of most small and medium sized enterprises. Such institutions were supplemented by contribution-based social insurance systems configured around protecting the standard of living of families supported by a single male breadwinner. That arrangement fed back positively into the employment system. By granting high levels of earnings-related compensation for labour market risks such as unemployment, it encouraged workers to make human capital investments in skills specifically valuable to a single industry or a single employer – for example, through vocational education.

As other articles in this volume show, the conditions that supported these arrangements have been eroded throughout Germany. But in East Germany such conditions were absent from the beginning and could not be created out of thin air by government in the 1990s. German unification therefore hastened the nationwide erosion of the German model. This section addresses the relevant issues one by one and then consider how federalism – as a potential technique to dissociate policies in eastern and western states – has helped or hindered efforts to address the unique problems of unification.

Wage Concertation

In the era of post-war growth, industry-wide peak-level bargaining between centralised employers' representatives and union representatives succeeded in organising a social class compromise. These negotiations resulted in the moderation of nominal wage increases, peaceful and predictable industrial relations for business and rising real wages for labour. The principal beneficiaries of the compromise were the very large, export-oriented German manufacturing companies that maintained high profitability and international competitiveness by pegging sectoral wages to the average conditions of firms in their sector. Furthermore, national wage leadership by the most export-oriented metal engineering sector throughout much of the post-war era ensured that unions and employers in the domestically oriented sectors could not ratchet up wages in ways that would endanger the international competitiveness of German business. Large firms also accepted institutions of 'co-determination' through factory-level works councils and firm-level workforce representation on company supervisory boards. Small and medium sized, mostly privately held businesses – an important ingredient of the West German growth and export machine – could swallow peak-level arrangements as long as domestic and international markets kept growing and did not require them to respond to tougher competitive environments with flexibility in the deployment of capital and labour.

The system of industry-wide peak-level wage bargaining was extended to East Germany just at the time when small and medium sized companies felt increasingly hard-pressed to accommodate such agreements. Moreover, East Germany lacked resourceful, large and profitable corporations in the aftermath of the dramatic de-industrialisation effected by the shocks of monetary union and privatisation under the Treuhandanstalt's regime of dismembering and down-sizing the old socialist holding companies and selling off the remaining marginally viable but generally unprofitable bits. Nonetheless, the first peak-level collective agreement negotiated by trade unions and employers' associations in 1991 resulted in a substantial wage increase despite generally low labour productivity. Consequently, firms either ignored the agreement or faced economic disaster. Although about 80 per cent of eastern enterprises – comprising almost 60 per cent of all wage earners – ignored the wage settlement, it set the standard for what union representatives advertised as 'fair' remuneration.

Because of the collapse of industry-wide wage contracts in the east, the unions began to tolerate firm-specific wage and working time agreements. So-called 'opening and hardship clauses' were introduced in collective agreements to improve factor flexibility. Innovative 'experimentalism'[12] became a standard means of coping with the rigidities of supra-firm-level collective agreements vis-à-vis the global competition.[13] While tight regulations were finally loosened in the west, belated institutional learning had little impact on the much poorer economic situation in the east. A key ingredient of 'model Germany' could not develop firm roots in the new Länder.

Wage Bargaining, Mittelstand and Industrial Policy

The institutional bias of German industrial wage bargaining in favour of large firms became dysfunctional for another reason as well. As early as the 1980s, large companies changed from being centres of job creation and instead became machines for high productivity growth through the insertion of capital-intensive, labour-saving technology and subcontracting with components manufacturers situated in low-wage countries. Innovative technology, new products and the rapid rise of business-related and private services fuelled a revival of small and medium sized enterprises (*Mittelstand*). Centralised industrial relations did nothing to nurture the take-off of small and medium sized companies in East Germany. Moreover, the imposition of western regulatory codes on an economic landscape in which only the massive creation of small companies could solve the problem of unemployment stifled factor flexibility and the entrepreneurial freedom required to stimulate the growth of small companies. While the federal government attended to the fate of the large, run-down socialist conglomerates, only a handful of members of parliament or representatives of business associations were campaigning to bring about a *Mittelstand*-friendly environment with effective incentives for venture capital and new entrepreneurs.

De-industrialisation and the collective bargaining system stifled the early emergence of a critical ingredient of the German 'system' – an infrastructure of intermeshed medium sized, competitive and export-oriented businesses. This deviation from the German model led policy-makers to adopt another deviation that reinforced economic rigidity and failure to adapt to new challenges: a defensive interventionist industrial policy. Expensive subsidies were paid to save as many jobs in the existing industrial plants as possible. Federal and state governments targeted subsidies primarily to areas in the 'old cores' of East German industry, where the shock of monetary union and marketisation had created particularly high unemployment. Because such policies consumed a large share of the disposable financial industrial aid, regions with a higher potential for growth in terms of human capital or infrastructure were left with too few incentives to attract a large volume of investments.[14] Clinging to an outmoded concept of industrial policy, governments proved unable to resist short-term labour market considerations. Thus, huge amounts of investment capital, both public and private, were allocated in inefficient ways.

The overall picture of state-subsidised investment is mixed at best. A telling example is the reconstruction of the GDR's chemical industry complex around the town of Bitterfeld. According to a promise made by Chancellor Kohl, the equivalent of 25 billion euros from federal and EU funds was marshalled to rebuild the run-down production sites. Several billion were given to the French investor Elf-Aquitaine, which is said to have redistributed a considerable share of the subsidy as bribes. A similar subsidy went to Dow Chemical, on the order of no less than 1.2 million euros for each of 1,800 jobs retained. Nonetheless, the unemployment rate in the state of Saxony-Anhalt continues at 20 per cent. Another famous case is the fate of the 'saved' company Zeiss Jena, one of the few high-tech firms of the former GDR. Instead of reconstructing the unprofitable site, the company's CEO, Lothar Späth (a former minister-president of Baden-Württemberg) dismantled the Jena-based workshop and stripped away nearly all of its workforce. At the same time, almost two billion euros in public subsidies were spent on the acquisition of already profitable firms in West Germany.

Overall, during the first decade after unification, policy-makers paid little attention to issues of structural reform, such as the creation of viable medium sized businesses. Macroeconomic problems left little time for them to consider microeconomic developments. The high debt generated by German unification became entangled in the imperatives of reducing public budgets in accordance with the Maastricht criteria for European Monetary Union. Minimal attention was paid to reconsidering the financial and social consequences of the unification process.

It was not until the mid-1990s that the debate over a renewal of Germany's institutional order resurfaced. Even then, as other contributions to this volume show, only meek initiatives were undertaken to revive economic growth. Little attention was paid to the special structural problems of East Germany. If anywhere, the accomplishments of reform after 1998 were concentrated in the area of 'post-materialist' issues such as environmental sustainability, citizenship and minority rights – all areas in which national rather than regional Eastern German constituencies guided the calculations of politicians.

Managing Risk through Social Insurance

As a result of the rapid de-industrialisation in East Germany, full coverage of its population by the same health care, pension and unemployment entitlements as their western counterparts was bound to lead to large revenue shortfalls. In order to pre-empt protests, the federal government had refrained from using unification as an opportunity to reform and retrench German social insurance benefits, and instead extended full coverage to all East Germans. As an immediate consequence, citizens in the east enjoyed a sudden increase in the quality of services and the level of income transfers. Whereas in 1990, pensioners in the east had received only 29 to 37 per cent of standard western pension, levels had risen to 79 per cent five years later.[15] Because benefit disbursements raced ahead of payroll tax receipts, employees' and employers' social security taxes had to be increased to 20.3 per cent of gross wages in 1997.

In the health care system, an analogous rise in expenses was triggered not only by the extension of benefits to East Germans, but also by institutional transfer from West Germany. The East German *Polikliniken*, with teams of salaried doctors working together in ambulatory care facilities, were a comparatively cost-efficient form of 'managed care'. With Eastern German doctors split over whether to keep this system or adopt the more expensive West German system of private medical practice – and with the federal Minister of Health remaining apparently neutral – the western doctors' special interest associations succeeded in extending the western system after carrying out a massive campaign among East German doctors. Instead of leaving the issue to western organised self-interest, the federal government could have strengthened its own and the public health care funds' position by adopting *Polikliniken* as a 'managed care' pillar of the German medical system. Failure to do so contributed to further cost escalation in the German health care system, evidenced by an increase in payroll taxes for health insurance from 12.6 per cent in 1990 to 14.2 per cent in 2002.

The collapse of the East German labour market in the aftermath of the currency shock contributed to deficits in the German welfare state, not only due to a surge of early retirees that had been forced out of the labour market and were compensated by generous pensions. There also was the drain of East German unemployment benefits and retraining measures on the German unemployment insurance system. Whereas many regard the overall results of the publicly funded labour market policies as 'a crushing disappointment',[16] the payroll tax for unemployment insurance rose from 4.3 per cent in 1990 to 6.5 per cent in 1995.

As Leibfried and Obinger report in this volume, the cumulation of all these expenses made German payroll taxes rise to record levels – from 35.6 per cent in 1990 to almost 42 per cent in 2002. The ensuing rise in labour costs further hurt the competitiveness of German business. Eastern Germans became beneficiaries of wage income replacement rates that had been set in the early 1970s, at a time when the single wage-earner family was still the norm. But in the 1990s, gainful employment by both men and women was the norm in East Germany, even more so than in the west. Hence, western benefits schemes translated into extremely high family compensations and weakened incentives for the beneficiaries to re-enter the labour market except for the lure of high wage rates. At the same time, because of the significance of high compensation levels for a large proportion of the East German population, any attempt at reducing their generosity would be political suicide for vote-seeking politicians. Nevertheless, it is clear that high payroll taxes and benefits drive up German labour costs and undercut efforts to stimulate growth and employment.[17]

Education System

Most citizens regarded the transfer of West German educational institutions to the new Länder as a more or less self-evident matter and, consequently, the issue did not gain much public attention. Of course, there were occasional misgivings because of the continued employment of GDR schoolteachers who were once required to display strong communist beliefs. Apart from this, however, the new East German institutions of primary, secondary and tertiary education replicate their western counterparts. Even the old western controversy about the proper organisation of secondary education – separated into three streams according to pupils' differing academic talents, or united as a comprehensive school for all children regardless of abilities – was carried over into the east. The only exceptional feature of eastern educational institutions remained the availability of kindergarten places for nearly all pre-school-aged children. General conformity to the western model can also be seen in the system of firm-based and state-organised vocational training.

Although the transfer of the western education system to the east may not be spectacular, it serves as yet another example of an area where the east adopted institutions just as they ceased to be unambiguously advantageous even in the west. Since 1990, signals indicating the declining performance of Germany's secondary schools and its vocational training and university systems have been frequent. Had it not been for the challenge of unification, the weakening performance of the West German educational system would have made it onto the political agenda earlier than it actually did, when the process of imposing the old western education system on its socialist alternative had finally come to an end.

Vocational education has long been a part of the German education system which seemed particularly indispensable for the proper operation of the German model. As Mayer and Hillmert indicate in this volume, efforts have been made to expand the menu of vocational education to include new occupations, but these efforts have been timid. Most of the 344 approved occupations are still defined by the sectoral and technological structures of the past. Some aspects of the system were already outmoded on the eve of unification. About two-thirds of all apprentices are trained for occupations in the shrinking sectors of manufacturing and *Handwerk*. At the same time, the system has failed to match employers' increasing demands for young people with broad basic competencies and special training in information technology and business-related services. Even East Germany's pressing need for jobs in innovative and growing business sectors has not been enough to trigger an adaptation of the system to its changing environment.

While the slow speed of reform in the system of vocational training appears to be a by-product of meso-level corporatist decision-making, the performance deficits attributed to German universities' inability to train students in new, highly marketable professions, long duration of degree programmes and effective time to completion, mediocre research productivity of university faculties stem from the interaction between the fiscal and organisational interests of the Länder administrations in governing their own university sectors and the self-interests of the corporate groups involved in the university system: professors, students and administrators. Limited self-governance on the part of the universities keeps a system in place in which all groups block change in order to preserve their entrenched privileges and material benefits. The Länder are unwilling to give universities more autonomy and responsibility, keeping control over admissions, faculty appointments, courses of study and degree requirements. Corporate groups inside the university block any change that would generate more competition for funds and status recognition among students, professors, faculties and entire universities. In turn, weak exposure of all of these groups to competition discourages innovators who might propose new professional curricula or avenues of research. Both the rewards for successful innovation and the punishments for failure in the pursuit of excellence are ineffectual. Universities have therefore seen little reason to adapt to the demands of external labour markets.

The inefficacy of the university system became particularly manifest when Chancellor Schröder came up with an unusual proposal. Since the universities had failed to train a sufficient number of information technology specialists, immigration laws should be relaxed to allow software experts from India and elsewhere to fill the available jobs. Although the debate on this subject was lively, consequences for the reorganisation of higher education were slow in coming. Such changes tend to be prompted by new Europe-wide agreements to organise higher education more efficiently in order to improve the comparability and equivalence of university certificates across Europe. Exactly the same slow pace of reform may result from the debate that has followed Germany's extremely low ranking in the Programme for International Student Assessment (PISA), a comparative survey of the school achievements of 15-year-old pupils organised by the OECD.[18]

The causes of the education system's declining performance are well known. They are representative of Germany's institutional conservatism, which is rooted in the anti-competitive predilections of occupational status groups as well as Länder governments. As Leibfried and Obinger argue in this volume, the social democratic-Christian welfare state in Germany has channelled funds away from the formation of new human capital to the care of holders of spent human capital. In 1999, Germany's overall public expenditures for education were slightly below the OECD average at 4.35 per cent, although overall social expenditures were near the top of the scale.

To make matters worse, the influence of occupational interest groups and political parties over education policy has biased the structure of expenditure and the educational governance regime away from the pursuit of excellence. Only the upper stratum of secondary education and the partly outmoded system of vocational training receive adequate funds because they enjoy sufficient external business backing or the attention of powerful status interests in the teaching profession. Furthermore, resource allocation favours teachers' and administrators' salaries at the expense of investments in buildings, teaching resources and media. The PISA survey demonstrates that the lower stratum of secondary and the whole of primary education are neglected both in funding and in management. As a result, the education system fails to provide the economy with a sufficient number of labour market entrants who are adequately prepared to thrive in a knowledge economy.[19] Not only the main political parties – which are beholden to powerful corporate interests dominated by people who care more about retirement and health care than about new human capital formation – but also the Länder governments, in whose jurisdiction much of educational reform would be located, lack the political incentives to develop a long-term investment perspective for education. Instead, they have treated educational and research budget lines as targets for fiscal austerity measures.

Federalism in Unified Germany

The logic of German federalism rests upon the notion of decentralised multi-level decision-making. But rather than providing a national framework for a market preserving federalism that enables sub-national units to compete with each other to find the most productive and democratically accepted innovative public policies, German *co-operative federalism* prescribes a complex web of interdependent decision-making that requires a broad consensus both at the national and the state level in order to enact change. Thus, the system handicaps reform initiatives emanating either from the centre or from the individual states. German federalism fragments jurisdictions, but does not create autonomy for bold initiatives. If innovation requires a consensual process involving both the states and the federal government, then the smallest common denominator among the many veto players determines the ceiling for reform efforts.

Unification enhanced the fragmentation of sub-national geographic jurisdictions in Germany. Although the GDR's new political elite had the option of joining the Federal Republic as a single additional Land, they chose to re-found five rather small Länder with a total of 14.5 million citizens that mirror the heterogeneous structure of the west. Germany now has 11 Länder with less than three million citizens each. Furthermore, the entry of the new states into the federation creates a new divide that cuts across the existing partisan and regional divisions in the Bundesrat. Here, majorities of the state governments can block federal policy initiatives in the many social and economic policy areas for whose governance the constitution prescribes co-operative federalism.

Co-operative federalism not only constrains the federal government but diminishes its control over public budgets as well. In accordance with the constitutional mandate to bring about 'equality of living conditions in the federation',[20] a substantial share of tax revenues is being redistributed from the wealthier to the poorer states. Because of the resulting high level of equalisation among individual state governments' tax receipts (*Länderfinanzausgleich*), the system has relieved the states from competing with one another for a more attractive business environment or more efficient public services. In particular, states and regions with aging traditional industrial sectors are tempted to free-ride on the prosperity of their luckier or pluckier neighbours.

For the new Eastern German states, becoming equal partners in the system of horizontal revenue redistribution in the mid-1990s has, therefore, been a double-edged sword. On the one hand, the comparatively poor eastern states gained access to badly needed resources they were unable to acquire through taxes or loans. On the other hand, however, a permanent role as recipients of other states' financial largesse has suspended the need for eastern state governments to reorganise social services and public infrastructure in ways that match expenditures to internal revenues in the foreseeable future. In fact, the eastern Länder are banding together to preserve or extend the federal system of fiscal redistribution in their favour.

The resulting system of power-sharing in Germany creates a strong bias in favour of the status quo[21] – accompanied by fiscal irresponsibility at the Land level, since sub-national jurisdictions are quite autonomous in their debt management. As a consequence, the federal government is forced to choose its fiscal policy within the boundaries of freedom left by the Länder after they have chosen their policies. Cutting across all of this are the political party interests of the Länder and federal governments. Since hardly a year goes by when state elections do not take place – and the loss of state election might impinge on the capacity of the federal government to shepherd its legislation through the upper house of the parliament – decision-making in the Bundesrat tends to generate not only fierce geographically based distributional conflict but also partisan divides motivated by state and federal politicians' desire to win elections.

UNIFICATION AND PUBLIC OPINION

Is public opinion potentially a force to counteract the political-economic reform blockages in Germany that have been exacerbated by national unification through the transfer of western institutions and the further entrenchment of organised interests? In other words, could the intensified crisis of 'Model Germany' cause a shift in public opinion that would, in turn, weaken the capacity of institutions and organised interests to resist innovation? Empirical evidence suggests instead that unification shifted the balance of public opinion towards more support for current German welfare state policies as well as for the status of organised interests in policy formation, especially that of the labour unions.

The achievement of unification after only a brief period of negotiations was facilitated by the complementarity of two sets of interests. The western elite's interest in institutional continuity was a perfect match for the easterners' desire to swap the miserly socialist system of social security for the much more generous welfare state of a leading OECD country. When faced with the East German citizens' expressed approval of an encompassing and redistributive welfare system, the proponents of unification refrained from retrenching and refashioning the existing German welfare state. Surveys throughout the 1990s have illustrated that underlying this social policy preference is a continued strong popular support for the socialist concepts of equality and redistribution in East Germany. Even seven years after unification, an 83 per cent majority of Eastern Germans considered socialism a good idea if implemented properly. When asked to choose between two basic values, no less than 75 per cent gave priority to the value of equality over the value of freedom. During the same period, the explicit preference for a socialist-type redistributive welfare state declined only slightly, from 76 per cent to 68 per cent. These figures put the Eastern Germans somewhat, though not dramatically, ahead of West German public opinion. In a survey conducted in the west in 1996, while only a 26 per cent minority of respondents endorsed socialist values, here, too, 51 per cent preferred equality over freedom. 61 per cent even identified socialism 'fully' or 'rather' as 'a good idea that was carried out badly'.[22]

Empirical evidence overwhelmingly indicates that the Eastern Germans' predominantly socialist sense of distributive justice translates into extraordinary levels of support for the status quo of the German welfare state. The organisation and experience of unification have reinforced the normative bases of an unsustainable welfare state. The federal government always faces a majority opposing social reforms and, in particular, cuts in benefits. In 1997, when public budgets and social insurance funds were already overburdened by financial transfers to the east, a two-thirds majority of German citizens was reported to oppose any change in existing entitlements. Only a tiny minority of 12 per cent in the west and one per cent in the east was willing to accept cuts.[23] A four-country survey on welfare state reform conducted in March 2000 found that Eastern Germans were the least willing to consider a reform of the pay-as-you-go public pension system by inserting a funded component. This response put the Eastern Germans' support of the national status quo slightly ahead of the Spanish support level, and more substantially ahead of that of the French, Italian and West German respondents.[24] East Germans were also significantly more willing than West Germans to call for a further extension of the welfare state through higher taxes.[25] The accession of East Germany thus broadened the majorities unwilling to consider far-reaching social policy reforms.

Support for comprehensive redistributive social policies and support for labour unions mutually reinforce each other. After having survived the mild economic liberalism of the West German centre-right government in the 1980s without much harm, German unions managed to extend their domain to the GDR even before unification. As strong supporters of the welfare state status quo, of equal pay and of substantial expenditures on active labour market policies, they soon won the broad acceptance of eastern blue- and white-collar employees. Although union density has fallen steadily since 1991, the unions have remained the unquestioned representative of the eastern skilled full-time employees in traditional industries such as manufacturing, construction and – above all – public administration and social services.

The unions' image as standard-bearers of the 'common good', combined with the prevailing socialist conceptions of distributive justice in Eastern Germany, effectively protected them from having to shoulder responsibility for high levels of unemployment in the east and increasing unemployment in the west. The unions successfully presented themselves as victims rather than co-authors of the persistent labour market malaise. Their privileged position in public opinion permitted them to act as defenders of the institutional order and to reject concessions within the framework of a proposed 'social pact' to benefit the unemployed. The refusal of German unions to make wage and social policy sacrifices for the sake of boosting employment stands in contrast to union conduct in post-communist Eastern Europe – as well as to that of unions in a number of European Union countries that had to reduce public deficits in order to qualify for participation in the European monetary union. Only in a climate of intensifying public dismay about the state of German public finances, further economic decline and the inability of the returning Red–Green coalition to propose a comprehensive reform policy after the September 2002 election, did German labour unions began to rethink their position and tolerate a labour market reform bill that passed the legislature in the winter of 2002/3. But with the extension of the unreformed West German welfare state to East Germany an accomplished fact, a full array of reforms will now be much harder to engineer politically than it would have been ten years earlier.

CONCLUSION

The international situation in 1989/90 – together with the institutional and electoral imperatives of the West German political elites – explains the hurried and wholesale transfer of West German institutions to East Germany during the unification process. With the benefit of hindsight, we can see that this pattern of unification has contributed to the weakening performance of the German political economy. Had international circumstances and domestic power relations been different, the elites might have seized upon unification as an opportunity to reform the basic parameters of the German institutional fabric. Now, after the turn of the millennium, the political elites find themselves in a situation in which this reform has become more urgent, but also even harder to achieve.

The opportunity costs of sticking to the status quo are rising as well. Past strategies for choosing a middle road between the Scandinavian social-democratic welfare state and the Anglo-Saxon liberal residual welfare state may now no longer be feasible.[26] The accumulation of performance problems – among them the generous extension of the western welfare state to East Germany – may now call for a market-liberal retrenchment of institutions and policies. But German political preferences and beliefs may change slowly enough to make this a long-drawn-out incremental process. In this situation, the proposal to shift policy jurisdictions to the Länder, release them from the strictures of co-operative federalism and unleash policy experimentation and innovation at the sub-national level is gaining credibility. As long as path-breaking policy changes at the federal level are unlikely, granting individual states the right to greater policy-making autonomy might be a useful detour on the way to improved economic performance.[27] Needless to say, even this institutional change presupposes an intensified sense of crisis among the population and the political elites –

one that makes them perceive doing nothing as more dangerous than engaging in some modest experimentation.

NOTES

1. G. Lehmbruch, 'Institutional Change in the East German Transformation Process', *German Politics and Society* 18/3 (2000), pp.13–47; R. Czada and G. Lehmbruch (eds.), *Transformationspfade in Ostdeutschland* (Frankfurt/New York: Campus 2000).
2. R. Pohl, 'The Macroeconomics of Transformation: The Case of East Germany', *German Politics and Society* 18/3 (2000), pp.48–93.
3. Pohl, 'The Macroeconomics of Transformation', p.51.
4. N. Werz, 'Abwanderung aus den neuen Bundesländern', *Aus Politik und Zeitgeschichte* 39–40 (2001), pp.23–31.
5. S. Bach and D. Vesper, 'Finanzpolitik und Wiedervereinigung – Bilanz nach 10 Jahren', *Vierteljahreshefte zur Wirtschaftsforschung* 69/2 (2000), p.203.
6. IWH (Institut für Wirtschaftsforschung Halle), 'Fortschritte beim Aufbau Ost: Forschungsbericht wissenschaftlicher Forschungsinstitute über die wirtschaftliche Entwicklung in Ostdeutschland', *Wirtschaft im Wandel* 8/7–8 (2002), pp.182–234.
7. Bach and Vesper, 'Finanzpolitik und Wiedervereinigung', p.204.
8. Empirical research revealed an opposite disposition among East German workers. See G.A. Akerlof *et al.*, 'East Germany in from the Cold: The Economic Aftermath of Currency Union', *Brooking Papers in Economic Activity* 1 (1991), pp.1–87.
9. The factors contributing to low productivity include comparatively low supply prices, the under-utilisation of capacities, a low capital intensity and – last but not least – over-employment in certain sectors. See Pohl, 'The Macroeconomics of Transformation', pp.67–69.
10. According to Chapter III ('Aufbau Ost') of the coalition agreement of 16 October 2002.
11. H. Wiesenthal, 'Post-Unification Dissatisfaction, or Why Are So Many East Germans Unhappy with the New Political System?', *German Politics* 7/2 (1998), pp.1–30.
12. W. Jacoby and M. Behrens, 'Experimentalism as a Tool of Economic Innovation in Germany', *German Politics and Society* 19/3 (2001), p.18.
13. As of 1996, almost half of the 120 largest German companies had made use of company-level agreements with work councils and/or trade unions. Max-Planck-Institut für Gesellschaftsforschung, *Arbeitsbeziehungen in Deutschland* (Köln: Max-Planck-Institut für Gesellschaftsforschung 2002)
14. F. Barjak, 'Regional Disparities in Transition Economies: A Typology for East Germany and Poland', *Post-Communist Economies* 13/3 (2001), pp.289–311.
15. M.G. Schmidt, *Sozialpolitik in Deutschland. Historische Entwicklung und internationaler Vergleich* (Opladen: Leske + Budrich 1998), p.141.
16. H. Feldmann, 'Labour Market Policies in Transition: Lessons from East Germany', *Post-Communist Economies* 14/1 (2002), p.76.
17. P. Manow and E. Seils, 'Adjusting Badly: The German Welfare State, Structural Change, and the Open Economy', in F.W. Scharpf and V.A. Schmidt (eds.), *Welfare and Work in the Open Economy*, Vol.II: *Diverse Responses to Common Challenges* (Oxford: Oxford University Press 2000), pp.264–307.
18. German 15-year-old students rank 21st among 30 countries in terms of their capabilities in reading, mathematics and science. OECD (ed.), *Measuring Student Knowledge and Skills: The PISA 2000 Assessment of Reading, Mathematical and Scientific Literacy* (Paris 2000).
19. M.G. Schmidt, 'Warum Mittelmaß? Deutschlands Bildungsausgaben im internationalen Vergleich', *Politische Vierteljahresschrift* 43/1 (2002), p.16.
20. Basic Law (Article 106-3, 2).
21. T. König, 'Bicameralism and Party Politics in Germany: An Empirical Social Choice Analysis', *Political Studies* 49/3 (2001), pp.411–37.
22. E. Roller, 'Erosion des sozialstaatlichen Konsenses und die Entstehung einer neuen

Konfliktlinie in Deutschland?', *Aus Politik und Zeitgeschichte* B29–30 (2002), pp.13–19; R.I. Hofferbert and H.-D. Klingemann, 'Democracy and Its Discontents in Post-Wall Germany', *International Political Science Review* 22/4 (2001), p.365.

23. R.H. Cox, 'The Social Construction of an Imperative: Why Welfare Reform Happened in Denmark and the Netherlands but Not in Germany', *World Politics* 53/3 (2001), p.493; E. Roller, 'Shrinking the Welfare State: Citizens' Attitudes towards Cuts in Social Spending in Germany in the 1990s', *German Politics* 8/1 (1999), p.26.

24. T. Boeri, A. Börsch-Supan and G. Tabellini, 'Would You Like to Shrink the Welfare State? A Survey of European Citizens', *Economic Policy* (April 2001), Table 10, p.28.

25. Ibid., Table 13, p.33.

26. M.G. Schmidt, 'Still on the Middle Way? Germany's Political Economy at the Beginning of the Twenty-First Century', *German Politics* 10/3 (2001), pp.1–12.

27. F.W. Scharpf, 'Mehr Freiheit für die Bundesländer', *Frankfurter Allgemeine Zeitung*, 7 April 2001, p.15.

Germany and European Integration: A Shifting of Tectonic Plates

CHARLIE JEFFERY and WILLIAM E. PATERSON

Alone among post-1871 German states, the Federal Republic has been internally stable and a contributor to wider European stability. At the foundation of the Federal Republic in 1949 this outcome looked extremely unlikely. Its future trajectory appeared more likely to be one of renewed instability. The defeat in 1945 had resulted in the division of Germany and the loss of substantial territories. Berlin was under Four-Power control and could not be the capital of the new polity. One-quarter of the population were recent refugees whose presence was resented by the host communities. War and defeat had bequeathed deep economic and social dislocation. The new West German state purposefully deconcentrated power away from central government in a new, institutionally plural separation of powers; this 'state without a centre'[1] seemingly lacked the capacity to deal with the challenges of dislocation and reconstruction. The residual powers of the wartime allies left West Germany with minimal capacity to act externally.

The weaknesses of central institutions, defeat and national humiliation, and the scale of the economic challenge of reconstruction seemed to suggest a reprise of Weimar. In the event, the Federal Republic rather quickly emerged as a state so notable for stability that it became seen as a model for liberal democracy internally and externally. The grounds for this transformation are multiple, but a number stand out. First and foremost, the geopolitical competition between the Soviet Union and the United States gave the US a vital interest in the stabilisation of West Germany. This was reflected in a security guarantee and the encouragement that the United States government gave to the development of joint fora, especially those of European integration, which would make acceptable an increase in the capacity of the federal government to act externally. Internally the fear of the perceived expansionist ambitions of the Soviet Union subdued the nationalist aspirations of the large refugee population and underlined the new state's Western orientation.

Second, the shaming and total nature of the defeat of Nazism in 1945, combined with a fear of communism perpetuated by the rival German Democratic Republic, helped internally to truncate the ideological spectrum and to support the emergence of a 'politics of centrality'.[2] Ideological conflict such as that which had undermined Weimar was no longer possible. The ground was established for a broad social consensus on the aims and means of domestic policy that evaded the potential for gridlock in an institutionally plural state structure. A series of long-term social compacts between business and labour – the new 'social partners' – pre-empted damaging distributional struggles. A comprehensive 'social state' was built up to express a commitment to social equity and solidarity. And the problem of economic reconstruction was dealt with by the long and sustained boom precipitated by the outbreak of the Korean war. The German model – *Modell Deutschland* – of economic governance and social cohesion became a success story for others to emulate.

In the creation of this stable, liberal-democratic path for the Federal Republic, European integration played a central role. An export-oriented economic structure gave West Germany a fundamental interest in the creation of frameworks for opening up international trade at the European level which would allow other European states, especially France, to gain sufficient confidence in the Federal Republic to lift post-war discriminatory provisions. The imperatives of bipolarity had already impelled the United States along this line of thinking. The situational logic of these founding years was captured in the distinction by Bulmer and Paterson[3] of the political importance of European integration as an arena of co-operation and its economic importance as an area of competition: 'Without European integration as a political arena of cooperation West German economic performance would have been perceived as a threat.'

Participation in European multilateral fora was complemented and deepened by the development of a privileged bilateral relationship with the European state which had originally been keenest to limit the external capacity of the Federal Republic: France. Focused initially on reconciliation, the Franco-German relationship became a vehicle for collective action bilaterally and in multilateral fora which made growth in German economic capacity acceptable. Economic growth in turn helped internally to strengthen popular attachments to the Federal Republic; initially conditional on economic success, these gradually diffused into a more fundamental allegiance to the West German state, 'post-national' in character and in part projected outward onto 'Europe'. This Europeanised state identity increasingly resonated at both mass and elite levels. The consensus on the desirability of European integration became a central element in the general political consensus that developed in the Federal Republic. It was largely perceived as part of a virtuous circle that transformed the Federal Republic into a stable, liberal-democratic state embedded at the heart of a wider (West) European stability.

FROM STABILITY TO CONGRUENCE: GERMANY AND THE SHAPING OF EUROPE

The dynamics of this virtuous circle have attracted considerable interest among scholars, not least because the Federal Republic did not seem to conform to the rationalist assumptions which drive most understandings of international relations. West Germany did not seek to articulate interests in national terms and pursue them unilaterally, but rather as multilateral or European interests shared with others and pursued in partnership, in particular with France and occasionally also with other West European states. This 'leadership avoidance reflex'[4] was underpinned by the institutional pluralism of domestic politics. Institutional pluralism further limited the capacity of the Federal Republic to pursue any kind of consistent, national grand strategy in European arenas; European policy-making was shaped by the dynamics of a highly sectorised and weakly co-ordinated ministerial apparatus in central government and in time fragmented further by the territorial dimension of German federalism and the role of key para-public institutions like the Bundesbank.

That the Federal Republic had a 'leadership avoidance reflex' did not mean it did not exert power in Europe. The Federal Republic's power was not, however, 'deliberate' power – the 'forceful articulations of interests, combined with … resources for articulating leverage'[5] – but rather 'soft' or 'institutional'. Soft power was expressed in particular through the supply of institutional models from the domestic arena which then set the institutional parameters for decision-making at the European level. The classic examples have included:[6]

- the role of German actors – public and private – in standard-setting in the European Single Market programme;
- the impact of the Bundesbank model in providing the parameters for monetary policy at the European level from the European Monetary System through to Economic and Monetary Union;
- the impact of the German Länder from the mid-1980s in securing recognition for the regional level in EU decision-making.

At times, this form of influence had to be lubricated by ratcheting up the German contribution to the EU budget in the form of side-payments, which were deployed to line up the preferences of other member states in a direction congenial to the Federal Republic. In some fields, notably social partnership in industrial relations and the commitment to a high-standard (and high-cost) social state, German actors had little success in replicating the German model at the European level. However, the overall impact of a pattern of institutional 'export'[7] was to establish a 'bias in the character of EU governance' and to produce a 'strikingly good fit' of the constitutional order, norms and conventions, patterns of meso-level governance and policy goals of Germany and the EU.[8] This bias completes a more nuanced version of the virtuous circle of German–EU dynamics suggested above:

- *A Europeanised identity*: multilateral co-operation in the EU was internalised over the post-war period as a normative value by German policy-makers.
- *Institutional power*: value-driven multilateralism meant that Germany became an instinctive *demandeur* for multilateral solutions. In doing so it frequently proposed and exported structures, norms and policy principles for the EU that were drawn from domestic German practice.
- *Congruence*: institutional export created an 'institutional setting [which] is remarkably familiar and natural for Germany', 'a milieu in which German actors can feel at home'[9] and which reinforced their Europeanised identity.

The Germany of the Federal Republic was one which had shaped 'the regional milieu'[10] in Europe in its own image. It was both deeply embedded in the EU and also 'nested' congenially in a wider European framework. Embeddedness and congeniality both underpinned and expressed the profound role that European integration had played in ensuring the stability of the Federal Republic.

As some of the examples mentioned above suggest, the interaction with the European integration process, which dated from its beginnings in the 1950s, persisted after German unification. The Federal Republic clearly did not conform to the expectations of those scholars who predicted that a post-Cold War international environment, the restoration of full external sovereignty and national unification would produce a more national, assertive and leadership-seeking Germany. In an influential study of the immediate post-unity era, Anderson and Goodman[11] could find no substantial evidence of change in the German approach to European integration, not least because the commitment to European co-operation had become so embedded after 1949 that they felt it was now 'ingrained, even assumed' among German policy-makers.

This continuity – confirmed in a range of other studies[12] – reflected the role of values in driving German European policy. Values rarely change in the short term. However, since 1990 both the internal and external contexts for Germany's engagement with the EU have undergone far-reaching change. United Germany is now more financially stretched, faces tougher economic challenges and has become politically more fractious than the old, pre-1990 Federal Republic. And the EU has taken on a raft of new policy challenges, not least EMU; is widening across the deep economic divide left by the Cold War; and is struggling to find a new institutional configuration capable of responding to these various challenges.

GERMANY AND EUROPE: THE SHIFTING OF TECTONIC PLATES

These are profound changes in the conditions facing policy-makers. A useful metaphor is to envisage German and EU politics as tectonic plates. The default position of tectonic plates is one of stability. However there is an underlying friction as the plates move imperceptibly. Periodically there are more substantial shifts of position – attended by considerable disruption – followed by a new period of re-equilibration and relative stability. To us the tectonic plates of German and EU politics appear to be shifting, opening up a critical juncture for change. Our hypothesis is that at this critical juncture the virtuous circle embedding Germany in a congenial environment of German–EU congruence is beginning to break down, forcing reconsideration of the values which had underpinned German European policy through to the 1990s.

Domestic Change

The major challenge in domestic politics has been economic. There remains a deep economic divide between east and west, and in the east a persistent problem of high unemployment despite a growing productive capacity based in greenfield investment. Some of the traditional core sectors in the west are also confronted with problems of modernisation in the face of transnational competition. The net result is a modest-to-stagnant growth pattern and a high burden of transfer expenditures which have brought with them an extended period of fiscal austerity. There is a sense of challenge to the consensus on the 'German model'[13] reflected in periodic soul-searching about the best properties for *Standort Deutschland* and pressures for deregulation which are less easily finessed in tripartite rounds of business, unions and government.

Public attitudes have become more critical of politics. Important east–west differences have emerged over questions such as the balance of market and state. Both factors have made the relationship between voters and parties more volatile. There are more unpredictable shifts between the major, establishment parties, but also at times away from them as protest parties of various kinds flash into prominence (and, normally, out of it again). There has also been a bifurcation of the party system, with only the CDU and SPD able to maintain a broadly uniform east–west presence. An important, yet often underestimated by-product of these developments has been the partial de-linkage of federal-level party competition from its equivalents in the Länder.[14] The result has been a growing territorialisation of political debate, with individual Länder, or groups of Länder with shared interests, increasingly ready to assert often quite narrow priorities in both domestic and EU politics with less regard than hitherto for the co-operative norms of the German federal system.[15]

The overall pattern is one of a harder-edged, less consensual, more fractious domestic political environment.

European Change

This changed Germany is now playing into a radically changed European context. The Federal Republic clearly did maintain its post-war approach to European co-operation into the post-unity era. The most striking outcome of this was the package agreed with strong German support at Maastricht. However, only now are the hard facts of decisions in principle taken at Maastricht – on EMU, foreign and security policy, and internal security – being realised. EMU was intended as a mechanism to impose German-style monetary rigour on the more profligate members of the Union. In practice it has become an unwelcome constraint on German fiscal policy when it needs to respond to persistent domestic economic malaise. In this instance at least, institutional export has had unexpectedly problematic consequences. Germany was locked into EMU at a disadvantageous DM–Euro rate, which has punished German exports. At the same time, the European Central Bank's policy has favoured fiscal tightness across the Euro area – reflecting pan-European conditions – in a period when high German unemployment would seem to require a looser fiscal policy. The ECB's 'one-size-fits-all' policy is now a problem for all, whereas in the early 1990s the DM-led model was imposed on all others, who had to adjust to German needs.

Elsewhere, the evolution of the Common Foreign and Security Policy and the addition of a European defence identity have challenged the inherited reservations about the use of military force on the part of the German 'civilian power'.[16] The controversies over the German position on the prospect of US-led military action against Iraq in 2002–3 reveal the acute tensions caused by the clash of historical memory and new demands for Germany to take on international 'responsibility'. And evolving European internal security policy has become highly politicised domestically amid concerns over economic migration from the east and burden-sharing on questions of asylum. More recently, international terrorism – not least the location in Germany of some of the groups involved in the 11 September 2001 attacks – has intensified German concerns that European-level justice and home affairs policy does not meet German requirements.

Eastern enlargement of the EU is, though, perhaps the biggest problem for Germany in the post-Maastricht EU. In the early 1990s, enlargement was self-evidently – in the abstract – a positive by-product of the end of the Cold War. But as the date of enlargement has neared, its concrete implications have begun to become visible. Enlargement is now perceived as a grave competitive challenge which German actors – especially those with interests close to the enlargement border – have sought to deflect or postpone through restrictions on the free movement of labour and on the extension of the single market in certain sectors. Notable here have been the protectionist impulses of the Länder. The Länder won new rights of input into German EU policy-making as a by-product of the Maastricht negotiations. They have increasingly used those rights to lobby for the protection of regional economic interests in the enlargement process[17] and, on a broader front, to claim a stake in the post-Nice debate on the future constitution of Europe.[18]

Enlargement also challenges inherited commitments in the Community *acquis*, such as the common agricultural and cohesion policies. These are policies that have traditionally been funded in large part by the German 'paymaster'. Without substantial policy reform enlargement will further increase the costs of those policies and by implication the burdens on the German budget. In a situation of domestic fiscal tightness – and after a decade in which the German contribution to the stabilisation of its Central and East European and Russian 'near abroad' has been immensely costly – this is not a congenial prospect. Others, for example at the 1999 Cologne Summit, still seem to view Germany as the classic broker of new steps of integration, made easier by German 'side-payments'.[19] This clash of expectations remains unresolved and is set to reappear as member states gear up for the 'Agenda 2007' debate on the EU budget.

In addition, the EU has continued to pursue a liberalising agenda beyond
the core achievements of the 1992 Single Market programme. The Single
Market programme was clearly congenial to Germany, especially when it
was combined with a standard-setting regime that strongly favours German
manufacturing sectors. But where market liberalisation has impacted on
service sectors – traditionally insulated in Germany from international
competition – it has brought the EU increasingly into conflict with German
economic interests. While the EU was earlier seen to be an overwhelming
positive force when it opened up other states' markets – one of the
foundations of German post-war recovery and consolidation – it is much
less welcome when it acts to open up protected German markets or limit the
scope of state economic intervention.[20]

A number of points of conflict have as a result emerged: on state aids to
industry; on the role of the *Landesbanken* in dispensing subsidised finance
to businesses in the regions; on public procurement procedures; on financial
markets, the organisation of the professions, and mergers and acquisitions
policies. The deterioration of relations between Germany and the European
Commission's Directorate General for Competition has been especially
striking. German unification is part of the story here. The enduring
problems of restructuring the East German economy have led the eastern
Länder persistently to test the limits of the EU state aids regime. But also in
the western economic heartland the Länder governments frequently and the
federal government more intermittently have sought opportunities to protect
and subsidise in the face of globalisation and associated pressures. As a
result, EU-level competence to make decisions about state aids has become
bitterly contested.

Liberalisation, in other words, now begins to hurt. It does so all the more
as it reveals through more open and transparent inter-state competition the
high non-wage costs attached to the German social state. These are not by
any means the highest in the EU. However, the failure earlier to export more
of the social dimension of the German model to Europe has exposed the
disadvantages of high levels of social provision, in part because of the wider
resource crunch caused by unification, in part because other member states
with a less comprehensive social policy – in particular the UK – have
pressed their alternative approaches increasingly strongly in EU debates.
High levels of social provision are essential components of the long-term
social compacts which we identified as the foundation of the stability of the
Federal Republic. EU-wide competitive pressures to reduce non-wage
labour costs clash with the historical foundations of domestic consensus.

The Grinding Plates

The German and European tectonic plates are, amid much subterranean grinding, clearly shifting position. The new tenor of domestic politics has had an impact on public attitudes to Europe. Initially analysts were struck by the limited nature of domestic change after unification. It had been feared that citizens in the five new Länder would not share the prevailing European consensus, but in the immediate post-unity period pro-European sentiments scarcely differed between west and east. From the mid-1990s, however, this has changed considerably. Generalised support for European integration has continued to fall, although in comparative terms it remains high in some policy areas, notably that of defence and security policy. This has reduced the 'wiggle room' for German policy actors, who can no longer rely on a permissive consensus in public opinion to allow them leeway in EU politics.

Among policy actors European integration has become more contested, in part as a result of shifts in public opinion and in part because key integration issues, especially enlargement, pose threats to territorial or group interests. The growing incongruence of those interests with the trajectory of EU policies has led policy actors to bridge elite–mass gaps and move closer to the concerns of affected constituencies. More generally, the long-term problems of the state of public finances have undermined both the capacity and the will of the Federal Republic to make the side-payments which were such a marked feature of the Kohl years. The increasingly assertive role of the Finance Ministry in EU affairs – which has grown through the various stages of EMU – has stiffened the post-unification resolve no longer to act as paymaster. Put simply, the costs of unification have consumed resources that might have been devoted to Europe.

Domestic political dynamics have in these ways clearly shaped a new German European politics. In some areas, the EU is still a self-evident arena for the pursuit of German interests, notably in the Second and Third Pillars of the EU (Germany is keen to maintain an Europeanised framework for its new military role; and Germany cannot keep full control over its numerous borders). Otherwise European policy is more and more constrained by domestic considerations. Old commitments have become hedged by new conditionalities, especially where domestic economic interests or budgetary questions are concerned. A new sense of calculation of cost and benefit – often designed to appeal back to domestic audiences – increasingly underlies German European policy thinking.

COST AND BENEFIT IN GERMANY'S NEW EUROPEAN DIPLOMACY

The emphasis on cost and benefit first emerged in the mid-1990s under the chancellorship of Helmut Kohl. It was pursued with greater consistency following the election of the SPD–Green coalition in 1998 under Gerhard Schröder. Schröder launched his chancellorship amid a flurry of path-breaking public statements. Under him, 'Germany standing up for its national interests will be just as natural as France or Britain standing up for theirs'.[21] One particular national interest was the German contribution to the EU budget: 'the Germans pay more than half the contributions which are frittered away in Europe'.[22] The implication that Germany needed to do more to protect its interests against its profligate and self-serving partners pervaded the early part of the Schröder chancellorship. It was reflected in:

• The (unsuccessful) attempt during the German EU Presidency in the first half of 1999 to rein in the German contribution to the EU budget negotiations by getting other states to contribute more (Britain via a cancellation of its rebate, France through a partial renationalisation of the Common Agricultural Policy, Spain by new limits on cohesion funding).
• The periodic attempt to suggest that progress on EU enlargement was conditional on progress on the Agenda 2000: 'The sooner the European Union gets to grips with the necessary reforms, the more quickly and smoothly the enlargement process will move on.'[23]

Elsewhere we have called this tendency a 'yes, but …' politics of European integration[24] which combines a reiterated commitment to the broader integration project with the application of conditions designed to soften the impact of integration on German interests. Further examples of this conditionality include:

• The insistence on the appointment of Günther Verheugen to the position of EU Commissioner for enlargement questions, that is, in an area of direct, national interest to Germany.
• The dogged attempts of German federal ministries, Länder and private sector interests to defend their 'possessions'[25] in the enlargement negotiations on such issues as border controls, environmental standards, 'social dumping', transitional structural aid, and the free movement of labour.
• Protectionism I: the attempts of firms and the Länder in which they are based or plan to locate to evade EU subsidy controls ('the right to protect

jobs through subsidies', as Bavarian Minister-President Edmund Stoiber put it in relation to the 1996 VW subsidy controversy in Saxony[26]).

- Protectionism II: the attempts of the Länder to re-designate various subsidised regional services as *öffentliche Daseinsvorsorge* ('essential public provision'), again to evade EU subsidy controls.
- Protectionism III: the role of Schröder in 1998–99 in overturning the implementation of a European directive on the recycling of cars at the end of their lives (against the wishes of his own environment minister), after successful lobbying by German car manufacturers.
- The role of various federal ministries (drawing support in part from the Länder) in vetoing moves to qualified majority voting in their fields of interest at the Amsterdam summit in 1996.[27]
- The concern at the 2000 Nice Summit that institutional reforms should ensure that Germany retained national 'weight' in the post-enlargement union.
- The debate pushed in the post-Nice process (in effect a replay of the Agenda 2000 issue) by several of the Länder, the SPD and the CSU to restrict and in part renationalise European competence especially in the fields of agriculture, regional policy and subsidy controls.

A further indication of this more calculated and conditional approach to Europe has been in Germany's partnership policy. For a number of reasons developments in the 1990s have led to a qualification of the commitment to Franco-German partnership, most obviously the shift of gravity of the EU to the east as enlargement approaches. The result has been a lesser sense of unchallenged exclusivity surrounding the Franco-German relationship. Though the centrality of that relationship is ritually reaffirmed and dramatised in flamboyant public statements, Franco-German relations have increasingly lost substance; the tendency is one towards a more contingent alliance strategy (a 'multiple bilateralism'[28]) in which Germany joins or creates issue coalitions on an *ad hoc* basis. While the debates in the European Convention may have brought a renewed focus on Franco-German joint initiative, the new logic of diversity is likely to be further embedded as enlargement is realised, and the Franco-German relationship is unlikely to be the vehicle for coalition-building and collective action that it was in a smaller, less complex EU. This point was dramatically demonstrated in the 'letter of eight' heads of government in January 2003, which rejected the Franco-German declaration on transatlantic relations and on the prospect of war on Iraq.

Two conclusions arise from this discussion. First, this cost–benefit German approach to Europe is largely a product of domestic circumstance.

It reflects a process of externalisation of the harder-edged domestic politics that have emerged since unification. That process has been reinforced by the fuller role a cost-conscious Finance Ministry now plays – in place of the integration-oriented Economics Ministry – in co-ordinating German EU policy. The downgrading of the Economics Ministry in European affairs after 1998 has allowed its overriding commitment to opening up competition to be challenged by particular sectoral interests. Similarly, key actors in federal government, the Länder and the private sector are seeking to respond to the heightened sense of distributional and territorial interests that has emerged among their constituencies since unification. Policy actors need to be seen to be protecting domestic interests; the old permissive consensus on Europe is now gone.

Second, the examples above relate to the activities of a large set of actors: individual federal ministries, various Länder and private sector actors. These do not act with any sustained sense of common purpose and institutional pluralism is alive and well. Reforms in recent years to the co-ordination machinery in the German federal government have not strengthened its capacity for concerted action.[29] There is still – and can be – no German grand strategy on Europe, but rather an accumulation of ill co-ordinated sectoral and institutional positions. The differences are that these positions are typically harder and more narrowly defined around calculations of national cost and benefit than they were ten years ago;[30] and that they are justified in the stance of a chancellor who has committed himself to a clearer identification and robust defence of German interests. The likelihood is that Chancellor Schröder – as has been typical for chancellors in their second term – will try to take on a more prominent role and place himself as a reference point and a broker for making institutional interests count, although the success of the Greens in delivering the wafer-thin coalition majority in the 2002 federal election allowed Foreign Minister Joschka Fischer to fend off Schröder's attempt to centralise EU policy co-ordination in the Chancellor's Office.

CHANGING EUROPEAN VALUES?

The fact that a range of actors engaged in European policy are individually moving towards a more instrumental approach suggests there is a common understanding of Germany's new role in a changing Europe. There is some indication in this of a value shift, a changed normative sense of how it is that Germany should engage with Europe. We suggested earlier that the drifting apart of the tectonic plates of Germany and Europe had opened up a critical juncture in which value change was possible. Such change is all the more likely to happen if 'transformational actors'[31] make and disseminate effectively an argument for change. The baseline for evaluating change in values on Europe is provided by Helmut Kohl. Through to 1998, he articulated a vigorous case for a set of values on Europe honed in the 1950s, in the period when the beginnings of European integration provided a context for the stabilisation and consolidation of the West German state. Kohl's history-laden narratives dominated the field in setting out what Germany should do in Europe. However, behind his 'smothering veil of rhetoric on continuity, the new challenges posed by post-1990 changes were being digested by Germany's pluralistic EU policy-making machinery, with new ideas of what Germany should do being formed and, gradually, expressed'.[32] Three transformational actors, representing a new generation of political leadership, emerged as especially significant after Kohl's departure:

- *Gerhard Schröder* has most clearly articulated the 'contingent' Europeanism discussed in the last section and has made respectable the expression of *national* interest. His personal association with the *Leitantrag* on Europe tabled at the SPD's party congress in 2001 gives clear expression to this more national view of Europe. Though in part proposing the strengthening of the supranational institutions of the EU, the *Leitantrag* also focuses on the delimitation of European competence, the renationalisation of competences in some fields, and a strong endorsement of the open method of co-ordination.[33] The latter is based not on the traditional Community method but on the European Council and leaves a far greater degree of discretion to national authorities. The stronger national focus in Schröder's view has qualified the centrality of the Franco-German relationship and underlined the shift towards a 'multiple bilateralism'. A key feature of this has been periodic closeness to the UK under Prime Minister Blair.

- *Joschka Fischer*, Schröder's foreign minister, has by contrast set out a modernised version of Kohl's narrative. On the one hand this has promoted policy change by using German history to justify – rather than prevent – a renewed German military capacity. On the other it has perpetuated the vision (as expressed in Fischer's Humboldt speech) of European federation and of a Franco-German *avant-garde*, a *Gravitationszentrum* of states committed to a maximal view of integration who would press ahead if necessary as a small, pioneering core. The Fischer vision – reminiscent of the Kohl-era Schäuble–Lamers paper – is, therefore, in part dissonant with that of Schröder. Fischer's membership in the European Convention – another prize arising from the Greens' strong showing in the 2002 federal election – has ensured a prominent platform for that vision.

- *Edmund Stoiber*, minister-president of Bavaria and unsuccessful CDU/CSU chancellor candidate in the 2002 Bundestag election, pronounced Kohl's Europeanism anachronistic as early as 1993.[34] Since then Stoiber and his Bavarian government have pursued with persistence a vision of European integration which is more decentralised, less interventionist and more respectful of national and regional autonomy.

A major research project in Germany has recently reported on how far significant change has filtered through in German European policy.[35] Its broad finding is that a continuity of inherited fundamental values (the Fischer position) co-exists with a growing tendency to make short-term calculations of cost and benefit (the Schröder position). On Stoiber there is barely a comment in a book of 864 pages.[36] This could have been extremely unfortunate had Stoiber won the 2002 election. Our view is that this is unfortunate *even though* he did not win, as the kind of position on Europe represented by Stoiber is now being articulated by a wider range of actors. The Stoiber vision of a rolled back European Union may have been overlooked because of its Bavarian origins. Bavarian ideas are at times not taken seriously enough by observers because so many of them dislike Bavarian politics or dismiss it as a form of narrow provincialism. But preconceptions about Bavaria should not lead to an underestimation of the Bavarian role in propagating new ways of thinking about the EU.

Bavarian thinking is about a rebalanced European federalism. It does not question the fundamental desirability of European integration. On the contrary, the Bavarian view can allow for further competences to be transferred to the European level (for example, on internal security) and even for a strengthening of supranational institutions. At the same time, though, those institutions would be much more tightly circumscribed by legal-constitutional limits to their scope of action. Moreover, there would be a tighter ring-fencing of national competence vs. European intervention combined with renationalisation of competences in agriculture, regional policy and subsidy controls.

This Bavarian position is arguably now the centre of gravity in German European debate (and the Fischer position the outlier). This does not imply that others necessarily support Stoiber, but rather that there has been a convergence of views on a recalibrated Euro-federalism. This certainly includes Schröder and the SPD; Schröder's *Leitantrag* to the SPD party congress in 2001[37] is remarkably similar to Bavarian policy papers from several years earlier on questions of renationalisation. The recent Schäuble–Bocklet paper[38] extends the Stoiber view to the wider CDU/CSU. Other prominents in the German Länder have also reiterated it, including former SPD Minister-Presidents Sigmar Gabriel[39] and Wolfgang Clement.[40] Clement has gone further than anyone else in setting out what a recalibrated Euro-federalism would look like – and in reaffirming that this would be a federalism with more tightly constrained European competence and more autonomy for the member states.

CONCLUSIONS: GERMANY AND THE RESHAPING OF EUROPE

The weight of views on a 'rolled back' Europe suggests to us that a value change is under way. It reflects and confirms that the virtuous circle of German–EU congruence which Bulmer and others identified has broken down. From the mid-1990s there was a shift that set the German and European tectonic plates apart from one another. From then the dynamics of German domestic politics were increasingly shaped by narrow sectional and territorial interests concerned about growing competition and market liberalisation, and by a resource crunch bequeathed by unification. In these circumstances a changing, more demanding Europe increasingly became a problem for Germany and was increasingly called so by a new generation of political leaders. Institutional export was succeeded by externalisation of hard-edged domestic interest politics in German European policy. The new German–EU *incongruence* led to a re-evaluation and recasting of traditional European values to incorporate greater emphasis on national interests and autonomy. Where Germany earlier shaped Europe in its own image, it is now trying to reshape Europe to hold it more at arm's length.

The trajectory is for Europe to be less congenial for Germany, and for Germany to be less embedded in European structures. This is not to suggest a future of German and European instability. The growing focus on costs and benefits and changing values of Europe are both attempts to rebalance Euro-federalism and create a new, different framework in which a different Germany can continue to feel at home. Policy shifts are part of a strategy to establish a new equilibrium between the tectonic plates of Germany and Europe and to restabilise Germany's relationship to the EU. In all of this there remains an underlying commitment to European co-operation as Germany lacks both the values and the institutional structures to pursue a unilateral strategy. It seems likely that Chancellor Schröder will play a key role in arbitrating between inherited but changing values and the pursuit of national interests. Existing and future member states will need to play their part in the process of re-equilibriation as they must learn to concede Germany more benefits and to rely less on (Franco)-Germany to drive and pay for further integration.

NOTES

1. G. Smith, 'The State Without a Centre', in G. Smith *et al.* (eds.), *Developments in German Politics* (London: Macmillan 1992).
2. G. Smith, 'West Germany and the Politics of Centrality', *Government and Opposition* 11 (1976), pp.387–407.
3. S. Bulmer and W. Paterson, *The Federal Republic of Germany and the European Community* (London: Allen & Unwin 1987), p.7.
4. W. Paterson, 'Muß Europa Angst vor Deutschland haben?', in R. Hrbek (ed.), *Der Vertrag von Maastricht in der wissenschaftlichen Kontroverse* (Baden-Baden: Nomos 1993).
5. S. Bulmer, 'Shaping the Rules? The Constitutive Politics of the European Union and German Power', in P. Katzenstein (ed.), *Tamed Power. Germany in Europe* (Ithaca: Cornell University Press 1997), p.73.
6. Cf. C. Jeffery and W. Paterson, 'Germany's Power in Europe', in H. Wallace (ed.), *Interlocking Dimensions of European Integration* (Basingstoke: Palgrave 2001).
7. S. Bulmer, C. Jeffery and W. Paterson, *Germany's European Diplomacy. Shaping the Regional Milieu* (Manchester: Manchester University Press 2000), pp.40–47.
8. Bulmer, 'Shaping the Rules?'.
9. P. Katzenstein, 'United Germany in a Unifying Europe', in Katzenstein (ed.), *Tamed Power*, pp.40–41.
10. Bulmer *et al.*, *Germany's European Diplomacy*.
11. J. Anderson and J. Goodman, 'Mars or Minerva? A United Germany in a Post-Cold War Europe', in R. Keohane, J. Nye and S. Hoffmann (eds.), *After the Cold War: International Institutions and State Strategies in Europe, 1989–1991* (Cambridge, MA: Harvard University Press 1993).
12. E.g. V. Rittberger *et al.*, *German Foreign Policy since Unification. An Analysis of Foreign Policy Continuity and Change* (Manchester: Manchester University Press 2001); Katzenstein (ed.), *Tamed Power*; S. Harnisch and H. Maull (eds.), *Germany as a Civilian Power* (Manchester: Manchester University Press, 2001).
13. R. Harding and W. Paterson (eds.), *The Future of the German Economy. An End to the Miracle?* (Manchester: Manchester University Press 2000).
14. C. Jeffery and D. Hough, 'The Electoral Cycle and Multi-Level Voting in Germany', *German Politics* 10 (2001), pp.86–93.
15. C. Jeffery, 'German Federalism from Cooperation to Competition', in M. Umbach (ed.), *German Federalism Past, Present and Future* (Basingstoke: Palgrave 2002).
16. H. Maull, 'Germany and Japan: The New Civilian Powers', *Foreign Affairs* 69/5 (1990), pp.91–106.
17. E.g. *Hofer 20-Punkte Katalog zur EU-Erweiterung*, Entschliessung der 2. Konferenz der EU-Grenzregionen am 24.–25. Juli 1998 in Hof, Munich, Bayerische Staatskanzlei.
18. Cf. U. Leonardy, *Europäische Kompetenzabgrenzung als Verfassungspostulat* (Baden-Baden: Nomos 2002), pp.236–326.
19. C. Jeffery and V. Handl, 'Germany and Europe after Kohl: Between Social Democracy and Normalisation', *German Studies Review* 24 (2001), pp.55–82.
20. It is highly significant in this respect that the Schröder government's flirtation with a Blairite, 'third way' agenda for the EU was so fleeting, and so quickly swept away in 1999 when jobs

were threatened by the Vodafone takeover of Mannesmann and the collapse of the Holzmann building concern. See C. Jeffery and V. Handl, 'Blair, Schröder and the Third Way', in L. Funk (ed.), *The Economics and Politics of the Third Way* (Hamburg: LIT Verlag 1999).
21. *Financial Times*, 10 Nov. 1998.
22. G. Langguth, 'Ein sozialistisches Europa? Ist die These "vom Ende des sozialdemokratischen Jahrzehnts" widerlegt?', *Politische Studien* 50 (1999), p.55.
23. G. Verheugen, 'Deutschland und die EU-Ratspräsidentschaft: Erwartungen und Realitäten', *Integration* 22 (1999).
24. Jeffery and Paterson, 'Germany's Power in Europe'.
25. 'Besitzstände'; see B. Lippert, 'Die Erweiterungspolitik der Europäischen Union', in W. Weidenfeld and W. Wessels (eds.), *Jahrbuch der Europäischen Integration 1997/98* (Bonn: Europa Union Verlag, 1998), p.38.
26. Quoted in *Focus*, 12 Aug. 1996, p.37.
27. Bulmer *et al.*, *Germany's European Diplomacy*, pp.83–4.
28. See W. Paterson, 'Britain and the Berlin Republic', *German Politics* 10 (2001), pp.201–24.
29. S. Bulmer, A. Maurer and W. Paterson, 'The European Policy-Making Machinery in the Berlin Republic: Hindrance or Handmaiden?' *German Politics* 10/1 (2001), pp.177–206.
30. See J. Anderson, *German Unification and the Union of Europe* (Cambridge: Cambridge University Press, 1999).
31. P. Cerny, 'Political Agency in a Globalising World. Towards a Structurational Approach', *European Journal of International Relations* 6 (2000), pp.435–63.
32. A. Hyde-Price and C. Jeffery, 'Germany in the European Union: Constructing Normality', *Journal of Common Market Studies* 39 (2001), p.697.
33. SPD, 'Keynote Proposal: Responsibility for Europe', Draft, National Conference of the Social Democratic Party of Germany (2001), at www.spd.de/english/politics/partycongress/europe.html.
34. *Süddeutsche Zeitung*, 2 Nov. 1993.
35. H. Schneider, M. Jopp and U. Schmalz (eds.), *Eine neue deutsche Europapolitik?* (Bonn: Europa Union Verlag 2001).
36. Cf. C. Jeffery, 'Auf den Spuren einer neuen deutschen Europapolitik', *Integration* 25/3 (2002), pp.244–8.
37. SPD, 'Keynote Proposal: Responsibility for Europe'.
38. W. Schäuble and R. Bocklet, 'Vorschläge von CDU und CSU für einen Europäischen Verfassungsvertrag' (manuscript, 2001).
39. S. Gabriel, 'Thesen von Ministerpräsident Gabriel für die politische und verfassungsrechtliche Struktur einer künftigen erweiterten Europäischen Union' (Hannover, Niedersächsische Staatskanzlei 2001).
40. W. Clement, 'Europa gestalten – nicht verwalten. Die Kompetenzordnung der Europäischen Union nach Nizza', *Forum De Constitutionis Europae* FCE 3/01 (2001).

PART II

LABOUR MARKETS, LIFE STYLES AND
POLITICAL PREFERENCES

New Ways of Life or Old Rigidities? Changes in Social Structures and Life Courses and their Political Impact

KARL ULRICH MAYER and STEFFEN HILLMERT

According to widely shared views, there have been profound discontinuities in the social structures of advanced societies during the last several decades. To mention but a few: the expansion of the service sector, technological advances and trans-national markets have reshaped the occupational structure; women have demanded and gained access to education and careers and have revolutionised the small worlds of families and the large world of demography; the inflow of migrant workers has dissolved local communities and created new ones.

Germany is no exception to these trends, but it is also a special case. Among other things, it underwent severe disruptions during and after the Second World War, including division into two states and their re-unification. Germany is also special in the sense that, up until the 1980s, it enjoyed a remarkable quality as a 'stable state' – a model case of high economic competitiveness, low industrial conflict, high levels of social protection, successful neo-corporatist co-ordination and political gradualism within a political framework of checks and balances. This German distinctiveness is now in question.

This study traces major changes in social structure over a period of roughly the last four decades. In particular, it will portray developments in the areas of population, the family, education, labour markets, class structures and life-course patterns. The aim is mainly to provide descriptive background information for the political processes that will be analysed in greater detail in other contributions to this volume. However, some analytical issues cannot be avoided. These include whether distinctions between historical periods that may be compelling for the political arena have counterparts in the social structure; what kind of social-structural changes have defined the political agenda and triggered political responses; and to what extent observed changes in social structures must themselves be understood as (intended or unintended) political outcomes. The second and major section of this article will address the empirical task, and the third section will tackle some analytical issues.

Let us begin with a description of the major social structures and life-course patterns prevailing in the two decades before and after 1980, respectively. These periods roughly correspond to government coalitions influenced or dominated by the Social Democrats (1966–82) and the Christian Democrats (1982–98). We will present two slightly different kinds of mappings. The first follows the conventional concept of social structure, that is, static distributions of social positions in various institutional settings as cross-sections of the population (see Tables 1 and 3). The second is aimed at the dynamic character of the various domains of the life course and is focused on the birth cohorts that experienced important transitions in their lives during these two periods (see Tables 2 and 4). As will become apparent, these perspectives complement each other. The summary descriptions in Tables 1 and 2 should be understood as 'stylised facts'. Where available, these are further backed up by empirical evidence (see Tables 3 and 4 and references in the text).

The 'Golden Age': The 1960s and 1970s

Demography, gender and family. The social structures in the first of the two periods is shown in column 2 of Table 1. As far as demographics are concerned, with the building of the Berlin Wall in 1961, the steady influx of East Germans into West Germany came to an end (3.8 million from 1950 to 1961).[1] During the 1960s, these people still had to find their way in the west.[2] Together with the inflow of foreign workers and their families, which continued throughout this period (1960: 0.32 million, 1980: 0.63 million), this contributed to positive population growth until 1973.[3] Population size, however, was most affected by the post-war baby boom, which started about 1957 and ended in 1966, with a peak in 1964 of 1.08 million new births. The baby boom was an echo effect of the large cohorts born around 1940, but also a consequence of early marriage and early first births. It can be seen as an expression of optimistic expectations based on high rates of economic growth. As a result, demographic discontinuities heavily affected the opportunities of young people moving from school to the labour market.

At least until the early and middle 1970s, this was a period when traditional family values prevailed. Women were almost universally engaged in gainful employment before marriage and the birth of the first

TABLE 1

SOCIAL STRUCTURES IN GERMANY IN THE
1960s–1970s AND THE 1980s–1990s

	1960s–1970s	1980s–1990s
Demography		
Population dynamics	Baby boom and fertility decline, beginning immigration	Population aging, fertility decline, immigration
Family	Almost universal marriage	Non-marital unions, pluralisation of family forms, legal recognition of non-heterosexual unions
Citizenship, national integration	Homogeneous	Immigration without assimilation, East/West cleavages
Education		
Qualifications and skills	Highly stratified education system, dual system of vocational training, educational expansion	Only modest educational inflation
Labour market		
Occupational structure	Upgrading, de-ruralisation, skilled industrial workers, expansion of white-collar work and qualified public service	IT-revolution, flexible and precarious work increases moderately
Labour markets	Segmented and segregated, high level of secure employment	High level of structural unemployment
Union organisation	High level of union membership	Decline of union membership
Income inequality	Stable and decreasing	Stable or increasing
Women	Gender division of labour within households	Increasing participation of women in the labour market
Social classes and social security		
Class structure	Middle class integration, status distinctions, rise of welfare state clientele, integrated social milieus	Increasing salience of cultural capital, social milieus heterogeneous by age and lifestyle
Voting behaviour	Stable normal class vote cross-cut by religious cleavage	Rise of new politics (Green party) and regional party (PDS), decreasing electoral participation
Social security	Expanding entitlements, universal coverage, old age poverty	Increasing contributions, declining entitlements, introduction of private insurance component
Social and political exclusion	Unskilled, small farmers	Immigrant workers, labour market outsiders

child, but labour force participation of married women was still low, intermittent and often part-time.[4] The women's movement and the student rebellion opened up a debate on the traditional family, but this started to have behavioural consequences only for younger women and men who were in their family formation phase after 1970. Gender relations were dominated by the division of labour and imbalance of power within households, families and partnerships, big differences in educational attainment, and a strong segregation between women and men with regard to vocational training, occupations and rank in firms.

Education. Education and training were characterised by the traditional institutions of a tripartite school system, the dual system of vocational training and a growing tertiary sector. Institutional reforms were often half-hearted due to conflicts between CDU/CSU and SPD-governed Länder – for example, over comprehensive secondary schools, comprehensive institutions of higher education, the establishment of the *Fachhochschulen* (polytechnics) as a second tier of higher education and the reform of vocational training (1969). However, participation grew rapidly at all secondary and tertiary levels, to the benefit of rural areas, women, Catholics and the middle and lower social classes. Human resource requirements after the 'Sputnik Shock', unequal opportunities and demographic pressures all contributed to massive educational expansion. Nevertheless, it should be noted that the modal qualification for German males was still compulsory school plus a craft or industrial apprenticeship, while for females it was compulsory schooling without an apprenticeship. Less than six per cent of the adult population had an advanced degree, but more than half had obtained either a vocational or a professional qualification.

Labour market. Labour markets in the 1960s and 1970s were marked by increasing numbers of jobs, low levels of unemployment, and shortages rather than a surplus of labour. Education, training and labour markets were closely matched and well co-ordinated. Segmentation lines in the labour markets corresponded to distinctions between the qualification levels of the unskilled and semi-skilled, the skilled manual, non-manual and professional, and between large and small firms.[5] The occupational structure changed rapidly with regard to sector, occupation and firm size. The primary sector was shrinking from 25 per cent (1950) to nine per cent (1970); the tertiary sector increased to 42 per cent in 1970; while industrial employment showed remarkable stability at around 45 per cent, peaking in 1970 at 49 per cent (see also Table 3). In contrast to many other highly industrialised societies, Germany maintained a large amount of mostly skilled employment in production, with an important role for skilled workers.

While many men who were made redundant in the rural sector or in traditional occupations (such as tailors and bakers) faced downward mobility into semi-skilled jobs, many more men with industrial and commercial apprenticeships experienced marked upward mobility into white-collar positions in sales, management and public service. Advances in the real wages of skilled workers were considerable and gave them a growing share in consumption. Still, there were even higher increases in the profits and incomes of the self-employed, and growing militancy in collective bargaining – for example, in the metal industry strikes of 1969. Just as inequality within the group of wage earners decreased, so did the gap between wage earners and the self-employed. Although some academic observers perceived a growing polarisation between skill levels,[6] in fact there was a continuous trend towards occupational upgrading.[7] This was due not least to a massive increase in highly qualified jobs in the public sector.

The linkage between wage incomes and net family incomes was increasingly weakened by transfers distributed via the welfare state – so much so that some observers introduced the notion of 'welfare classes' as social classes whose income was directly or indirectly derived from the public purse.[8] At any rate, to the extent that the proportion of GNP spent on social transfers increased, the welfare state assumed growing significance for both material well-being and socio-political integration. As far as social policy was concerned, the major problem of this period was old-age poverty in women who had not been able to build up sufficient pension entitlements.[9]

Social classes. The major building blocks of the class structure were not difficult to identify. First of all, families rather than individuals were the units exposed to market opportunities and risks of various kinds. While the class cleavage between wage earners and the self-employed persisted, it was modified by the growing importance of joint stock companies. More important, however, were the traditional class distinctions based on skill and qualification. Here, the skilled workers as the quantitatively dominant category, and the academically trained professionals and civil servants as another fairly visible and distinctive group, were complemented by the intermediate classes of manual supervisors, *Meister* and qualified white-collar employees. At the other end of the spectrum were the unskilled and semi-skilled workers. The shrinking category of the farmers was maintained by the public subsidisation of medium sized family farms. Increasing relative gains in earnings and consumption and protective labour legislation enhanced the legal status of manual workers and made actual class differences less visible, thereby reducing conflict potential.[10] Employment in the social services grew to such an extent that it came to be recognised not only as a distinct class and status category, but also as an important carrier of special attitudes and interests. Inter-generational social mobility was widespread due to the shifting occupational structure. On balance, this mobility was upward, although relative mobility distances and probabilities were fairly stable and clearly patterned in a strong hierarchical manner.[11] Except for deficits in access to education, opportunity differences were overwhelmingly perceived as legitimate, since they were seen as being mediated by personal ability and effort.[12]

Although the massive influx of expellees, refugees and foreign workers introduced heterogeneity into formerly tightly knit social milieus and communities, integrated settings still predominated. Here, class, religion and region coincided in defining the boundaries of social networks and made new groups into outsiders who were only barely accepted. The political parties could rely on stable voting blocks defined by class and religious cleavages and connected via the intermediate organisations of trade unions, professional associations and churches.

Life-course patterns. Life-course patterns in the first historical period are shown in the second column of Table 2. Their development in Germany after the Second World War is usually constructed as two phases which roughly coincide with the two periods used here: a phase of institutionalisation and standardisation which lasted until the early 1970s, followed by a phase of de-institutionalisation, pluralisation and de-standardisation. The latter is assumed to continue up to the present with accelerating and accentuating tendencies.[13] When tying life-course patterns to historical periods, one should, however, be aware of a number of complications. Such periods cover different age and birth cohorts. People enter them with life courses shaped by earlier times, such as the pre-war, war and immediate post-war periods. We can assume that period changes should become most visible in differences between cohorts making the transition into adulthood.[14]

If we take the end of schooling and entry into the labour market as boundary transitions, the 1960s and 1970s were the formative years for the cohorts born between the late 1940s and late 1950s. These cohorts profited from the expansion and reform of the educational system. For the first time

TABLE 2

LIFE-COURSE PATTERNS IN GERMANY IN THE 1960–1970s AND THE 1980–1990s

	1960s–1970s	1980s–1990s
Demography		
Family formation and dissolution	Early, universal marriage and childbearing; low divorce rate	Initial non-marital unions, delayed and partial marriage, increasing risk of divorce
Age at leaving home	Decreasing	Increasing
Education		
Education	Persistent inequalities in opportunities	Prolonged, interrupted educational careers; multiple training periods
Age at leaving school/ training	Medium, stratified by qualification	Delayed, high variance
Labour market		
Labour market entry	Early, continuous, low youth unemployment	Delayed, increasing transition difficulties
Working lives	Long firm tenure, occupational stability, upward mobility	Between firm/between occupation mobility, episodes of unemployment
Women's careers	Pre-marriage, pre-birth employment, discontinuous careers	Increasing long-term participation, but mostly part-time
Age at retirement	Low variance at legal ages	Early retirement, high variance
Political alignment		
Political life course	Generational imprinting and continuity	Decreasing life-course political alignment
Social security		
Precarious life-course stages	(Women's) old age poverty	Single mothers, young families with children, early adult marginality

in German history, modal educational trajectories went beyond compulsory schooling and vocational training and showed – for girls as well as boys – a sequential pattern: kindergarten and pre-school, elementary school and secondary school up to *Mittlere Reife* (intermediate leaving certificate) or *Abitur* (higher leaving certificate), followed by vocational training or higher education. At the same time, education became the gateway not only to employment and occupational careers, but to opportunities in the marriage market as well. It also had important effects on fertility behaviour as well as civic and political attitudes. Longer education spells and further education were facilitated by the removal of student fees for secondary schools and universities and the extension of public financial support to students (*Honnefer Modell, BAföG*).

The transitions from schooling to training and from training to first job were swift in their timing and mostly successful due to a good match between training and employment.[15] Youth unemployment was the lowest among all industrialised countries, because apprenticeships served as an efficient bridge into working life.[16] The occupational careers of men were characterised by continuous employment, permanent work contracts, long firm tenure, occupational stability, upward career mobility and progressive real-wage trajectories. Expansion of the higher salary groups of the civil service opened up career opportunities for middle-aged civil servants and employees, but opportunities for university graduates were declining in the second half of the 1970s. Women extended their employment beyond marriage until the birth of the first or second child, but re-entered only partially after their childcare phase. The welfare state guaranteed wage replacement in case of illness, provided for paid maternity leave and introduced subsidised parental leave. Pensions were tied to net real wages and the pension system standardised the legal retirement age and offered high replacement rates. The public and private sectors – especially larger firms – and manual and non-manual labour markets converged in regard to employment protection, sick leave and paid vacation. Since sectoral, qualificational and occupational restructuring was mainly achieved through exits and new entries rather than by reallocation of workers, opportunities for labour market entry and careers were generally good.

Age at marriage and at first birth dropped and the number of children per family increased with a sharp reversal in both nuptuality and fertility in the first half of the 1970s. Divorce rates were low by international standards and in comparison to the immediate post-war period. In addition to a good job and a family, home ownership became an important and increasingly realistic life goal, subsidised and encouraged by loans and tax regulations.[17]

Up until the mid-1960s, life courses tended to become more orderly, continuous, differentiated in their sequential patterns and more standardised in regard to the age grading of important life transitions.[18] In the eyes of some observers, the standardisation and institutionalisation of the life course replaced the class structure as the most salient social structure.[19] The subjective significance of the life-course regime underwent a marked change. For the older cohorts, their subjective biography meant material progress as a contrast to the dire conditions just after the war – but also conformity to traditional roles in the economy and the family. Social identities were well defined and stable, deviant behaviour such as having illegitimate children was consensually identified and sanctioned. For the cohorts born after around 1955, material security began to be taken for granted. As a result, the quality of work and of life in general became more valued. Behavioural norms underwent remarkable changes: the acceptance of premarital sex, the rise of non-marital unions, delayed age at marriage and first birth, declining fertility and increasing divorce rates indicated a new sense of the value of the individual and his or her autonomy.[20]

New Challenges: The 1980s and 1990s

The previous section described the social structures of a period which is often termed the 'Fordist regulation regime',[21] the 'Golden Age'[22] or an 'exceptional period of prosperity'.[23] If there was a 'Golden Age' for Germany, however, it was amazingly short. Its onset was delayed by the enduring impact of the Second World War and the long era of the Adenauer government, and it was cut short by the first oil shock of 1973. Nevertheless, as a social-institutional model it extended well into the 1980s. What has changed in German social structures in the 1980s and 1990s in comparison with the two previous decades (Table 1, column 3)? Above all, unification. By merging west and east, Germany has become more Protestant and atheist, more elderly (as a result of early retirement), more unequal in income distribution and more dependent on the welfare state. For the purposes of this discussion, we will concentrate on West Germany and West Berlin for the 1980s and on the united Germany for the 1990s.

Demography, gender and family. With regard to population dynamics, demographic ageing was both a fact and a topic of public debate in the 1980s and 1990s. Continuous low fertility and higher than expected rises in longevity increased the proportion of elderly in the population. With an actual retirement age of around 60,[24] forced retirement in the east after unification beginning with age 54, and an actual age at labour market entry of 22, the relationship between social security contributors and dependants begun to deteriorate. The proportion of those 60 years and older changed from 20 per cent in 1971 to 23 per cent in 2000 for the whole of Germany, and is expected to rise to 29 per cent in 2020 and to 36 per cent in 2050. The old age dependency ratio, defined as the proportion of people aged 60 and older to those aged 20–59, rose from 40 per cent in 1971 to only 41 per cent in 2000, but it is expected to rise to 53 per cent in 2020 and to 75 per cent in 2050. Demographic ageing spurred debates on the financing of the pension system, leading to increased contributions and the introduction of a supplementary private insurance programme in a formerly pure pay-as-you-go system.

The population grew from 61.7 million in 1980 to 66.7 million in 1998 in the west, and from 78.4 to 82.0 million in Germany as a whole[25] due to influx of migrant workers and their families, East Europeans of German descent (2.5 million between 1988 and 1998), citizens of European Union countries – and of course, most significantly, the incorporation of 16 million East Germans. Another several hundred thousand persons are probably working in Germany illegally. Lack of public support for childcare – but also changed gender relations – go a long way in explaining the continuous decline in fertility. In East Germany, the number of first births halved after unification and has come back up only slowly. As of the present, the former eastern level has not been recaptured, and even the West German level has been reduced.[26]

With regard to private life, the experiments and exceptions of the 1970s became the new standard. This has been the case for non-marital unions, which have become an accepted stage before marriage. Marriage is now contemplated when the first child arrives or is wanted. Some observers speak of a dualisation of family behaviour: one part of the population aiming at families with two children; the other, growing, part not wanting any children at all.[27] Lifelong childlessness is now estimated to have risen above one-fifth of all women. Divorce rates have been increasing continuously. However, there is more continuity than is usually apparent. About four-fifths of all children still grow up with a father and mother and at least one sibling.

Education. The qualification structure in terms of educational distribution shifted massively upwards between 1980 and the turn of the century. While the shift towards secondary education continued, enrolment in higher education fell back in the 1980s – both in absolute numbers and in proportions of cohort or of those with *Abitur* – and then rallied in the 1990s.[28] Women have overtaken men in their share of general education and have greatly increased their mean occupational qualifications. The PISA study demonstrated major deficits in educational outcomes. Even the upper segments of the highly stratified school system performed poorly in international comparisons. Thus, Germany may well lose its century-old distinction as one of the most educationally competent nations. A growing element has been that of further training after the start of the occupational career,[29] but this has remained confined to a period of a few years up to about age 35. Continuing education has served to reinforce educational advantages rather than to compensate for educational deficits.[30] The segregation between male and female vocational training has persisted in regard to both institutions (dual apprenticeships vs. vocational schools) and occupations. There was a noticeable shift towards service occupations, and new training occupations were developed – but in comparison to demand, far too many young men were still being trained in industrial occupations.[31] Following the business cycle, the middle of the 1980s, the early 1990s and the most recent years were difficult times, both for access to vocational training and for entry into the labour market. The dual system of training came under considerable pressure due to the declining willingness of employers to offer training places. Whether educational returns declined or actually increased remains controversial.[32]

Labour market. With regard to sectoral dynamics and occupational structures, shift analyses show that the rate of change was clearly higher in this historical period. This was partly due to the reorganisation of firms where many industrial services (information services, financial services, training) were out-sourced. Services now comprised the largest share of the labour force with 45 per cent. Despite considerable shrinkage and out-migration of industrial production, this was still higher than in comparable nations.[33] East Germany, of course, suffered a huge loss of industrial employment (more than two million workers or almost a fifth of the total labour force of the GDR in 1989). As in other advanced societies, with the shrinking of the production sector, it became increasingly difficult for the unskilled and semi-skilled to find employment. Tightening public budgets led to a reversal in the growth of public sector employment. The agriculture share was further diminished in the west and dramatically reduced in the east (from about one million, or ten per cent, of the working population at the end of the GDR to 250,000, or four per cent, in the mid-1990s).[34]

The loss of credibility of the German model[35] was most dramatic in regard to labour market performance. Unemployment increased from 0.76 million in 1980 to 3.9 million in 1998.[36] Despite a moderate decline to September 2001, it reached this level again in 2002. Worse still, structural unemployment increased from one business cycle to the next, leading to a very high share of long-term unemployed. The full amount of real unemployment is still masked by shifts between unemployment and training, as well as by early retirement. Nonetheless, the construct of an insider–outsider labour market[37] can only claim partial validity; women actually strongly increased their labour market participation.[38] However, they still frequently worked in segregated, non-career jobs with less pay (resulting in wage gap of about 20 per cent[39]) and, if married, they often worked part-time. Despite significant changes in attitudes and political measures to promote equal opportunity, most women in the west were still secondary breadwinners. Women in the east clung to their full-employment model, even if they could not often realise it.

In the 1980s and 1990s, several observers saw the decline of the lifelong occupation and a breakdown of the normal work biography. Clearly, there are trends in this direction, but their amount and significance has probably been over-rated. Fixed-term contracts have increased somewhat for both low and highly skilled positions, and especially for first jobs. Temporary work is still limited, and rather than being deregulated, it has been regulated by law and collective agreements. The same is true for marginal employment in terms of working hours, which did increase.

Particularly in contrast to the Anglo-Saxon countries, there was no comparable increase in wage inequalities. In West Germany, there was a slight decline in the 1980s and a limited increase in the 1990s.[40] Income inequality has been smaller in East Germany.[41] With regard to the welfare state, the expected backlash has hardly occurred if we consider the social budget as a percentage of the GNP.[42] With the introduction of old age care insurance in 1996, the system has even expanded. The costs of German unification were financed to a large extent by integrating East Germans into the West German social insurance funds. The major social risks shifted from old age poverty in the first period to young families with more children, single mothers and the long-term unemployed in the second. An ever larger share of social assistance was claimed by residents of foreign descent or citizenship, including the so-called *Aussiedler*.

Social classes. Starting as early as the late 1970s, many social scientists began to question the continuing salience of economically based class distinctions. In addition to the emergence of 'new inequalities' of age, generation, gender and ethnic origin,[43] social milieus were seen as overriding or replacing class as a determinant of identity, life chances, behaviour, interests and attitudes. 'Individualisation' was a notion that found wide acceptance as a self-image of society – including in the media and in political parties. The 1990s, however, brought the harsher realities of class-based advantages and disadvantages back home to many individuals and families. Risks of unemployment and income loss, high housing costs, poor health and the chance to find adequate treatment, life expectancy and children's educational opportunities continued to be tied to class. The expansion of dual-earner families tended to increase income gaps between households.[44] Employment in the public sector and the accompanying social protection, earnings opportunities and pension entitlements became even greater privileges at a time when employment and income trajectories in the private sector were becoming less secure and less stable. Inheritance, especially of real estate, increased class inequalities as more and more members of the post-war generations passed their accumulated savings on to their children and grandchildren.[45] More significantly, the chance to inherit real estate or capital differed dramatically between east and west. The pension rights of the elderly, often augmented by savings, came to constitute a new kind of privileged class situation vis-à-vis the middle-aged and the young.

Although this phenomenon was scarcely noticed, social mobility research showed remarkably constant inequalities of opportunity through the decades since the 1960s, and showed Germany to have the strongest links between class origin, educational attainment of parents and children's educational opportunities of all the OECD countries.[46] The PISA results revealed this to an attentive public. Among the 32 countries studied, Germany exhibited one of the largest variations in competence based on social class. Work-life mobility declined, not least because initial educational achievement had improved. The probability of downward mobility also increased – dramatically in the east,[47] but also in the west.

Immigration from non-EU countries – including *Aussiedler* and war refugees from the Balkans – increased considerably during this period and was severely restricted thereafter. The debate over citizenship, multiculturalism and assimilation intensified and reached a preliminary conclusion with the controversial draft of a *Zuwanderungsgesetz* (Immigration Act) in 2002. Foreign-born residents and their descendants were disproportionately unemployed and living on social assistance. Their low language skills and lack of training threatened them with persistent social exclusion. Exclusion was also an important theme with regard to East Germans, who, to an increasing degree, no longer compared their lives with their situation in the GDR, but rather with those of the better-off West Germans. Very real discrepancies and cleavages emerged. This was partially softened by the relative gains of East Germans in real labour and social wages[48] and by the integration of the PDS as a legitimate political force.

Life-course patterns. We now look at the life-course patterns in the 1980s and 1990s – a period which has been termed 'post-Fordist', 'post-industrial' and pluralised.[49] Although such a dramatic view is hardly borne out by the available data, there is little dissent about the tendency of life-course organisation to shift from the collective units of families, households, partnerships and social status groups to the individual. It is also apparent that individuals were expected to take control of their own lives at ever younger ages. Economic conditions, labour market recession, rapid structural change – and, for the East Germans, unification – led to increasing differences in life courses and inequalities in life chances (see Table 2, column 3). In general, the life courses of women changed more markedly during this period.

Looking at the various life transitions in diachronic fashion, the first remarkable fact of the 1980s and 1990s was a further rise in the average age at leaving school and at leaving occupational training and entering employment (see Table 4). Several factors contributed to this – among them, greater participation in upper secondary education, longer transition times between school and training, spells of unemployment, waiting periods until the start of military or civil service, more unsuccessfully completed

TABLE 3

STRUCTURAL CHANGE AND MARGINALISATION IN THE LABOUR MARKET,
WEST GERMANY 1970–95

	1970	1975	1980	1985	1990	1995[1]
Labour force participation rates (% of population)						
Men	59.1	57.1	58.4	60.3	60.8	57.8
Women	30.2	30.9	32.6	35.9	39.2	40.9
Labour force composition (% of all employed)						
Men, full-time	65.0	62.0	61.0	60.0	58.0	53.0
Women, full-time	26.0	26.0	27.0	27.0	26.0	27.0
Men, part-time	1.0	1.0	1.0	1.0	2.0	3.0
Women, part-time	8.0	11.0	11.0	12.0	14.0	17.0
Unemployment (%)						
Total unemployment rate	0.7	4.7	3.8	9.3	7.2	9.3
Unemployment rate: without training	–	6.1	5.9	14.9	13.3	20.0
Unemployment rate: non-Germans	0.3	6.8	5.0	13.9	10.9	16.6
Social budget (in % of GNP)	25.9	33.3	32.0	31.3	28.8[1]	33.2

Note: 1 West and East.

Sources: Official statistics (Labour force participation and composition, social budget: Arbeits-
und Sozialstatistik 2002; Unemployment by qualification: IAB; Total unemployment
and by nationality: Bundesanstalt für Arbeit: ANBA-Jahreszahlen.)

TABLE 4

SELECTED LIFE-COURSE INDICATORS (IN YEARS) FOR THE BIRTH COHORTS
1950–71 (WEST GERMANY AND GERMAN CITIZENS ONLY)

Birth cohort	1950	1955	1960	1964	1971
Median age (first job): men	18.8	19.5	19.9	20.3	21.1
Median age (first job): women	18.1	18.9	19.7	20.3	20.9
Median age (first stable job): men	20.2	21.3	21.7	21.8	23.9
Median age (first stable job): women	19.0	20.0	21.0	21.7	22.3
Median job duration (first stable job): men	4.3	5.3	5.3	6.6	5.5
Median job duration (first stable job): women	4.6	4.8	5.2	5.3	5.3
Median occupational duration (first stable job): men	>9	>11	>9	13.1	>8
Median occupational duration (first stable job): women	6.2	7.7	7.6	7.4	6.4
Median age at first marriage: men	25.0	27.0	30.0	29.0	–[1]
Median age at first marriage: women	21.0	23.0	26.0	26.0	–[2]
Median age at leaving home: men	25.0	24.0	23.0	23.0	24.0
Median age at leaving home: women	22.0	21.0	21.0	21.0	22.0

Notes: First stable job: minimum duration of two years.
    1. Less than 25% have married by age 27.
    2. 25% have married by age 24, but less than 50% by age 27.

Sources: Own calculations; Data: German Life History Study.

apprenticeships, multiple training periods and longer durations of study.[50] With regard to some of these, the unstable situation of training and labour market entry were more significant than long-term trends.[51]

Working lives now more commonly started with fixed-term contracts, especially for very low and very highly skilled workers. Although there was much talk about the decline of occupations, occupational stability and matches between training and employment did not change significantly.[52] Firm tenure decreased slightly for men, but increased for women.[53] Median labour income trajectories became flatter due to low or negative real growth and the reduction of wage shift. Careers became more contingent on the economic fortunes of the employing firm;[54] therefore, heterogeneity between working lives increased. The age at the end of the working life decreased markedly, and the proportion of men working between the ages of 60 and 65 dropped from 44 per cent in 1980 to 31 per cent in 2000. The rate for women remained stable at 13 per cent. The proportion of men working between the ages of 55 and 59 dropped from 83 per cent to 79 per cent; for women, in contrast, it rose from 39 per cent to 58 per cent.[55] This also increased the variance in age of retirement, not least due to early retirement programmes.

Age at leaving home changed very little, and oscillated with the business cycle and labour market opportunities. The age at forming non-marital unions stagnated or decreased somewhat, while age at marriage and at first birth increased markedly. This meant, in effect, that at age 30 almost half of the men and one-third of the women were not yet married, and that half of the women and two-thirds of the men were not yet parents. Divorce affected about one-third of all first marriages. While non-marital unions became widespread before marriage – and also became acceptable for the middle-aged, divorced and widowed – children were still normally expected to be raised by married partners. However, this was less true for East Germany, with over ten per cent of first births occurring before marriage.

The subjective perception of the new life-course regime was probably rather hedonistic for the young adults of the more advantaged section of the population, where people expect to have their own life designs and life projects. For the other part of the population, subjective life courses have meant the adaptation of expectations to insufficient incomes.

STRUCTURAL CHANGES AND POLITICAL CONSEQUENCES

This final section addresses the question of how the described changes in social structures may have affected interest formation, political cleavages, political agendas and policies. Here, the answers are necessarily more tentative than conclusive. On the one hand, there is less systematic evidence – or at least it cannot be developed here in sufficient empirical and methodological detail. On the other hand, there are many and increasing uncertainties as to how the theoretical link between social-structural change and political change can adequately be constructed. What we can do, however, is to select some particularly crucial facts and develop their potential implications. We will concentrate on three points:

Do we see a temporal correspondence between structural changes and political periods? The periods invoked by writers on politics and the political economy – for example, before and after the first and second oil shock – have only limited meaning for the observer of changes in social structure. First, despite political, social and economic turmoil and widespread feelings of dramatic change, it is characteristic for Germany that a number of structural and institutional continuities prevail. One such major continuity lies in the educational and training system. Vocational and academic credentials still define boundaries and distances between social status groups and, to a large extent, also determine income and life chances.

If politics has played an active role in this field in the last decades, it has been in maintaining these structures rather than in changing them, seeking incremental adaptation without threatening the German model as such. Second, major structural changes appear to be long-term, gradual and robust. This applies to educational upgrading and expansion as well as to the advances made by women in social, political, educational and employment participation. In hindsight, the 1960s and 1970s were a major turning point in these areas. Third, major structural discontinuities, especially demographic change, only partially coincide with political periods. For instance, the baby boom cohorts born in the early 1960s put great pressure on training and labour markets in the 1980s and triggered massive political responses, but in retrospect this period appears to have been relatively stable and prosperous.

The question is, then, will the 1990s mark a more significant turning point? Will the coincidence of unification, rapid technological and organisational change and the exposure to transnational markets also imply structural ruptures? Will the more deregulated labour markets of East Germany become the model for Germany as a whole? So far, the normal and largely protected work biographies have eroded only at the fringes – for example, with regard to fixed-term contracts and early retirement.

Has structural change affected interest formation and political cleavages?
During the 1980s and 1990s, the political party alignment of social classes and status groups underwent a dramatic change in the eyes of both academic and political observers. Voting volatility and voting abstention increased, and the 'normal vote' appeared to be much less reliable than in former times. All parties – with the possible exception of the Greens and the PDS – competed for centrist policies and the middle class, with the SPD paying more attention to industrial and public service workers and their unions, the CDU/CSU to the self-employed, and the FDP to the professions. Increasingly, personalities, media performance and the skills of political gamesmanship seemed to be more relevant than class interests and their articulation and representation.

However, if one asks to what degree these assumed changes can be attributed to structural changes occurring after 1980, the answer is probably very little. Research on political values and quantitative electoral research have demonstrated some tendencies toward restructuring, but also remarkable continuities in class coupling.[56] It is a safe assumption that significantly better educated and informed voters are less likely to form an ultra-stable electorate, and that educated and employed women are less likely to simply follow the voting preferences of their husbands. It is a puzzling question whether and how the expansion, educational upgrading and redistribution of white-collar positions with regard to gender and sector affected the formation of political orientations and interests. As Müller[57] has shown, the service class is split in its political alignment according to the differentiation between white-collar positions, with the private sector (mostly managerial) tending towards the CDU/CSU and the public sector (mostly social services) tending towards the SPD. When this distinction is introduced, political class alignments turn out to be much more stable than many observers believed.

There is also little evidence that new structural groups such as the elderly, the e-boom generation of the 1990s or the globalisation losers are aggregating into visible and distinct collective political actors. The established parties still rally around their traditional organised interests. The reduction of the industrial workforce and of employment in the public sector reduced union membership and should have weakened the political power of the trade unions. However, the dependence of the Social Democrats on union support has limited that impact up to now. Labour market rigidities testify to the persistent political strength of the trade unions, despite heavy losses in membership.

How responsive have politics been to structural changes? Parties, politics and even unions responded more quickly than the general public to the issue of equal opportunity between women and men. 'Gender mainstreaming' and related policies have started to respond to the demands of well-educated, well-trained and self-confident women. This may have undermined a traditional organisation of interests and class cleavages based on males and their stages in life. The new educational equality of women has also affected their family and fertility behaviour and posed policy challenges ranging from childcare to pensions and old age care. However, institutional adaptation has been extremely slow, as shown in areas such as the provision of kindergarten and pre-school places, the lack of full-day schools and the very slow shift of social benefits from the old to young families.

Another major structural change that has come to dominate the political agenda is demographic ageing. The burdens posed by increasing longevity, low fertility and higher health and pension costs were visible in the 1980s and 1990s, but policy reactions were slow – as in the case of the introduction of a private component in old age insurance – or counterproductive, as in early retirement. Old age reinforced the distribution of inequalities in comparison to the active years. Birth cohorts in or close to retirement enjoyed high pension entitlements, could accumulate savings, were the recipients of considerable inheritances (in the west), and benefited from the introduction of chronic care insurance. Although their collective interests lacked organisation, the threat of withdrawal of electoral support was sufficient for defending their entitlements.[58]

A third major structural change was more gradual and less visible, at least with respect to its consequences: the delayed transition to the full responsibilities associated with adulthood, as shown in the median and variance of the age of entry into employment, marriage and first birth. Partly, this was a consequence of the upgrading of schooling and training, but it was also due in part to the increasing numbers of young men and women combining training and higher education or higher education and employment. Again, there has been a lack of institutional adaptation enabling advanced degrees to be reached in a shorter time – such as, for example, a shortening of the *Gymnasium*, a combination of training and higher education, and especially the introduction of short degrees (BA) in universities and polytechnics.

Three theses can be put forward in summing up and generalising these examples. First, the changes in social structures and life-course patterns which Germany experienced over the last four decades have been much more consequential as challenges for political action than as conditions for a restructuring of collective interest formation and political cleavages. Changes in social structures did not lead to a major reorganisation of collective interests. This might be due to the fact that the established parties effectively integrated and accommodated emerging new interest groups.

Second, the new political challenges probably originated to a greater extent from changes in age and gender than from the macroeconomic forces of internationalisation and industrial restructuring. There can be little doubt that the competitive pressures resulting from European market integration and from the expansion of financial and product markets will restructure the employment system sooner or later. So far, however, it seems that the protection provided by labour market regulations and redistribution via the welfare state have prevented the rise of new kinds of employment as well as the formation of new interest groups. Political attention is focused on the more indirect problems of financing the welfare state – in particular, old age pensions, unemployment insurance, rising health costs and social assistance.

Third, in spite of the challenges mentioned, the absence of institutional adaptation or increased flexibility is much more conspicuous than change, at least as far as West Germany is concerned. Some outstanding examples of continuity are the institutional stratification of education; the predominance of the dual system of vocational training; the close links between education, employment and occupation; the persistence of occupational and firm labour markets; the incomplete inclusion of women in the labour market; the rigidities and privileges of public service employment; the relatively comfortable material situation of the elderly; and high employment protection. In the past, many of these features have been seen as assets rather than liabilities of the German model. One might wonder, however, whether continuities of this sort should not be better interpreted as rigidities – that is, as indicating a lack of adaptive capacity. Another example of this is the primarily administrative division of labour between departments and policies.[59] It seems obvious that structural changes do not find their way into the political economy on their own.

NOTES

1. R. Herden and R. Münz, 'Bevölkerung', in B. Schäfers and W. Zapf (eds.), *Handwörterbuch zur Gesellschaft Deutschlands* (Opladen: Leske + Budrich 2001), pp.75–88.
2. P. Lüttinger, *Integration der Vertriebenen. Eine empirische Analyse* (Frankfurt am Main: Campus 1989).
3. Statistisches Bundesamt, *Lange Reihen zur Wirtschaftsentwicklung 1998* (Wiesbaden: Statistisches Bundesamt 1999).
4. A. Willms-Herget, *Frauenarbeit. Zur Integration von Frauen in den Arbeitsmarkt* (Frankfurt am Main: Campus 1985).
5. W. Sengenberger (ed.), *Der gespaltene Arbeitsmarkt – Probleme der Arbeitsmarktseg-mentation* (Frankfurt am Main: Campus 1978); H.-P. Blossfeld and K.U. Mayer, 'Labour Market Segmentation in the Federal Republic of Germany: An Empirical Study of Segmentation Theories from a Life-Course Perspective', *European Sociological Review* 4/2 (1988), pp.123–40.
6. H. Kern, *Industriearbeit und Arbeitsbewusstsein* (Frankfurt: Europäische Verlagsanstalt 1970).
7. W. Müller, 'Wege und Grenzen der Tertiarisierung: Wandel der Berufsstruktur in der Bundesrepublik Deutschland 1950–1980', in J. Matthes (ed.), *Krise der Arbeitsgesellschaft? Verhandlungen des 21. Deutschen Soziologentages in Bamberg 1982* (Frankfurt am Main: Campus 1983), pp.142–60.
8. J. Bergmann et al., 'Herrschaft, Klassenverhältnis und Schichtung', in T.W. Adorno (ed.), *Spätkapitalismus oder Industriegesellschaft? Verhandlungen des 16. Deutschen Soziologentages* (Stuttgart: Enke 1969), pp.67–87.
9. J. Alber, C. Behrendt and M. Schölkopf, 'Sozialstaat/Soziale Sicherheit', in Schäfers and Zapf (eds.), *Handwörterbuch zur Gesellschaft Deutschlands*, p.656.
10. J. Handl, K.U. Mayer and W. Müller, *Klassenlagen und Sozialstruktur. Empirische Untersuchungen zu Strukturen sozialer Ungleichheit und Prozessen sozialer Mobilität in der Bundesrepublik Deutschland* (Frankfurt am Main: Campus 1977).
11. W. Müller, 'Klassenlage und Lebenslauf' (Habilitationsschrift, Universität Mannheim 1978).
12. K.U. Mayer, *Ungleichheit und Mobilität im sozialen Bewußtsein. Untersuchungen zur Definition der Mobilitätssituation* (Opladen: Westdeutscher Verlag 1975).
13. M. Kohli, 'Die Institutionalisierung des Lebenslaufs. Historische Befunde und theoretische Argumente', *Kölner Zeitschrift für Soziologie und Sozialpsychologie* 37 (1985), pp.1–29; K.U. Mayer and W. Müller, 'The State and the Structure of the Life Course', in A.B. Sørensen, F.E. Weinert and L.R. Sherrod (eds.), *Human Development and the Life Course: Multidisciplinary Perspectives* (Hillsdale, NJ: Lawrence Erlbaum 1986), pp.217–45.
14. K.U. Mayer and J. Huinink, 'Age, Period, and Cohort in the Study of the Life Course: A

Comparison of Classical A-P-C-Analysis with Event History Analysis or Farewell to LEXIS?' in D. Magnusson and L.R. Bergman (eds.), *Data Quality in Longitudinal Research* (Cambridge: Cambridge University Press 1990), pp.211–32.

15. D. Konietzka, *Ausbildung und Beruf. Die Geburtsjahrgänge 1919–1961 auf dem Weg von der Schule in das Erwerbsleben* (Opladen: Westdeutscher Verlag 1999); S. Hillmert, *Ausbildungssysteme und Arbeitsmarkt. Lebensverläufe in Großbritannien und Deutschland im Kohortenvergleich* (Wiesbaden: Westdeutscher Verlag 2001).

16. D. Soskice, 'Reconciling Markets and Institutions: The German Apprenticeship System', in L.M. Lynch (ed.), *Training and the Private Sector. International Comparisons* (Chicago: University of Chicago Press 1994), pp.25–60.

17. Mayer, *Ungleichheit und Mobilität im sozialen Bewußtsein.*

18. K.U. Mayer, 'Gesellschaftlicher Wandel, Kohortenungleichheit und Lebensverläufe', in P.A. Berger and P. Sopp (eds.), *Sozialstruktur und Lebenslauf* (Opladen: Leske + Budrich 1995), pp.27–47.

19. Kohli, 'Die Institutionalisierung des Lebenslaufs', pp.1–29.

20. M. Buchmann and M. Eisner, 'Geschlechterdifferenzen in der gesellschaftlichen Präsentation des Selbst. Heiratsinserate von 1900 bis 2000', in B. Heintz (ed.), *Geschlechtersoziologie, Sonderheft 41 der Kölner Zeitschrift für Soziologie und Sozialpsychologie* (Wiesbaden: Westdeutscher Verlag 2001), pp.75–107.

21. R. Boyer and J.-P. Durand, *After Fordism* (Basingstoke: MacMillan 1997); J. Myles, 'Is There a Post-Fordist Life Course?' in W.R. Heinz (ed.), *Institutions and Gatekeeping in the Life Course* (Weinheim: Deutscher Studien-Verlag 1993), pp.171–85.

22. G. Esping-Andersen, *The Social Foundations of Postindustrial Economies* (Oxford: Oxford University Press 1999).

23. B. Lutz, *Der kurze Traum immerwährender Prosperität. Eine Neuinterpretation der industriell-kapitalistischen Entwicklung im Europa des 20. Jahrhunderts* (Frankfurt am Main: Campus 1984).

24. VDR, Verband Deutscher Rentenversicherungsträger (ed.), *Rentenversicherung in Zeitreihen – Juli 2002*, DRV-Schriften, Vol.22 (Frankfurt am Main: VDR 2002), p.115.

25. Herden and Münz, 'Bevölkerung', pp.75–88

26. M. Kreyenfeld, 'Employment and Fertility – East Germany in the 1990s' (Dissertation, Universität Rostock 2001).

27. J. Huinink, *Warum noch Familie? Zur Attraktivität von Partnerschaft und Elternschaft in unserer Gesellschaft* (Frankfurt am Main: Campus 1995).

28. K.U. Mayer, 'Das Hochschulwesen', in K.S. Cortina et al. (eds.), *Das Bildungswesen in der Bundesrepublik Deutschland* (Reinbek: Rowohlt forthcoming).

29. S. Hillmert and M. Jacob, 'Bildungsprozesse zwischen Diskontinuität und Karriere: das Phänomen der Mehrfachausbildungen', *Zeitschrift für Soziologie* 32/4 (2003).

30. R. Becker and K. Schömann, 'Berufliche Weiterbildung und Einkommenschancen im Lebensverlauf: Empirische Befunde für Frauen und Männer in West- und Ostdeutschland', in D. Beer et al. (eds.), *Die wirtschaftlichen Folgen von Aus- und Weiterbildung* (München: Rainer Hampp 1999), pp.93–121.

31. L. Alex, 'Diskrepanzen zwischen Ausbildung und Beschäftigung insbesondere im Facharbeiterbereich', paper presented at the Jacobs Foundation Conference *The Transition to Adulthood: Explaining National Differences*, Schloß Marbach, Oct. 1999.

32. M. Tessaring, *Training for a Changing Society. A Report on Current Vocational Education and Training Research in Europe* (Thessaloniki: CEDEFOP 1998).

33. F.W. Scharpf and V.A. Schmidt (eds.), *Welfare and Work in the Open Economy. From Vulnerability to Competitiveness*, Vol.1 (Oxford: Oxford University Press 2000).

34. Statistisches Bundesamt, *Schriftenreihen zu Methodenfragen. Heft 14: Erwerbstätige 1950 bis 1989* (Wiesbaden: Statistisches Bundesamt 1994); Statistisches Bundesamt, *Bevölkerung und Erwerbstätigkeit. Fachserie 1. Reihe 4.1.1.* (Wiesbaden: Statistisches Bundesamt 1997).

35. W. Streeck, 'German Capitalism: Does it Exist? Can it Survive?' *New Political Economy* 2 (1997), pp.234–56.

36. Statistisches Bundesamt, *Statistisches Jahrbuch für die Bundesrepublik Deutschland* (Wiesbaden: Statistisches Bundesamt 1981, 1999, 2001).

100   GERMANY: BEYOND THE STABLE STATE

37. A. Lindbeck, *The Insider-Outsider Theory of Employment and Unemployment* (Cambridge, MA: MIT 1989).
38. H.-P. Blossfeld and C. Hakim (eds.), *Between Equalization and Marginalization. Women Working Part-Time in Europe and the United States of America* (Oxford: Oxford University Press 1997).
39. H. Brückner, 'The Dynamics of Social Stability: Gender Inequality in the Labour Market in West Germany 1975–1995' (Dissertation, University of North Carolina, Chapel Hill 2000).
40. Statistisches Bundesamt (ed.), *Datenreport 2002: Zahlen und Fakten über die Bundesrepublik Deutschland* (Bonn: bpb 2002), p.583.
41. R. Hauser, 'Einkommen und Vermögen', in Schäfers and Zapf (eds.), *Handwörterbuch zur Gesellschaft Deutschlands*, pp.157–70.
42. Alber *et al.*, 'Sozialstaat/Soziale Sicherheit'. See also Table 3.
43. R. Kreckel, *Soziale Ungleichheiten* (Göttingen: Schwartz 1983); P.A. Berger and S. Hradil (eds.), *Lebenslagen, Lebensläufe, Lebensstile (Sonderband 7 der Sozialen Welt)* (Göttingen: Schwartz 1990).
44. H.-P. Blossfeld and S. Drobnic (eds.), *Careers of Couples in Contemporary Society. From Male Breadwinner to Dual-Earner Families* (Oxford: Oxford University Press 2001).
45. Favouring sons more than daughters. See R. Braun *et al.* (eds.), *Erben in Deutschland* (Köln: Deutsches Institut für Altersvorsorge 2000).
46. Y. Shavit and H.-P. Blossfeld (eds.), *Persistent Inequality. Changing Educational Attainment in Thirteen Countries* (Boulder/San Francisco/Oxford: Westview Press 1993).
47. K.U. Mayer, 'Soziale Mobilität und Erwerbsverläufe in der Transformation Ostdeutschlands', in W. Schluchter and P.E. Quint (eds.), *Der Vereinigungsschock. Vergleichende Betrachtungen zehn Jahre danach* (Weilerswist: Velbrück Wissenschaft 2001), pp.336–65.
48. Hauser, 'Einkommen und Vermögen', pp.157–70; M. Diewald *et al.*, 'Back to Labour Markets – Who Got Ahead in Post-Communist Societies after 1989? The Case of East Germany', *European Societies* 4/1 (2002), pp.27–52.
49. See also M. Corsten and S. Hillmert, 'Bildungs- und Berufskarrieren in Zeiten gestiegener Konkurrenz. Eine lebenslauftheoretische Perspektive auf den Wandel der Arbeitsgesellschaft und ihr theoretischer Ertrag', *Zeitschrift für Berufs- und Wirtschaftspädagogik* 99/1 (2003), pp.42–60.
50. D. Konietzka, 'Die soziale Differenzierung von Übergangsmustern in den Beruf', *Kölner Zeitschrift für Soziologie und Sozialpsychologie* 54/4 (2002), pp.645–73.
51. S. Hillmert, *Kohortendynamik und Konkurrenz an den zwei Schwellen des dualen Ausbildungssystems*, Arbeitspapier Nr. 2 des Projekts Ausbildungs- und Berufsverläufe der Geburtskohorten 1964 und 1971 in Westdeutschland (Berlin: Max-Planck-Institut für Bildungsforschung 2001).
52. S. Hillmert, 'Stabilität und Wandel des "deutschen Modells" Lebensverläufe im Übergang zwischen Schule und Beruf', in M. Wingens and R. Sackmann (eds.), *Bildung und Beruf. Ausbildung und berufsstruktureller Wandel in der Wissensgesellschaft* (Weinheim: Juventa 2002), pp.65–81.
53. A. Mertens, *Labour Mobility and Wage Dynamics: An Empirical Study for Germany in Comparison with the United States* (Aachen: Shaker 1998).
54. Dramatically so in East Germany. See A. Goedicke, *Beschäftigungschancen und Betriebszugehörigkeit: Die Folgen betrieblichen Wandels für ostdeutsche Erwerbstätige nach 1989* (Wiesbaden: Westdeutscher Verlag 2002).
55. Statistisches Bundesamt, *Statistisches Jahrbuch für die Bundesrepublik Deutschland* (1981, 2001).
56. W. Müller, 'Class Cleavages in Party Preferences in Germany – Old and New', in G. Evans (ed.), *The End of Class Politics? Class Voting in Comparative Context* (Oxford: Oxford University Press 1999), pp.137–80; F. Brettschneider *et al.* (eds.), *Das Ende der politisierten Sozialstruktur?* (Opladen: Leske + Budrich 2002); Kitschelt in this volume.
57. Müller, 'Class Cleavages in Party Preferences in Germany – Old and New'.
58. See also Leibfried/Obinger in this volume.
59. See on structural similarities of problems for social and educational policy, J. Allmendinger, 'Bildungsarmut: Zur Verschränkung von Bildungs- und Sozialpolitik', *Soziale Welt* 50/1 (1999), pp.35–50.

The Crumbling Pillars of Social Partnership

WOLFGANG STREECK and ANKE HASSEL

Stable relations of mutual recognition, institutionalised co-operation and regulated conflict between organised labour, organised business and government were core elements of the post-war political economy of West Germany. Social partnership came to its peak in the *Modell Deutschland* of the 1970s, with unions strengthened by the worker revolt of 1969 and by favourable legislation on workplace participation. Employers accommodated union strength by investing in skills, advanced technology and quality-competitive products. The social-liberal government depended on union co-operation in keeping the national economy competitive.

First fissures in the West German industrial order were observed in the 1980s when unions divided over how to respond to persistent unemployment. Opposing the reduction of weekly working hours pursued by the left wing of the union movement, the Kohl government invited employers, works councils and dissenting unions to rely on the social security system for reducing the supply of labour. Simultaneously it took steps to curtail union power. For a short time, unification restored tripartite co-operation as government, business and labour worked hand in hand to transfer West German institutions to the new Länder of the east. The ensuing economic crisis, which was exacerbated by the accelerated internationalisation of European economies, drove a wedge in the employers' camp, caused a mismatch between institutionalised union strength and economic conditions, and forced the government to do something about rising social security expenditures and public debt. When in 1996 government attempts at consensual labour market and social security reform failed – mainly due to opposition in the government camp demanding more aggressive intervention – a solution was sought by unilateral legislation. Causing unprecedented union protest while falling short of business demands, it contributed to Kohl's defeat two years later.

While the Schröder government succeeded in setting up the tripartite Alliance for Jobs (*Bündnis für Arbeit*) that had eluded its predecessor, it failed to break the deadlock over reform and Schröder had to end his first term almost empty-handed. In part, the political stagnation of the first Schröder term reflected a progressive erosion of the organisational capacities of business and labour especially in the 1990s. With unions declining and business leaders having to pay more attention than ever to small and medium sized companies (*Mittelstand*), tripartite meetings were little more than public rituals. Incremental adjustments were made at the level of individual firms, by modifying and undercutting central agreements, while erosion of the labour market regime made unions all the more tenacious in its defence. Also, unions were unenthusiastic about the government retreating from the early retirement policies of the 1980s that continued to be highly popular with their members. In the end, the Alliance resulted in little more than two years of union wage restraint, which had to be purchased by the government with inactivity on labour market reform.

The discussion will proceed as follows. Starting with a brief recapitulation of the origin and the architecture of post-war German social partnership, it will examine the emerging conflicts of the 1980s and the crisis caused in the 1990s by unification and European integration and then trace the erosion of the organisational strength of business and labour that began in the 1980s and rapidly accelerated in the 1990s. Next, it will recount the experience of the Schröder Alliance and end with a few tentative conclusions on the changing character and significance of tripartite relations between government, business and labour in Germany.

SOCIAL PARTNERSHIP IN POST-WAR WEST GERMANY

Like other capitalist democracies, the post-war settlement in West Germany for the first time in the history of the country safely institutionalised union rights to free collective bargaining and political participation. Recognition of organised labour as a co-equal partner of business and the state in the governance of the West German political economy was facilitated by reorganisation of the politically divided unions of the Weimar Republic as industrial unions (*Einheitsgewerkschaften*). The 1950s witnessed the gradual establishment of a sectoral collective bargaining system and a stable division of labour between the bargaining autonomy of unions and employers (*Tarifautonomie*), on the one hand, and government social policy, on the other. Unions also achieved a recognised role in the administration of the social security system (*Selbstverwaltung*) and in the management of individual firms (*Mitbestimmung*).

Again as in other countries, the unofficial strikes of the late 1960s boosted union power and recognition. Under the Grand Coalition and the social-liberal governments of Brandt (1969–74) and, less so, Schmidt (1974–82), German unions moved into the centre of political power. Regular meetings between government ministers, unions and business representatives on the economic situation in the framework of 'concerted action' (*Konzertierte Aktion*) visibly established tripartism in government economic policy and were, if nothing else, of high symbolic significance. Co-determination at the workplace was extended in two landmark pieces of legislation in 1972 and 1976, legislation that is still on the books. Public recognition and institutional support for union organising efforts produced an unprecedented increase in membership during the 1970s. Unions were able to maintain good working relations also with the conservative opposition, which has a strong labour wing.

West German tripartism was distinguished by a conjuncture of a weak and fragmented 'semi-sovereign' state with a strong organised and centralised society.[1] Its condition of semi-sovereignty, which applied in domestic just as in foreign affairs, constrained the West German state to cultivate more subtle means of governance, which could be found in and further developed out of long-standing corporatist traditions, rather than direct state intervention. West German political and economic success resulted in large part from the fact that semi-sovereignty protected the post-war German state from illusions of omnipotence still held by other states, and promoted a policy style that happened to be better matched than state intervention to post-war problems of social integration and economic management.

Due to limited state capacities for direct control, post-war West German statecraft consisted, more than in other countries, of arranging deals with and between well-organised independent actors in civil society commanding their own sovereignty which the state could not ignore or circumvent. The high art of government in West Germany was to turn social organisations with guaranteed autonomy and independent power into agents of publicly licensed self-government, in the context of a negotiated public order within which the state was just one participant among others. Where this was successful, social autonomy was transformed into delegated public responsibility, and organised interest groups became quasi-public agencies more competent and legitimate in governing their constituents than state agencies.

More specifically, social order and economic governance in post-war West Germany depended not on the strength of the state, but on a politically managed *balance of power* between social groups as well as on a *corporatist pattern of social organisation,* together holding organised private interests accountable to public purposes. As to the former, while the German state was constitutionally barred from a statutory incomes policy, its political and economic institutions have, over the years, provided a framework that enabled the fine-tuning of the relative power of unions and employers' associations in such a way that wage settlements never strayed too far from a path of high growth, low inflation and stable employment. Carefully balanced rights of unions to strike and of employers to lock out, combined with co-determination at the workplace allowing for moderate wage drift, externalising distributional conflict to the sectoral level, protecting the strike monopoly of industrial unions and enabling co-operation between management and workforces in pursuit of high productivity and international competitiveness, were central elements of this regime. At the same time, the autonomy of the Bundesbank protected unions in particular from Keynesian illusions and located responsibility for employment within the system of free collective bargaining. The strict refusal of the Bundesbank after 1974 to accommodate inflationary wage increases required tight discipline, which could only be delivered by wage bargaining institutions sufficiently centralised to contain wage pressures from sheltered sectors.[2]

Second, the West German state, through a variety of legal and other means, helped insure that social interests were represented by a small number of encompassing organisations that could effectively and legitimately speak on behalf of their constituents, covering the society as a whole and not excluding any significant social category. Such organisations, described as 'neo-corporatist' by the literature of the 1970s,[3] define their interests in such a way that they take the public interest sufficiently into account[4] to enable a semi-sovereign state to stay out of industrial conflict. Rather than intervening directly, semi-sovereign governance relying on corporatist intermediation tries to arrange for social interests to be represented by non-competitive encompassing organisations, externally inclusive to make it impossible for them to impose the costs of their policies on outsiders, and internally heterogeneous to force them to integrate divergent special interests and learn to align them behind a broad, centrist compromise.

THE 1980s: FIRST FISSURES

Under the West German financial regime there never was a place for a Keynesian monetary policy. Faced with rising unemployment, the government of Helmut Schmidt placed its hopes on internationally co-ordinated fiscal reflation at the Bonn summit of 1978. However, in an unexpected turn, American economic policy at the end of the Carter administration abandoned the 'locomotive' strategy and left Germany with high public debt and, after another oil shock, even higher unemployment. In 1982, Schmidt was succeeded by Kohl, who began a cautious policy of fiscal consolidation and union retrenchment. In turn, the metalworkers' union, IG Metall, embarked on a campaign to restore full employment by a reduction of weekly working hours through collective agreement. This resulted in a split in the national union confederation, the DGB, as five other unions under the leadership of the chemical workers – the 'Gang of Five' – sought early retirement instead.[5] The split among the unions was exploited by the government, which supported the more politically moderate unions. Increasingly the social security system was relied upon to cut the labour supply.

In 1984, IG Metall won a national strike, the last major strike in Germany, for a gradual introduction of the 35-hour week. The union had to pay dearly for its success as it had to accept an increase in working-time flexibility. As a result, unions and works councils lost control of the wage-effort bargain at the workplace. In subsequent years, cuts in working hours were compensated by employer-driven productivity increases, and the same was true for high wage settlements, at least in large firms. Where cost and productivity increases caused by wage settlements and working-time cuts reduced labour demand, early retirement offered employers and works councils an easy way out, paid for by public money.

Developments in the 1980s changed the balance of power between business and labour and pulled the state into the management of the labour market. Government support for reducing labour supply relieved the pressure on the social partners to behave responsibly. While workplace flexibility increased the power of employers on the shop floor, it weakened employers' associations. Companies lost interest in fighting wage increases and resisting strikes by lock-out – given that they could respond to high wage settlements by reorganising production and shifting redundant workers into rapidly expanding early retirement schemes.[6] Social policy began to play the role that Keynesian demand management had played outside Germany in the 1970s. It accommodated and underwrote wage settlements that jeopardised employment. This was the beginning of a new configuration between the state and organised interests that we have elsewhere called 'welfare corporatism'.[7]

The strike and its settlement also set in motion a trend towards decentralisation of collective bargaining, with works councils and individual employers regulating a growing share of wages and working conditions at the firm level.[8] Meanwhile, relations between the Kohl government and the unions deteriorated. The bankruptcy of the trade union-owned real estate company Neue Heimat gave the Kohl government an opportunity to undermine the political legitimacy of the trade unions in the 1987 election campaign.[9] In 1988, the government set up a deregulation committee to introduce flexibility in the labour market. It also retaliated against IG Metall's strike strategy, with legislation barring unemployment benefit being paid to workers laid off as an indirect consequence of a strike. While all this prevented a return to the amicable relationship of the 1970s, continuing union strength kept the Kohl government from adopting a more Thatcherist anti-union policy. It did not, however, prevent a slow attrition of union power.

THE 1990s: UNIFICATION, RECESSION AND THE END OF CONSENSUS

German unity halted the decline of social partnership and temporarily restored and re-centralised co-operation between government, business and labour. The Kohl government was eager to mend its fences with the unions and found an ideal ally in the leader of the chemical workers' union, Hermann Rappe, who had always been adamant in defending his union's independence from IG Metall. In part, reconfirmed recognition of unions, as one of three main pillars of public order in Germany, was to prevent an increase in the strength of the union left-wing due to the accession of East German members and officials. It also was needed for managing the disastrous economic consequences of unification, first in the east and then in Germany as a whole.

The overriding objective of the Kohl government, after initial hopes for a fast recovery of the East German economy did not materialise, was to avoid raising taxes while containing the increase in the national debt. Still, between 1992 and 1996 public debt as a share of GDP grew by 20 percentage points, to 66 per cent. The price unions had to pay for their place at the court was that a large part of the costs of unification was imposed on the para-fiscal social security funds that paid, among other things, for vast early retirement and labour market programmes. To secure union support for his unification strategy, Kohl was willing to accept tensions with business, whose representatives increasingly accused him of a lack of understanding of economic affairs.

The unification boom was followed by the worst recession since the Second World War. Half a million jobs were lost within a year in the manufacturing sector in 1992/93. The recession was exacerbated by the restrictions that came with European economic integration. In many ways, integration had suited the German industrial order perfectly. German industry had been a strong competitor on world markets and did not have to fear the internal market. The outstanding performance of the German currency during the 1970s combined with industrial strength had made the German economy a role model for the rest of Europe. However, the high costs of unification, the Bundesbank's strong reaction to high wage settlements, and the liberalisation of previously sheltered sectors put a heavy burden on the labour market and on German business, which was already under strain from the competitive pressure of emerging economies.

By the mid-1990s at the latest, a political-economic crisis had matured that had long been developing. Centralised collective bargaining continued to produce both high wages and an egalitarian wage structure, and rising productivity kept unit cost increases moderate and provided for monetary stability and international economic competitiveness. Gradually, however, the expansion of national and international markets paying for high-cost labour of the German sort had begun to lag behind the continuing increase in German wages and productivity. As a consequence, the number of workers employable by the German economy began to shrink. Rather than changing the institutions governing the labour market, the state had agreed early on to take surplus workers out of the labour market. Meanwhile, firms continued to respond to wage increases by augmenting their productivity and trimming down their workforces. Whether or not the emerging combination of high productivity and low employment, or of 'high equality and low activity', would have been socially viable in the long term may be an open question. It soon ceased to be economically viable, however, since the German welfare state, which bore the costs of defensive labour supply management, is funded by payroll taxes. As a result, the more labour was taken out of the market, the higher became the cost of labour, forcing further productivity increases which, in turn, required even more workers to be laid off.

It was the employers who first began to press for a departure from the new 'German model'. Rising non-wage labour costs had become a burden on the international competitiveness especially of small and medium sized firms. *Mittelstand* employers became ever more vocal and began to contest the leadership of large companies in employers' and business associations. After the last of the tripartite Chancellor's Rounds (*Kanzlerrunden*) on German unity in 1995, employers asked for new talks, this time on labour market reform, cost reduction and generally the competitiveness of the German economy (*Standortdebatte*). Divisions showed between the confederation of trade associations, BDI, which openly pressed for a neo-liberal course, and the national association of employers' associations, BDA, whose affiliates have to deal with the unions in collective bargaining. The more militant employers connected with the small coalition partner, the FDP, and with a growing opposition to Kohl in the Christian Democratic Union, especially with the leader of its parliamentary group and potential Kohl successor, Schäuble.

The unions, for their part, were soon to experience the drawbacks of institutional strength in a time of economic distress. The surprise victory of the metalworkers in the *Bayern-Streik* in 1995 documented the vulnerability of employers under just-in-time production and the declining ability of their associations to organise a lock-out.[10] It also had the unexpected effect of a revolt inside the employers' camp. Smaller firms began to leave the employers' associations and collective bargaining coverage declined, especially in the east, where collective agreements were disregarded by large numbers of firms. In big companies a wave of concession bargaining forced works councillors to sign away bonuses that companies paid on top of collectively agreed wages, which questioned the authority of the union on wage bargaining.[11] In 1995, the leader of IG Metall, Klaus Zwickel, called for an 'Alliance for Jobs' (*Bündnis für Arbeit*), under which unions were to make wage concessions if employers promised more employment and the government agreed to forgo social policy cuts.

The government, however, was internally divided. Negotiations with unions and employers took place and an agreement was almost reached in early 1996. But then the internal opposition in the government camp – especially the FDP in alliance with the BDI – raised the stakes and demanded more radical changes, especially in sick pay, which the unions could not accept. Predictably they walked away from the bargaining table and the government was both free and forced to take unilateral action. Various legal measures were passed, but the cut in sick pay, which was the most visible, did not take root since sick pay in Germany is regulated not just by law, but also by collective agreement. Large firms like Siemens and Daimler quickly caved in to union resistance and left their associations and the government holding the bag. The rift between government and unions, as documented by a large union protest rally in May 1996, was not healed until the election in September 1998. Kohl lost to Schröder, having failed at both consensual and unilateral reform.

EROSION OF ORGANISATIONAL CAPACITIES

From the mid-1980s, core elements of German social partnership started to show signs of accelerating decay, among them the organisational capacities of unions and business associations, the stability of the collective bargaining regime and the ability of the government to bring the special interests of unions and employers in line with the public interest.[12]

Disorganisation of business and labour reinforced the destructive effect on tripartite co-operation of their changed balance of power. *Trade union membership* dramatically declined in the 1990s, in East as well as West Germany. In 2000, there were no more union members in united Germany than there had been in West Germany in 1990. More than four million members, equivalent to the entire membership increase after unification, were lost within ten years (Table 1). Union membership among those under 25 dropped to about ten per cent, and density among white-collar workers went down to less than 13 per cent (Table 2). Unions became increasingly locked in the declining group of blue-collar workers. By the late 1990s, pensioners accounted for 19 per cent of DGB membership. Excluding the retired and the unemployed, overall union density in the private sector of the German economy fell from 27.3 per cent in 1980 (West Germany) to no more than 17.3 per cent in 2000.

The bleeding was not stopped by the union mergers of the 1990s. Low union membership reflected low employment as much as, especially in East Germany, high unemployment. It was also related to the growth of the informal economy and of non-standard forms of employment, caused mainly by high costs of labour. In addition, general demographic change and reluctance of younger workers to join unions – due to different employment conditions, work experiences and career expectations –

TABLE 1

TRADE UNION MEMBERSHIP (IN 1,000), 1970–2000

	West			West and East	
	1970	1980	1990	1991	2000
DGB	6,713	7,883	7,938	11,800	7,772
DAG	461	495	505	585	451
CGB	195	288	309	330	305
DBB	721	819	799	1,053	1,200
Total	8,207	9,484	9,552	13,768	9,728

Source: Ebbinghaus, 'Dinosaurier der Dienstleistungsgesellschaft? Der Mitgliederschwund deutscher Gewerkschaften im historischen und internationalen Vergleich', MPIfG Working Paper 02/3 (2002).

TABLE 2

NET UNION DENSITY (%), DGB ONLY, BY STATUS, SEX AND AGE, 1970–2000

	West			West and East	
	1970	1980	1990	1991	2000
Total	25.4	27.3	24.2	28.1	17.31
Blue collar	40.7	47.3	48.4	48.1	36.9
White collar	12.6	16.3	15.1	16.1	12.6
Women	13.6	17.5	18.8	27.1	16.2
Under 25	20.4	21.1	20.5	22.6	10.2

Note: Net union density: members in employment, in per cent of all employees in the respective category.

Source: See Table 1.

resulted in a rapid increase in the average age of union members while early retirement raised the proportion of pensioners among the membership.[13] At the same time, new divisions emerged in the employers' camp as a consequence of the internationalisation of product markets and production systems. Facing unprecedented price competition in domestic and international markets, large and increasingly multinational firms responded to cost increases by asking their domestic suppliers for price reductions. Sometimes this directly followed wage rises conceded by the large firms, in their capacity as leaders of the employers' association, not just on their own behalf, but also on that of their small suppliers. Generally, declining resistance of large firms to wage demands, due to both foreign competition for market share and the new opportunities to compensate wage rises by productivity increases, convinced many small and medium sized employers that the large companies used the employers' associations to secure labour peace for themselves at their expense.

By the mid-1990s, after the end of the unification boom, an unprecedented revolt was under way inside the system of business associations. In the 1970s, Hanns-Martin Schleyer, the president of the BDA, was elected president of the BDI. During his double presidency, which coincided with the Schmidt government, the corporatist centralisation of German business associations reached its peak, and so did the role of employers as compared to trade associations. One-and-a-half decades later the situation had almost reversed. After the short interlude of national unity following 1989, the more specialised and less encompassing trade associations came to serve as representatives of the interests of smaller firms, and their most forceful and militant spokesman, Hans-Olaf Henkel, became the president of the BDI. Using neo-liberal rhetoric hitherto unheard from a German business leader, Henkel became highly visible by publicly confronting his counterparts at the BDA, first Klaus Murmann and then, after causing Murmann's resignation, Dieter Hundt.

Radicalisation among employers coincided with declining membership in employers' associations (Table 3). While large firms wanted to preserve sectoral bargaining since it protected them from having to pay wages in line with their economic performance, small and medium sized firms began to defect in rising numbers, especially after the 1995 strike in Bavaria.[14] Employers' association membership was particularly low in the east, where most firms had never joined an association in the first place.

Union decline and employer divisions contributed to a progressive *encapsulation* of the traditional system of industrial relations, in both a sectoral and generational sense. Co-determination and sectoral-level collective bargaining remain increasingly confined to industries, large firms and workers who came of age in the 1970s, with prospects for a further

TABLE 3

MEMBERSHIP DENSITY (%) METAL INDUSTRY EMPLOYERS' ASSOCIATION
(GESAMTMETALL)

	Companies		Employees	
	N	Density	In 1,000	Density
1993	8,863	42.8	2,663	63.1
West	7,752	44.0	2,459	63.3
East	1,111	35.7	204	60.0
1998	6,810	31.8	2,167	62.2
West	6,307	34.1	2,079	64.8
East	503	17.1	88	32.2

Sources: Gesamtmetall, Statistisches Bundesamt, own calculations.

TABLE 4

PLANTS AND EMPLOYEES NOT COVERED BY COLLECTIVE BARGAINING,
1998–2000

	Plants (%)		Employees (%)	
	West	East	West	East
1998	48	67	24	37
1999	52	74	27	43
2000	52	73	30	45

Note: Including workplaces in the public sector.

Source: IAB Betriebspanel.

gradual but steady decline of their reach. Survey data show that between 1998 and 2000 the percentage of West German plants not covered by collective agreements increased from 48 to 52 per cent (Table 4). In East Germany, where industry-wide collective bargaining never really took root, the share of plants without a collective agreement increased from 67 to 73 per cent.[15] Moreover, collective agreements were increasingly company agreements. In 2000, about 39 per cent of all collective agreements were company agreements, as compared to 27 per cent in 1990 (Table 5).

Coverage by works councils in the private sector had decreased already in the 1980s (Table 6). The decline accelerated in the 1990s and coverage fell from 50.6 per cent in 1981 (West Germany) to 39.5 per cent in 1994.[16] In the domain of IG Metall, coverage declined by five percentage points between 1994 and 1998, from 68 to 63 per cent. This adds up to an overall decline between 1984 and 1998 of 15 percentage points.[17]

Within the shrinking core of the German system of industrial relations, older tendencies towards *decentralisation* to the plant level continued to operate with new force. Works councils took over a growing share of the subject matter that used to be regulated in industrial agreements, and unions and employers' associations began to write industrial agreements that have left broad space for workplace parties to negotiate customised workplace-

TABLE 5

NUMBER OF COLLECTIVE AGREEMENTS
(COMPANY AGREEMENTS AS % OF ALL AGREEMENTS)

	West	East	Total
1990	33,449 (26)	670 (64)	34,119 (27)
1997	40,066 (33)	7,268 (46)	47,334 (35)
2000	46,277 (37)	8,663 (49)	54,940 (39)

Source: Federal Ministry of Labor and Social Affairs, *Tarifvertragliche Arbeitsbedingungen im Jahre 2000* (Bonn 2001).

TABLE 6

PLANTS WITH ELECTED WORKS COUNCILS, PRIVATE SECTOR;
EMPLOYEES COVERED BY WORKS COUNCILS
(% TOTAL PRIVATE SECTOR EMPLOYMENT), 1981–94

	1981	1984	1987	1990	1994
Number of plants	37,650	36,492	35,687	35,198	38,425
% employees covered	50.6	49.4	47.9	45.4	39.5

Source: A. Hassel, 'The Erosion of the German System of Industrial Relations', *British Journal of Industrial Relations* (Sept. 1999), pp.484–505.

level arrangements. Of the few forms in East Germany that are covered by an industrial agreement, a growing number pay less than the official wage, often with the consent of works councils desperate to protect employment in their workplace.[18] Paying below the going rate as set by a collective agreement (*unter Tarif*) has spread to firms under distress in the west, and so has the practice of more or less tacit concession bargaining between employers and works councils.[19]

De facto decentralisation of industrial relations is forcing unions to rethink their role with respect to the new bargaining arenas at the workplace, where workers are represented not by unions but by works councils. Local autonomy is causing unprecedented diversity of working conditions between firms, as reflected particularly in a wave of so-called production site agreements (*Standortvereinbarungen*) between works councils and managements, often tolerated and sometimes co-signed by industrial unions. *Standortvereinbarungen* contain workforce concessions, often involving derogations from collective agreements, in exchange for employment guarantees or management commitments to future investment at a given production site. Agreements of this sort have the strong support of employers' associations, which refer to them as local *Bündnisse für Arbeit* and ask for changes in the law on collective agreements to make them easier to negotiate and safer from legal challenge.[20]

Unions, and especially IG Metall, have helplessly watched the de facto decentralisation of collective bargaining, sometimes trying to prevent it, sometimes condoning it under pressure from the membership, and often looking the other way. Ironically, decentralisation is in part another outgrowth of the 1984 working-time settlement, which gave works councils and individual employers the task of setting the details of working time regimes, thereby preparing the institutional arena for the new workplace bargaining of the 1990s. Under pressure from works councils, unions agreed to insert clauses in industrial agreements that allowed individual employers, with the consent of the works council or of the social partners, to suspend wage increases, extend working hours, or cut working hours at reduced pay (so-called hardship or opening clauses). As a result, reform of the sectoral collective bargaining regime is very much under way, although more or less surreptitiously. So far, national unions are still puzzling over their response. In 2002, IG Metall rejected a proposal by its leader for differential wage settlements for firms in different economic conditions.

THE SCHRÖDER DEADLOCK: WEAK STATE, WEAK ASSOCIATIONS

When Schröder came to power in the autumn of 1998, he had seen Kohl fail twice in attempts to deal with the – mutually intertwined – crises of the labour market and the social security system. First, when he tried in vain for a negotiated consensual approach and, second, when he was forced to take unilateral action, which led to his defeat at Schröder's own hands. As a social democrat, Schröder might have thought he had a better chance than his predecessor to get the unions to support the necessary changes. In any case, the social-democratic Left, which had never liked him, and in particular his rival Oskar Lafontaine still controlled the party. Already during the campaign Schröder promised to create the *Bündnis* that Kohl had been unable to forge in 1996. This was not least to avoid answering questions about his employment policy, which, as he repeated again and again, was a matter for discussion in the new *Bündnis*. Otherwise, deep disagreements inside his camp, both within the party and between party and unions, would have been revealed.

The Left, however, was less than enthusiastic about tripartism. Their sentiment was shared by powerful forces inside the unions, which did not see why they should share with the employers access to a government that had come to power mainly because of their political and financial support. Moreover, almost from the beginning, major government ministries regarded the Alliance as a barely concealed instrument of the Chancellery to centralise government decision-making by controlling external relations with business and labour. This was true in particular for the Ministry of Labour, which was to be just one participant among others in the government delegation, and for the Ministry of Finance. In addition, the parliamentary party of the SPD was concerned about tripartite agreements that it would be expected to execute unchanged. Other than Schröder and his circle, only the employers were really interested in an alliance as it promised them formal and regular contacts with a chancellor who was not a member of their political family.

In December 1998, the Alliance for Jobs, Training and Competitiveness was formally instituted.[21] Operated out of the Chancellor's Office, it started with a long declaration of intent, in many points similar to the document Kohl had tried to get accepted, which promised far-reaching reforms aimed at increasing employment.[22] The first on a long list of measures for this purpose was a 'fundamental reform of the social security system'. An elaborate system of committees was set up, overseen by a 'Steering Committee' chaired by the head of the Chancellery, at the time a cabinet minister and Schröder's closest aide. Soon it became apparent that the

Alliance had a much harder time to get into operation than the chancellor might have hoped. Difficulties abounded on all three sides of the bargaining table; indeed, they rather increased than subsided in subsequent years.

As far as the government was concerned, it never achieved the internal unity that would have been required for hard bargaining with unions and employers. Lafontaine, by and large, boycotted the meetings; publicly he and his secretary of state encouraged high union wage claims which, they argued, were needed to increase demand and thereby improve employment.[23] Other ministers insisted that Alliance committees dealing with issues under their jurisdiction had to be chaired by them – which meant that the ministries' established advisory bodies continued to operate as before, under new names but still out of the Chancellery's sight. The Ministry of Labour, which traditionally was the bridgehead of the unions in the federal government structure, continued to control the Federal Employment Office (Bundesanstalt für Arbeit), the largest of all clientelistic structures as it was governed by a board of delegates of employers' associations, trade unions and the three levels of government, *Bund*, Länder and local communities.[24]

At least equally important, however, was the fact that the social-democratic Left was adamant that the party keep its election promises to the unions. As a result, Schröder had to scrap all of Kohl's social security reforms by January 1999, without having a chance to extract anything in return from the unions, for example concessions on labour market reform. Moreover, the party immediately proceeded to legislate on a number of other issues dear to the heart of the unions, like higher social security contributions for low wage earners and curbs on the so-called 'pseudo self-employed' (*Scheinselbständige*), many of whom were by law declared wage earners, thus becoming liable to pay social security. None of this ever came to the Alliance bargaining table, and all of it was handed to the unions for free.

Employers, for their part, were satisfied with having a foot in the door of the new government and looked the other way when the Alliance, almost immediately after it had been set up, was circumvented by bilateral agreements between government and unions. In the longer term, employers regarded the Alliance as an opportunity to push for wage moderation – or, more precisely, to involve the chancellor in wage negotiations where, given the economic situation, he could not but be supportive of their position. Obviously the unions, insisting on the constitutional principle of free collective bargaining, immediately threatened to walk out if wages were mentioned in any other than the most general way. Being able on their own to get what they wanted from the Ministry of Labour and their friends in the SPD parliamentary party, they saw no reason to talk about wage restraint. The most obvious case in point was the amendment of the Works Constitution Act in 2000, which was to prevent a further erosion of the organisational position of unions at the workplace. This bill never came on the agenda of the Alliance, nor was it in any way part of a tripartite or, for that matter, bipartite *quid pro quo*.

Employers, too, had pet projects that they were averse to seeing discussed in context, let alone in that of a joint policy pledged to increasing employment. While the unions and the Labour Ministry became obsessed with raising money to save the pension system and fund labour market policy, business concentrated its efforts on the reform of corporate taxation, which it strongly preferred to pursue on a bilateral basis.[25] The Labour Ministry, for its part, tried increasingly single-mindedly to get a pension reform passed. Both tax reform and pension reform were dealt with on their own terms, in intense political wrestling between government and opposition in the Bundestag and especially in the second chamber, the Bundesrat. At no point during Schröder's entire first term was there an attempt at a comprehensive discussion, not to speak of a trilateral give-and-take, in the *Bündnis für Arbeit* of the relative merits or the interdependence of these two central government projects from the perspective of employment.

This is not to say that bargaining with the unions over pension reform was anything other than contentious. At first the issue was complicated by its linkage to early retirement and labour market supply management. Once *Rente mit 60* had been cleared out of the way, the government proposed an obligatory supplementary pension scheme, fully funded by worker contributions only, to compensate for declining benefits under the existing pay-as-you-go system. When the opposition rejected compulsory participation, the government had to throw in high subsidies as an inducement to subscribers. As a concession to the unions, cuts in public pensions had to remain far below what had originally been intended. Moreover, unions and employers managed to convince the government to make the public subsidies available also to occupational pension schemes provided by employers, and to exempt worker contributions to these from social security taxes if made under a collective agreement. In the end, Schröder's and Riester's pension reform not only involved significant future commitments of tax money, but also cut public pensions less than deemed necessary, while at the same time reducing the revenues of the public pension system.

Not a single package deal cutting across the jurisdictional boundaries of different ministries ever came to pass. After two years, the Bündnis had become an empty shell. Meetings provided photo opportunities for a chancellor who, at the end of 1999, had been pronounced politically dead and was rescued only by the party finance scandal caused by his predecessor. Alliance committees produced papers and nothing else, apart from minor changes in labour market policy that were enacted in early 2002 but soon overtaken by the dramatic developments later that year. Tripartite meetings were convened every half year, and always under threats from unions or employers, and in the end also from the chancellor, no longer to take part. It seemed the only reason why unions and employers allowed the Bündnis to continue was that they needed it to threaten each other and the government with resigning from it.

The one major accomplishment with which the public credited the Alliance was the moderate two-year wage settlement in early 2000.[26] It is true that Schröder, like all his predecessors who used to hold private discussions with the main players in critical wage rounds, was involved in circumventing the peak associations and talked directly to the sectoral associations. While the unions, clinging to the sacred principle of *Tarifautonomie*, denied such talks had taken place, insisting that they could in no way be binding for them, the employers to the contrary celebrated the moderate settlement as a triumph of the Alliance, so as to assuage their *Mittelstand* members who had grown ever more sceptical about tripartite talks which excluded wages. The government was helped by the division in the union camp between IG Metall and the chemical workers' union, IG BCE, which settled ahead of IG Metall at a level that was generally considered moderate.[27]

Two years into his four-year period of office, Schröder found himself in the same situation as Kohl at the end of his reign, in that both unilateral and negotiated solutions to the labour market crisis had eluded him. Indeed his party and the electorate, in a sequence of Länder elections, had made it clear that they would not stand for effective unilateral measures to lower non-wage labour costs or increase labour flexibility. As a result, Schröder's bargaining power with the unions – which had proven in the 1998 campaign that they were capable of punishing a hostile government at the polls – was probably lower than Kohl's in 1996. Government weakness, exacerbated by Schröder's early loss of his Bundesrat majority, was complemented by declining organisational strength of the social partners. Among employers, BDI and BDA watched each other suspiciously, the personal relations between their leaders poisoned beyond repair. Making concessions to unions and government even more difficult, neither of them could afford any longer to set aside the interests of the increasingly vocal small and medium sized firms.

On the union side, the peak association DGB was less than ever able to speak for IG Metall, which was immersed in a lasting succession crisis. Moreover, IG Metall was desperately looking for a way to extricate itself from its historical demand for further cuts in weekly working hours, which had become thoroughly unpopular with the membership. To conceal its *volte face*, the union demanded a lowering of the legal age of retirement from 65 to 60. As much as the government might have been willing to oblige, this was out of the question given the demographic situation. The government did, however, include in its pension legislation the possibility for unions and employers' associations to regulate occupational pensions by collective agreement and use them to fund early retirement. Meanwhile, Alliance meetings finally took on a ceremonial character. From the summer of 2001 on, the Bündnis was kept alive only for public consumption.

At the beginning of the election year, all the old problems the government might have hoped would be covered up by a few more months of the bubble economy began to return with a vengeance. Unemployment again approached four million. The supplementary pension system, the pride of Schröder's social policy, was only slowly being taken up. Non-wage labour costs were not falling; in fact, all the pension reform and the energy tax had accomplished was to keep them from rising, and only for a short breathing space. Both the health care and the pension systems would soon need fresh money. At the same time, large cuts in corporate taxes, designed to please business and thereby force the opposition to let them pass the Bundesrat, were starving the budgets of the federal government, the Länder and the local communities. As the government was unable to cut expenditures even further, it was getting in conflict with the budget consolidation targets under Monetary Union. As a result, the European Commission was getting ready to put Germany on notice for breaching the Stability Pact. Politically this would undercut Schröder's only remaining claim to fame – beginning to reduce the national debt.

In this situation, Schröder all of a sudden dropped all previous pretensions at tripartite consensus and abruptly switched to unilateral action, skilfully exploiting the approaching campaign and using his weakness in the opinion polls as a source of strength. A scandal was revealed in the Bundesanstalt für Arbeit, where it had become common practice for officials to falsify their job placement statistics. While this was not news among insiders or in the Chancellery or the Ministry of Labour,

Schröder used a secret report by the government accounting office to fire the leadership of the Bundesanstalt and appoint a close confidant as its president. The government also pushed through the Bundestag legislation that curtailed the influence of the social partners on the Bundesanstalt and fundamentally reorganised it, to make the speedy placement of job seekers its principal activity. With the election approaching, SPD and unions could not but close ranks behind the Chancellor, no matter how much they may have disliked the new policies he imposed on them.

Moreover, to design a long-term reform of labour market policy, Schröder appointed a commission under the VW personnel director, Peter Hartz, which was to report in August, a month before the elections. The composition of the Hartz Commission represented a break with the tripartite philosophy of the Alliance for Jobs in that its 21 members included no more than two union representatives and only one official of a – small firm – business association, the Federation of Craft Associations (Zentralverband des Deutschen Handwerks). Behind the scenes, the Chancellery remained deeply involved in the work of the commission, quite unlike the aloof position it had taken in relation to the various bodies of the Alliance. Having publicly committed himself at the outset to full implementation of whatever the commission proposed, Schröder pressed the unions and his party to profess their support for Hartz throughout the campaign and to allow the commission to issue a unanimous report. Not knowing whether Schröder's last minute manoeuvre would cut any ice with the voters, and in any case expecting to be able to renege after the election, Schröder's followers reluctantly acquiesced in his exercise in state unilateralism.

Once the election was won, the SPD parliamentary party and the unions began to chip away at the Hartz proposals. However, when the new coalition agreement between the SPD and the Greens was gradually revealed,[28] the continuing financial crisis of the state and the social security *parafisci* came back to the attention of an electorate that, under the influence of Schröder's campaign rhetoric and hardly disturbed by an exceedingly cautious opposition candidate, had spent the summer in a happy condition of collective amnesia. A series of stop-gap measures, such as an increase in social security and health insurance contributions as well as in various taxes, had a devastating impact on an unprepared public and caused an unprecedented loss of government support in the opinion polls that was to last well into 2003.

Perhaps anticipating that he might have to spend the rest of his second term defending an unending string of improvised emergency measures to an increasingly impatient electorate, Schröder returned to his approach of before the election. In a surprise move, he dissolved the Ministry of Labour, assigned labour market policy to the jurisdiction of the Ministry of Economic Affairs, and appointed a political heavyweight and proven right-winger, Wolfgang Clement, to the new *Superministerium*. Having deprived the unions of their bridgehead inside the state and facing two major regional elections, the government announced a series of painful labour market and social security reforms that rendered the new coalition agreement meaningless. Replaying Hartz, it appointed another commission, under the economist Bert Rürup, to propose a reform of the health care system within a year, pre-empting the minister in charge who was an exponent of the conservative wing of the SPD parliamentary party. Also, with the help of the opposition, the government passed various pieces of legislation derived from the Hartz proposals but in part going beyond them, for example on temporary work and low-wage employment. In effect, it replaced the restrictive legislation of early 1999 with measures that were exactly its opposite. With a new and unproven DGB leader, the unions looked on in bewilderment.[29]

OUTLOOK: FROM STABLE STATE TO STALEMATE?

In its heyday, *Modell Deutschland* disciplined business and labour and forced them to work with each other, pursuing their respective interests in ways that did not interfere with the sustainability of the existing industrial order. With hindsight, it appears that this accomplishment was conditional on a range of factors which were beyond the control of the parties involved. Foremost among these were world markets that not only put a premium on the comparative advantages of the German labour market regime, but also allowed for near-full employment in Germany at high and relatively egalitarian wages. This condition slowly began to wither away in the late 1970s and finally came to an end in the years after unification, when high unemployment combined with low labour market participation became the signature characteristic of the German economy.[30]

While social partnership had been a solution to the problems of the 1960s – which were problems of political institution-building, social integration and industrial modernisation – it became itself a problem in the 1980s and 1990s. As unemployment increased and turned into a permanent condition, the government of the weak German state was unable and unwilling to reorganise the labour market – unable because of strong unions and employers bent on avoiding industrial confrontation, and unwilling for fear of electoral retaliation. Instead, corporatist social partnership responded to the national and international monetarism of the 1980s through large-scale early retirement and costly labour market policy programmes. This practice reached its peak after unification in the early 1990s when it underwrote tripartite consensus on preserving the West German model by transferring it wholesale to the east.

That consensus, however, was bound to break up. With the shrinking of the core of *Modell Deutschland*, and the corresponding need to pay for a growing number of casualties, resistance to consensus and its costs increased among employers. Also, high and persistent unemployment sent union membership into a tailspin, and unions and co-determination became encapsulated in a still highly productive but inevitably shrinking industrial sector. Wage and employment policies that had been inclusive and encompassing in the past became insider policies, leaving it to the government to take care of the outsiders. Too weak to take risks and too strong to give way, German unions turned into a thoroughly conservative political and industrial force opposed to experiments of any kind and defending, with industrial and political-electoral means, the accumulated entitlements of an ageing core membership. Just as their weakness made unions unwilling to make concessions, it encouraged employers to demand deeper changes than even a conservative government could make without endangering its electoral support.

The deadlock that began in the final years of Kohl is not likely to be overcome any time soon. Public finances are overdrawn, the European Union effectively enforces fiscal austerity and the limits of taxation have long been reached, especially with respect to social security contributions. There is, therefore, little if anything a government could offer unions in exchange for co-operation in labour market reform. Improved workplace participation, as demonstrated by the controversy over the minuscule changes in the *Betriebsverfassungsgesetz* passed by the Red–Green government in 2000, is bound to antagonise employers, especially of the *Mittelstand*, given continuing pressures for industrial restructuring. Macroeconomic reflation is out of the question in the Europe of Monetary Union. More employment requires more flexible labour markets, but flexibility endangers the security unions are committed to defending. 'Flexicurity', the new magic formula for consensual change, is still no more than a word. Nobody knows what a new sort of security could look like that would be both supportive of flexibility and acceptable to the unions.

During his first term Schröder was in the same situation as Jospin, Prodi, d'Alema and other social-democratic modernisers searching for something attractive to offer their union supporters to make them give up their resistance to more flexible labour markets. Schröder's experiment with unilateral reform shortly before and then again after the 2002 election may signal the final end of his hope for a politically safe consensual solution. Business, including its associations, showed no gratitude for the corporate tax reform the government had handed them. Instead, it openly sided with the opposition in the election campaign, and may have convinced Schröder further that if he was to accomplish anything, he had to accomplish it unilaterally.

In early 2003, having failed in his first term to cajole the unions into co-operation within a tripartite setting, Schröder appeared to have given up on the Bündnis and seemed to be seeking an alliance with the opposition instead. The CDU victory in the February 2003 Länder elections having cemented opposition dominance over the Bundesrat, Schröder found himself having to convince the CDU/CSU that they had to share responsibility for reforms, while convincing his party that anything other than joint policies had become impossible. But it remained questionable at best whether the SPD parliamentary party and the social-democratic Left would support the sort of reforms that Schröder and Clement hoped to negotiate with the opposition. Given the congenital weaknesses of the semi-sovereign German state, the prospects of government unilateralism, short of a Grand Coalition, seem in the end not much better than those of the old politics of consensus.

NOTES

1. P.J. Katzenstein, *Policy and Politics in West Germany: The Growth of a Semisovereign State* (Philadelphia: Temple University Press 1987).
2. See F.W. Scharpf, *Crisis and Choice in European Social Democracy* (Cornell University Press: Ithaca 1991); W. Streeck, 'Pay Restraint without Incomes Policy: Institutionalized Monetarism and Industrial Unionism in Germany', in R. Dore, R. Boyer and Z. Mars (eds.), *The Return of Incomes Policy* (London: Pinter Publishers 1994); P. Hall and R. Franzese Jr., 'Mixed Signals – Central Bank Independence, Coordinated Wage Bargaining, and European Monetary Union', *International Organization* 52/3 (1998), pp.505–35.
3. See P.C. Schmitter, 'Still the Century of Corporatism?', *Review of Politics* 36 (1974), pp.85–131; P.C. Schmitter and G. Lehmbruch (eds.), *Trends toward Corporatist Intermediation* (Beverly Hills, CA: Sage 1979).
4. M. Olson, *The Rise and Decline of Nations: Economic Growth, Stagflation and Social Rigidities* (New Haven, CT: Yale University Press 1982).
5. In addition to the chemical workers, the 'Gang of Five' included the miners (IG BE), the food workers (NGG), the construction workers (IG BSE) and the textile and garment workers (GTB).
6. On the expansion of early retirement see C. Trampusch, 'The Blurring of Divisions between Institutional Stability and Institutional Change: The Case of Germany's Early Retirement Policy', in W. Streeck and K. Thelen (eds.), *Continuity and Discontinuity in Institutional Analysis* (forthcoming).
7. W. Streeck, 'From State Weakness as Strength to State Weakness as Weakness: Welfare Corporatism and the Private Use of the Public Interest', in S. Green and W. Paterson (eds.),

Semisovereignty Revisited: Governance, Institutions and Policies in United Germany (forthcoming).

8. K. Thelen, *Union of Parts. Labor Politics in Postwar Germany* (Ithaca, NY/London: Cornell University Press 1991).
9. The government set up a parliamentary investigation committee on the bankruptcy of *Neue Heimat* in order to highlight the economic incompetence of trade unions. This was unprecedented since these committees are designed to deal with wrongdoings of governments not of private firms.
10. K. Thelen, 'Why German Employers Cannot Bring Themselves to Dismantle the German Model', in T. Iversen, J. Pontusson and D. Soskice (eds.), *Unions, Employers, and Central Banks* (Cambridge: Cambridge University Press 2000), pp.138–172.
11. A. Hassel and B. Rehder, *Institutional Change in the German Wage Bargaining System: The Role of Big Companies*, MPIfG Working Paper 01/9 (Cologne: MPIfG 2001).
12. A. Hassel, 'The Erosion of the German System of Industrial Relations', *British Journal of Industrial Relations* 37 (1999), pp.483–505.
13. The median age of members of IG Metall was 38 years in 1979, 44 in 1994, and 48 in 2002 (own calculations based on IG Metall membership figures).
14. See Hassel and Rehder, *Institutional Change in the German Wage Bargaining System*. For data on resignation from employers associations, see W. Schroeder and B. Ruppert, 'Austritte aus Arbeitgeberverbänden. Motive – Ursachen – Ausmaß', *WSI-Mitteilungen* 49 (1996), pp.316–29.
15. See S. Kohaut and C. Schnabel, 'Tarifbindung im Wandel', *IW-Trend* 26/2 (1999).
16. Unfortunately, there are no comparable data on the results of the works council elections in 1998 and 2002 for the private sector as a whole.
17. A. Hassel, 'The Erosion Continues. Reply', *British Journal of Industrial Relations* 40/2 (June 2002), pp.309–17.
18. I. Artus, *Das deutsche Tarifsystem in der Krise. Erosion des Flächentarifvertrags in Ost und West* (Opladen: Westdeutscher Verlag 2001).
19. R. Bispinck, 'Überreguliert, undifferenziert, unbeweglich? Zum Flexibilitätspotential des Tarifvertragssystems und zu den Anforderungen an die künftige Tarifpolitik', in T. Dieterich (ed.), *Das Arbeitsrecht der Gegenwart. Jahrbuch für das gesamte Arbeitsrecht und die Arbeitsgerichtsbarkeit. Nachschlagewerk für Wissenschaft und Praxis* (Berlin: Erich Schmidt Verlag 1997), pp.49–67.
20. B. Rehder, 'Pfadwechsel ohne Systembruch. Der Beitrag betrieblicher Bündnisse für Beschäftigungssicherung und Wettbewerbsfähigkeit zum Wandel der Arbeitsbeziehungen in Deutschland' (Ph.D. Dissertation, Humboldt University Berlin 2002).
21. See on the conduct of the Alliance for Jobs W. Eichhorst, '2002: Bündnis für Arbeit – Chancen vergeben?', *Sozialer Fortschritt* 51, special issue 'Bilanz der rot-grünen Arbeitsmarkt-, Sozial- und Steuerpolitik' (2002), pp.274–8; S. Blancke and J. Schmid, 'Bilanz der Bundesregierung Schröder im Bereich der Arbeitsmarktpolitik 1998–2002: Ansätze zu einer doppelten Wende?', in C. Egle, T. Ostheim and R. Zohlnhöfer (eds.), *Das rot-grüne Projekt. Eine Bilanz der Regierung Schröder 1998–2002* (Wiesbaden: Westdeutscher Verlag 2003); A. Hassel, 'The Problem of Political Exchange in Complex Governance Systems: The Case of Germany's Alliance for Jobs', *European Journal of Industrial Relations* 7/3 (2001), pp.305–23.
22. Presse- und Informationsamt der Bundesregierung, 1998: Gemeinsame Erklärung des Bündnisses für Arbeit, Ausbildung und Wettbewerbsfähigkeit vom 7. Dezember 1998, www.buendnis.de
23. IG Metall, 'Costly Deal Averts Strikes for Now', *International Herald Tribune*, 19 Feb. 1999.
24. C. Trampusch, 'Die Bundesanstalt für Arbeit und das Zusammenwirken von Staat und Verbänden in der Arbeitsmarktpolitik von 1952 bis 2001', MPIfG Working Paper 02/5 (Cologne: MPIfG May 2002).
25. 'Bosses to the Barricades', *Financial Times*, 6 March 1999.
26. 'Schroeder Hails Accord with Unions Over Wages', *International Herald Tribune*, 10 Jan. 2000.
27. See A. Hassel, 'The Problem of Political Exchange in Complex Governance Systems: The

Case of Germany's Alliance for Jobs', *European Journal of Industrial Relations* 7/3 (2001), pp.305–23.

28. SPD/Bündnis'90/GRÜNE, '2002: Erneuerung – Gerechtigkeit – Nachhaltigkeit. Für ein wirtschaftlich starkes, soziales und ökologisches Deutschland. Für eine lebendige Demokratie' (Berlin, 16 Oct. 2002).

29. Michael Sommer, an official of the former union of postal workers was elected chairman of the DGB in May 2002.

30. W. Streeck, 'German Capitalism: Does it Exist? Can it Survive?', in C. Crouch and W. Streeck (eds.), *Political Economy of Modern Capitalism: Mapping Convergence and Diversity* (London: Sage 1997), pp.33–54.

Political-Economic Context and Partisan Strategies in the German Federal Elections, 1990–2002

HERBERT KITSCHELT

Policy preferences articulated by German voters on the political demand side have evolved from 1990 to 2002 and so have policy options offered by competing German parties on the supply side. But have they changed in such ways as to facilitate the eventual adoption of innovative economic policies that would address the performance problems generated by the persistence and gradual crumbling of established institutions and practices associated with the German model? Looking back at the most recent federal elections, this article submits empirical evidence to provide a negative answer to this question. The profile of the winning electoral coalition is increasingly that of a social protectionist majority with a strong preference to defend the traditional German political-economic model as much as possible. Looking forward, however, the opposition minority begins to configure more and more around groups dissatisfied with that status quo and leaning towards a revision of the German model, a trend that ultimately might result in majority government consisting of reform-oriented parties.

The geographical divide between Eastern Germany, where the social protectionist majority is hegemonic, and Western Germany, where the social protectionist majority has a thin lead, is only a special case of a broader emerging partisan realignment between regions, economic sectors and voters separating those with preferences for social protectionist policies from those that favour more market-liberal reforms. The continued evolution of this realignment, accelerated by economic stagnation and crisis as a catalyst, may render it possible that a more sharply contoured market-liberal reformist party alliance may eventually prevail at the national level. The electoral rule that only parties with five or more per cent of national electoral support or three single member district mandates can claim a proportionate share of legislative seats may facilitate this outcome. The Party of Democratic Socialism (PDS), in particular, which still attracts a substantial segment of the social protectionist electorate in Eastern

Germany, may continue failing to clear the national five per cent hurdle of legislative representation, as it did in the 2002 federal election.

Although the dynamic of voter flows from the 1998 to the 2002 elections primarily appears to relate to the economic situation, the changing alignments among German voters have also socio-cultural causes. Both economic and socio-cultural realignments cross-cut conventional class divides and contribute to the emergence of a new landscape of polar opposites and affinities among electoral constituencies as well as political parties that may eventually even make a Christian Democratic–Green reform alliance possible.

The system of democratic supply and demand undergoes dynamic change resulting from two sources. In the short run, vote- and office-seeking politicians work with basically fixed policy preferences among the critical segment of the electorate that monitors and responds to programmatic policy appeals, but strategically adapt their parties' issue position in response to their competitors' moves in the issue space. Of course, valence issues based on a retrospective performance of the economy under a party's government ('competence' to achieve universally desired economic objectives), and non-issue signals (candidate personality, incorruptibility, and so on), and the unthinking identification of a large segment of the electorate with a given party also play a role. In the long run, the voters' issue preferences themselves are subject to dynamic change originating not only in exogenous social and technological processes, but also in endogenous policy-making and politicians' issue leadership. In particular, the profile of the welfare state and of political-economic institutions affects the distribution of economic and social policy preferences through the outcomes they deliver in terms of citizens' life chances.

The German model shaped a popular preference distribution overwhelmingly oriented towards the maintenance of the current political status quo. The corresponding feature on the political supply-side is a centripetal competition of the two major German parties, the Social Democrats (SPD) and the Christian Democrats (CDU and CSU) with only marginally differentiated economic policy positions. The question now is whether the interaction of exogenous economic and social developments with status quo-preserving policies, resulting in economic drift and slow growth since the early 1990s, will stimulate both a gradual change in the demand-side for economic policy *and* new incentives for politicians to reconfigure the supply of alternatives in the future. This article claims that, in fact, the development of electoral alignments in German politics from the 1990s to the 2002 election signals that this process is under way, even though a reform-oriented coalition has not yet won a majority. The article sketches West and East German demand and supply conditions for political alignments from the 1970s to the turn of the century. It then gathers empirical indicators from the 1998 and 2002 federal elections that reveal elements of changing electoral alignments and corresponding party strategies. The conclusion returns to the prospects of economic reform under the conditions of an unravelling of competitive centripetalism in German politics.

CHANGING DEMAND AND SUPPLY CONDITIONS IN GERMAN POLITICS

Political Demand Conditions: Economic and Socio-Cultural Preferences

In the economic dimension, citizens divide over the extent to which governments should accept the spontaneous market allocation or redistributive intervention on behalf of the less fortunate. The former position is often labelled 'right', the latter 'left' in current political semantics. In the socio-cultural dimension, citizens hold different normative conceptions of appropriate behaviour that range from a libertarian extreme – featuring personal autonomy, tolerance for difference, gender equality, multicultural expressiveness, and participatory self-governance in collective choices – to an authoritarian extreme – with insistence on the authority of binding collective norms and a particular image of 'social decency', uniformity and conformity enshrined in the model of the paternalist family and its sexual code, religious and linguistic homogeneity, and deference to the authority of political elites. In popular political semantics, the libertarian position is often identified with the left, the authoritarian position with the right.

In the economic dimension, the role of class – defined either in Marxist terms as ownership or non-ownership of means of production or in social stratificationist terms as the difference between manual wage earners and the white-collar salariat as well as the self-employed – in structuring political interests gives way to sectoral-occupational affiliations and individual human capital endowments, characterised by the level and field of educational training, age and gender.[1] Generally, citizens prefer spontaneous market allocation of scarce goods to authoritative economic and social policies if they (1) work in private sector firms with hard budget constraints, particularly those exposed to domestic or international competition, (2) have human capital endowments that allow them to adjust flexibly to changing labour market conditions (for example, higher education, especially in technical, financial and legal fields with little educational 'asset specificity'), and (3) have demographic attributes that enhance market adaptation, such as youth or male gender, still resulting in less commitment to adaptation-impeding family obligations to children and the elderly in current Western family systems.

In socio-cultural terms, those with high cognitive and social skills embrace libertarian views of tolerance for diversity and participatory collective decision-making instead of authoritarian views of collective conformity and top-down command. Libertarians tend to (1) have acquired above average education and work in (2) dialogical, client-interactive occupations (such as in education, culture, social services) drawing on knowledge and technology with uncertain cause–effect relations and relying on the input of the clients themselves. They also tend to be (3) female, possibly because of self-selection into client-interactive employment sectors. Citizens with less education and/or in object- and document-processing, monotone work situations employing technology with more definite knowledge about cause–effect relations, in contrast, tend to subscribe to more rigid, intolerant codes of individual conduct and collective decision-making processes which insist on conformity and authority.[2]

What are the political-economic parameters that influence the distribution and configuration of political preferences? Three historical constellations obviously idealise the conditions of mature welfare states in the 1970s and 1980s of which the West German political economy was one prominent example; the change of these conditions accelerated in the 1990s and after the turn of the millennium (post-industrial 'new' economy). A further complication is the political economy of post-communism (the former GDR) adding to Germany's configuration in the second phase. Demographic shifts have also begun to assert themselves in the distribution of political preferences of wealthy post-industrial polities.

In the first phase of the 1970s–1980s, *mature comprehensive welfare states* created a left-wing and libertarian constituency of highly skilled white-collar employees in client-interactive domestically sheltered and often public or quasi-public organisations. A job-creating or at least job-preserving and internationally competitive manufacturing sector and a limited dependency ratio of elderly and unemployed people kept these arrangements viable. Moreover, the system generated sufficient resources to compensate declining groups of small business independents (especially farmers) and low-skill manual and clerical wage earners, despite the fact that some elements of these groups crystallised around right-authoritarian political appeals in the 1980s. Whereas both constituencies embraced socio-cultural authoritarianism (including a rejection of immigration and multiculturalism), it was obviously the small business constituency more so than the marginal working class supporters who embraced a market-liberal critique of the welfare state.

In the second phase, characterised by the *expansion of a post-industrial political economy based on new information technology and services* from the 1980s onwards, (1) de-industrialisation with human capital intensive productivity improvements in manufacturing and administration and (2) the changing geographic distribution of comparative advantages in global markets resulted in the redundancy of increasing numbers of industrial workers and a structural crisis of the welfare state in the advanced capitalist welfare states of Europe.[3] Highly skilled labour market entrants are now more likely to be absorbed by the private, market-exposed sector than by non-profit welfare state organisations. This increases the proportion of the right-libertarian clientele, particularly among younger age cohorts.[4]

While the educated white-collar 'middle class' leans towards libertarian socio-cultural sensibilities, the less educated clerical and manual wage earners tend to be more authoritarian. The latter, however, are internally divided between social protectionist and market-liberal tendencies. Particularly among the younger age cohorts, those with occupational success in market- and export-exposed firms tend to embrace market-liberalisation and social reform policies to secure the continued competitiveness of their employers. They affiliate less with labour unions and social democratic parties than older workers, particularly in sheltered and domestically oriented industries and generally stronger union and social democratic ties. Young unskilled marginal entrants into the labour force may look for more radical alternatives. With socialist political options having become unviable, they may not vote on economics at all, but support an extreme authoritarian right with 'welfare chauvinist' demands to halt immigration and limit social policy benefits to the indigenous population. Since the 1990s, right-wing authoritarian parties have had incentives to tone down their market-liberal rhetoric in favour of a more selective welfare chauvinism, corresponding to their rising popularity among working class and clerical voters.

Figures 1 and 2 graphically illustrate the changing distribution of the main voter preferences from the heyday of the welfare state to the post-industrial political economy emerging in the new millennium.[5] Politicians now face a two-dimensional competitive arena in which it is all but impossible to find a strict equilibrium strategy, if the formal theory of spatial party competition applies. What constrains parties is their reputation

FIGURE 1

DISTRIBUTION OF POLITICAL PREFERENCES FROM THE POST-WAR DECADES
TO THE 1970s AND 1980s

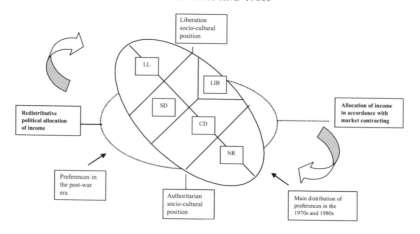

FIGURE 2

DISTRIBUTION OF POLITICAL PREFERENCES FROM THE 1980s
TO THE TURN OF THE MILLENNIUM

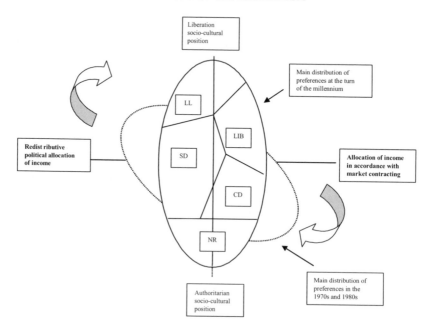

based on their past track record and programmatic appeal in government or opposition, their ability to update such appeals only incrementally without losing core voters, and the costs sunk in the parties' organisational structures and stock of cadres. Political parties encounter strategic dilemmas in this space of competition described for the German case below.

A further complication in the second phase was the addition of East Germany's formerly *sheltered, regulated import-substituting planned economy* to the West German arrangements. Such planned economies almost completely eliminated efficiency-stimulating domestic or international market competition among firms. Moreover, socialist economy skill levels and profiles were inferior to an advanced capitalist economy. As a result of market liberalisation after communism, therefore, most workers and employees in state-owned companies feared for their jobs and almost automatically joined a 'Left' social protectionist camp. The exception were young, highly educated individuals who tended to embrace markets and socio-cultural libertarianism. At the aggregate level, the advocates of market-liberalism were stronger in countries with greater experience with past capitalist development and better prospects of inserting themselves into the Western capitalist economies.[6]

In the third phase, beginning around the turn to the new millennium, the *political and economic consequences of the demographic revolution* start to gain centre-stage. As the share of elderly people in all advanced capitalist democracies rises in the first several decades of the new millennium, distributive struggles will intensify. Older people demand the bulk of transfer payments and public or non-profit social services. Their discount rates are too high to accept welfare state cutbacks and market liberalisation now in order to increase economic growth later. Moreover, the current elderly generation is less educated and more culturally authoritarian. They resist immigration on cultural and economic grounds. If major established parties with whom they identify move away from protectionist social policies, these groups could become available to a populist, redistributive authoritarian party. At the opposite end of the political spectrum are young, highly educated people in the market-exposed sector who endorse both multiculturalisation and market liberalisation.

Political Supply Conditions: Strategic Options and Dilemmas for Political Parties

Political parties affect voters by issue appeals. Even though some voters respond to such appeals in their electoral choice, issue appeals are obviously not the only mechanism deciding electoral contests. Some citizens vote on the economic performance under the incumbent government (retrospective voting). Most citizens cast their votes on habit, emotion or social conformism. They have either too hazy and vague a structure of personal programmatic policy positions to be affected by parties' issue appeals or they are too rigidly ideological to respond to new messages. Hence, strategic politicians can focus only on a subset of intermediately informed and ideologically sophisticated voters who actually can be swayed by political appeals.[7] Such voters behave instrumentally in a spatial sense and vote deliberately. They support the party close to their own ideal point on salient issues, when compared to other viable party alternatives. Even if these voters amount to no more than 10–20 per cent of the electorate, they constitute the systematic component that affects the aggregate response patterns of electorates and structures voter-partisan alignments over time.

In Germany, both CDU/CSU and SPD could take credit for crafting and extending the comprehensive welfare state. Hence, both parties were able to attract large constituencies supportive of this arrangement. Until recently, the SPD's followers were concentrated among unionised wage earners in manufacturing. In the past, the CDU/CSU drew its welfare state constituency especially from the ranks of pensioners. Both parties experienced internal divisions over socio-cultural issues. All in all, the SPD was only moderately more libertarian than the CDU/CSU.

In Western Germany, a small liberal party, the Free Democrats (FDP), has traditionally supplemented the two parties. It has combined a mildly civil libertarian position with a support for market liberalisation, tempered by special interest group advantages for the professions. Since the 1980s, the left-libertarian Greens have expanded this party system, capturing welfare state constituencies, particularly younger, well-educated non-profit sector employees. An extreme right, under the label of the Republicans (REPs) and combining marginalised working class and small business constituencies, which was on the verge of succeeding in the late 1980s, ultimately failed because of infighting over the political message of the party. Moreover, German unification enabled the CDU/CSU to adopt the mantle of national unification, depriving the extreme right of an important issue. In the 1990s, the German extreme right was divided into several small parties, and it has not won even moderate electoral support since then except in a handful of isolated state elections.[8]

The incorporation of Eastern Germany in 1990 made it difficult for the West German parties to promote a unified all-German winning electoral formula to all voters. Socio-cultural libertarian politics were unpopular in Eastern Germany and anti-immigrant feelings ran higher than in Western

Germany, even though the resident population of foreigners was very small. After the exceptional unification election of 1990, the libertarian Greens and the FDP lost most of their voters in Eastern Germany. Because East German voters are highly averse to market-liberalism, SPD and CDU/CSU appeals in the east must be even more social protectionist than in Western Germany. Even so, social protectionism and anti-capitalism in the east have still enabled the successor of the former communist ruling party, the Party of Democratic Socialism (PDS), to garner a substantial share of the vote and increase it in the federal elections of 1994 and 1998.

What, then, are the strategic options of the various parties in the new decade to confront the declining economic performance combined with rising unemployment and the prospect of demographic change, all of which make it increasingly hard to maintain the existing welfare state and associated institutions of the German model? As the problems of the German political economy become more pressing, politicians may no longer hope to win elections by simply playing down economic reform issues, embracing bland middle-of-the-road status quo-oriented economic policy appeals and focusing on socio-cultural appeals and non-issue attributes (politicians' personalities, valence issues, competence, leadership).

European party systems display either a rather clear bipolar competition between focal parties in a social-democratic leftist camp and a distinctly market-liberal camp with one major liberal party attracting more than 20 per cent of the vote – such as in Britain, Denmark, the Netherlands or Sweden – or a centripetal competition between a moderate social-democratic party and a large conservative centrist party that organised a political-class compromise around institutions of the welfare state after World War II.[9] Examples of this latter configuration are Austria, France, Italy and Germany. In this second competitive format, conservative parties with a positive reputation for social protectionism can engage in market-liberal reforms only at the risk of losing a substantial share of their established voters, especially pensioners and other net beneficiaries of the welfare state. They could make up for this loss only if market-liberal policies attracted a large portion of blue- and white-collar wage earners situated in the market-exposed sectors of the economy from the social-democratic camp, as well as younger professionals with a market-liberal disposition. In Germany, while the blue- and white-collar constituencies tend to be socio-culturally middle of the road or more authoritarian, younger professionals affirm distinctly libertarian positions and are thus inclined to vote for small liberal parties, such as the FDP or a Green party with less social protectionist emphasis. In any case, the realignment of conservative electorates around market-liberal policies would create huge risks for centrist conservative parties accompanied by internal strains that could break them up. The experience of Italy and Japan in the 1990s, but also the gradual decline of traditional conservative parties in Austria, Belgium, the Netherlands and Switzerland may serve as illustrations.[10] Only a serious economic and political-electoral crisis might make such conservative parties see the risk of rupture with past programmatic appeals as less severe than the continued support of incrementally adjusting the policy status quo.

Social democratic competitors to centrist conservative parties also have little incentive to embrace vigorous market-liberal reform. When social democrats in government engineer market-liberal reforms, a centrist conservative opposition party with a track record of building the welfare state can credibly oppose such unpopular policies and 'leapfrog' to the left of the social democrats in order to alienate social protectionist voters from the governing party. Because conservatives are credible defenders of the welfare state, labour unions would not acquiesce to market-liberal reform, but would threaten to defect to the opposition.[11] This would further electorally weaken the social democrats.

In party systems with centripetal competition, both social democrats and centrist conservatives thus have to choose between unpalatable strategic options when the welfare state enters a structural crisis. Either they engage in only marginal, incremental economic reform, but risk lacklustre economic performance that prompts an electoral backlash based on retrospective economic voting. Or they embrace vigorous reform, which would in turn enable the major opposition party to adopt the mantle of social protection and attract some of the governing party's now alienated core constituencies.

In contrast, small niche parties, such as the left-libertarian Greens and the right-libertarian FDP, in principle face less sharp trade-offs. In both instances, differentiation from the mainstream parties is an imperative. Left-libertarian parties achieve this by sharply contoured positions on socio-cultural issues. As the uni-dimensionality of party competition in the era of 'model Germany' gives way to a two-dimensional competitive space and as more highly libertarian voters endorse centrist or market-liberal economic positions, left-libertarians and Greens may moderate their economic policies and even move towards market liberalism, provided they can continue to attract their social protectionist wing with strong socio-cultural issue credentials. In a similar vein, right-wing libertarian parties, such as the FDP in Germany, stand to gain from accentuating their market-liberal credentials at the expense of their economic special-interest reputation.

Compared to other European countries, the German party system has one unique component, the post-communist PDS, which faces difficult strategic dilemmas in the competitive party configuration. A radical social protectionist economic stance *without* pronounced libertarian socio-cultural appeals wins a substantial electorate in Eastern Germany, but none in Western Germany. It confines the party to the status of a regional pressure group. Moreover, in Eastern Germany post-communists and social democrats can form state-level governments. Thus the party has little bargaining power because it has no realistic alternative coalition partner. If the party makes too many concessions to the SPD and has no pronounced issue areas of differentiation from its coalition partner, such as the Greens do with libertarian issues, voters sooner or later will see no reason to prefer the PDS to the SPD.

Finally, extreme rightist parties also face dilemmas under the conditions of political economic change at the turn of the millennium. As the share of economic modernisation losers in their electorate – particularly low-skill and many craft-trained workers and clerical employees – increases, they find it hard to maintain a combination of authoritarian and market-liberal demands. For the sake of their growing constituencies of economically marginalised working class supporters, these parties tend to back-pedal on liberal reform or confine themselves to liberal demands for tax cuts that do not obviously infringe on the welfare state's social security net. As the experience of the Austrian Freedom Party and the Italian Northern League shows, once in government such parties cannot manage the internally diversity of their electoral support alliance. Their mainstream conservative coalition partners typically make them sacrifice much of their authoritarian agenda – whether in the realm of immigration policy, European integration, the family or the environment – but uphold their agenda of market liberalisation that alienates especially the blue-collar extremist electorate.

Except for the small liberal party, none of the other parties in the German party system can obtain an unambiguous electoral advantage from stridently market-liberal policies. Of course, there are other elements of the German polity that reinforce the tendency towards political-economic stasis, such as federalism and bicameralism. The upper house of the German parliament often has a different partisan majority than the lower house. In a divided polity, CDU/CSU and SPD block each other's efforts to engineer political-economic reform. The importance of the upper house of the German parliament for most domestic politics also forces politicians almost continuously to engage in electoral campaigns for state elections staggered throughout the term of the federal parliament.

GERMAN PARTY STRATEGY AND ELECTORAL PAYOFFS, 1990–98

The evolution of party strategies since the unification election in 1990 highlights the logic of party competition under conditions of centripetal multipartyism. However, the new political economic challenges begin to create voter alignments that undercut the parties' strategic capacities to maintain established patterns of competition.

In 1990, the incumbent government's achievement of rapid national unification was a virtual guarantee of victory. The Helmut Kohl government promised a warm shower of subsidies to East Germans and a painless transition to market economics. In contrast, the SPD and Green opposition parties predicted higher tax and a costly, arduous unification process. This negative outlook at a moment of national triumph sealed the parties' defeat in the east, despite being quite popular in the west.

By 1994, the Kohl government, which had worn thin its social protectionist credentials in Eastern Germany, lost voters that joined the PDS and the SPD camps. The parties with an emphasis on civic libertarian positions, the Greens and the FDP, saw most of their eastern voters defect to other parties. In the west, the Social Democrats and Greens engaged in a strategy of moderate left-libertarian appeals that almost deprived the Kohl government of an overall legislative majority.[12] What saved the Kohl government was a vigorous economic upturn in the election year. Even if SPD, Greens and PDS had captured a majority of parliamentary seats they would have been unable to craft a workable legislative and executive majority to displace the incumbent CDU/CSU–FDP coalition.

In 1998, the Red–Green opposition renewed its centrist appeals under Gerhard Schröder's leadership. Its electoral victory followed the Christian democrats' efforts to break out of the centrist economic policy mould and adopt more distinctly market-liberal reforms of sickness benefits and public pension plans in 1996 and 1997.[13] Social protectionist voters, such as pensioners, punished the CDU for welfare state retrenchment, particularly in Eastern Germany. In the end, the SPD captured the median voter, while the CDU remained dominant only among those with more rightist and authoritarian positions. The East German PDS thrived among leftist and distinctly authoritarian voters.[14]

STRATEGIC AMBIGUITY: GERMAN PARTIES BEFORE THE 2002 ELECTION

The interplay of politics and economics in the elections of the 1990s taught the German parties that weak economic performance was detrimental to the governing parties' electoral fortunes, but so were market-liberal reform initiatives. Especially in 2002, politicians anticipated that the election would hinge on economic policy performance and issue positions, but less so on socio-cultural issues such as the environment, gender relations or immigration and multiculturalism. Such issues were either the preserve of the Greens or were likely to benefit otherwise weak and divided extreme rightist parties.

In the election period 1998–2002, the Red–Green coalition presided over four more years of mostly anaemic economic performance, particularly in Eastern Germany. As a result, the unemployment rate in 2002 was almost as high as in the months leading up to the 1998 election. Furthermore, the Red–Green government reversed the previous government's pension reform, but only in order to put its own unpopular pension reform in place, which cut back on the pay-as-you-go benefits scheme in favour of a supplementary contributions-defined, funded pension component. Together with a fairly tight fiscal policy, a corporate tax cut and an abolition of the capital gains and wealth taxes, these measures constituted the main liberal reform policies of the electoral term. They were counterbalanced by concessions to the governing parties' labour wing, especially guarantees to back up pension shortfalls with general government revenue and a further extension of workers' participation in the governance of private companies. Most importantly, the government stayed away from a liberalisation of labour markets that was dreaded by the unions.

In addition to this ambiguous retrospective record, the SPD added more vagueness in the campaign through its prospective promises. On the one hand, it engaged in social protectionist rhetoric and depicted the CDU/CSU–FDP opposition as a danger to Germany's welfare state. On the other, when faced with declining support among centrist voters in the run-up to the election date, it embraced a commission proposal to liberalise German labour markets. Although it was a compromise that included a large programme of government loans for firms creating new jobs, particularly in Eastern Germany, the proposal was meant to demonstrate the SPD-led government's ability to generate new ideas about economic reform.

Interestingly, it was the formerly most leftist Greens who moved most unambiguously towards a market-liberalising reform agenda in the 1998–2002 term and in their pre-2002 election rhetoric, as evidenced by the party's stance on pension reform, fiscal policy and labour market liberalisation. Several reasons may have motivated this. First, much of the economic reform retrenchment has a generational edge to it. Fiscal austerity and pension reform, in particular, but also labour market reform, enhance the well-being of younger voters who are over-represented in the Green electorate. Moreover, new young highly educated voters with libertarian socio-cultural leanings often have a more liberal economic outlook and work in the private sector. They constitute an electorate the Greens cannot leave to the FDP. Finally, the established Green left-libertarians working in non-profit and public social services vote primarily on socio-cultural issues. Thus they do not see the SPD as an attractive alternative preferable to the Greens, as long as the latter have good prospects to clear the threshold of legislative representation.

How could the opposition exploit the predicament of the governing parties to maintain their social protectionist coalition, but also signal capacity for reform in a time of weak economic performance? Because of its own centripetal disposition and complex electoral coalition, the CDU/CSU could not thrive on the economic problems of the government to the extent it might have hoped for. On the one hand, the market-liberalising track record of the last Kohl government on pension reform and sickness funds, and the new rhetoric of the party's chancellor-candidate, Edmund Stoiber, to reduce income and payroll taxes as well as public expenditures, shored up the party's market-liberal credentials. On the other hand, so as not to frighten the party's social protectionist constituencies, the party promised a whole menu of new expenditures for which it did not disclose how funding would be provided. Among them were new subsidies for Eastern Germany, a quadrupling of monthly family subsidies for child rearing, the establishment of all-day schools for all children in Germany by 2008 and a promise not to cut unemployment benefits.

The FDP's electoral campaign enhanced the strategic ambiguity of the opposition. The party's new leader, Guido Westerwelle, correctly identified the combination of market-liberalism and libertarian politics as his party's most promising winning formula to attract younger highly educated professionals. The party's focus on economic competitiveness and educational reform, however, was counteracted by a one-man campaign against Israel's policy towards Palestinians waged by the party's deputy leader Jürgen Möllemann. Regardless of Möllemann's intentions, right-authoritarian voters lacking a viable extreme right-wing vehicle for their position could not help but interpret this campaign as a subterranean appeal to anti-semitic, nationalist and xenophobic constituencies. Such a message was likely to alienate precisely those libertarian, right-wing, young and well-educated professionals the FDP's leadership had targeted in favour of voters otherwise distant from the FDP because of their authoritarian and intolerant leanings. Clearly, Möllemann took the Austrian Haider or the

Italian Bossi as his models to open up new electoral constituencies for his party.

All in all, the CDU/CSU and FDP most likely came across as somewhat more sincere market-liberalisers than the governing Red–Green coalition. From the vantage point of the German median voter, harbouring a continuing strong preference for social protectionism,[15] the incumbent parties had a track record of pushing only mild reforms. In contrast, the CDU/CSU and especially the market-liberal FDP promised to be a riskier bet. Both the conservative-liberals' late conversion to more vigorous market reform in the final years of the Kohl government and some of Stoiber's rhetoric in the 2002 campaign increased the risks that a new conservative-liberal government would indeed get more serious on liberal reforms. Thus, while the opposition parties scored higher on perceived economic policy competence than the governing parties, they were not particularly palatable alternatives for voters with social protectionist inclinations.

This is not to suggest that the CDU/CSU and FDP lost the 2002 election because of their economic issue stances. Had it been a retrospective evaluation of economic performance alone, conditions might have been sufficiently bad to push out the incumbent Red–Green coalition in favour of a mildly more market-liberal, 'Black–Yellow' alternative. In the final analysis, the election was won and lost on a host of unanticipated and non-issue developments. Among them were the chancellor's personal popularity advantage when compared to his challenger from Bavaria who was particularly unpopular in northern Germany; the government's competent handling of major floods in Eastern Germany in the summer of 2002; and the government's opposition to Germany's participation in a United States-led military campaign against Iraq. Military engagement was intensely unpopular in Germany and the CDU/CSU waffled on this issue. Taking all these developments together, the governing coalition barely survived the 2002 election with a paper-thin advantage over the CDU and FDP. As Table 1 shows, the Red–Green coalition managed to garner 47.1 per cent of the vote (down 0.5 per cent) compared to the Black–Yellow coalition's 45.9 per cent (up 4.6 per cent). If we were to add the PDS into the equation as votes in favour of social protectionism, then the social protectionist quasi-coalition in German politics would still have a sizeable advantage, which, however, would not convert into legislative seats because in 2002 the PDS fell short of the five per cent electoral threshold.

From a broader, long-term social science perspective, however, it is not vital who won or lost the 2002 election. What is more interesting is to analyse voter movements and what they reveal about the support coalitions

TABLE 1

NATIONAL ELECTION RESULTS OF THE GERMAN FEDERAL ELECTIONS,
SEPTEMBER 1998 AND SEPTEMBER 2002[1]

	1998	Change 1994–98	2002	Change 1998–2002
Voter turnout	82.2	+3.2	79.1	–3.1
SPD	40.9	+5.8	38.5	–2.4
Greens	6.7	–0.6	8.6	+1.9
PDS	5.1	+0.7	4.0	–1.1
All social protectionist camp	52.7	+5.9	51.1	–1.6
CDU/CSU	35.1	–6.3	38.5	+3.4
FDP	6.2	–0.7	7.4	+1.2
All conservative camp	41.3	–7.0	45.9	+4.6

Note: 1. Turnout as percentage of eligible voters, party support as percentage of valid votes.

of the competing parties. Only because the broad social protectionist tendencies in German politics are still sufficiently strong was it possible that a host of short-term issues could enable the Red–Green coalition to cross the victory hurdle, if only barely so. At the same time, the 2002 election, in combination with voter movements in previous elections, suggests that a realignment of German politics that leads beyond centripetalism associated with the 'German model' is under way.

THE STRUCTURE OF THE GERMAN PARTY SYSTEM AND POLITICAL
ECONOMIC COALITIONS IN THE 2002 ELECTION

In order to gauge longer term trends in German elections, the results of 2002 need to be placed in the framework of longer term tendencies, a task this article cannot achieve with preliminary data for 2002. If the 2002 election follows a pattern of realignment in which the major parties reconfigure around a regional, sectoral, occupational, age and gender divide between more social protectionist and more market-liberal elements that displace the cross-cutting alliances inside SPD and CDU/CSU in the past, the following three propositions should be true. First, East Germans should be much more likely to vote for the governing Red–Green parties in 1998 and 2002. Change rates of support should be such that they defect less from the social protectionist coalition than West Germans. Second, within West German states and electoral districts with a higher proportion of non-profit and public sector employment should vote more Red–Green than those with more private sector employment. Third, at the individual level, elderly people should leave the less social protectionist parties, FDP and CDU/CSU, while younger individuals should congregate towards FDP, CDU/CSU and Greens. The new alignment should also open up a gender gap with women preferring the social protectionist parties. The social democrats' advantage among blue-collar workers should shrink and disappear, with some of them moving to the extreme right and others to the more market-liberal parties.

Of course, all of these hypotheses apply only as a statistical tendency. Only a minority of voters update their party preferences based on issue positions. Furthermore, political preferences come in complex bundles so that new political-economic cues make a difference only at the margin.

East–West Differences in German Partisan Alignments

In order to place the 2002 election in context, trends of party system fragmentation and electoral volatility as well as the disparity in the support for parties in East and West Germany need to be taken into account (see Table 2). In West Germany, the 2002 election confirms the long, gradual increase in the effective number of parties from a low in 1972 to the 1994–2002 level. Western Germany is now a 'four-and-a-half party system' with SPD, CDU/CSU, FDP, Greens and a scattering of extreme rightist splinter parties. In Eastern Germany since 1990, party fragmentation has been higher because of the additional presence of the post-communist PDS. In Eastern Germany, electoral volatility in a 'young' party system has been higher than in the west, though declining over time, as one might expect in consolidating democracies.

The divergence between the East and West German party systems, as measured by the sum of the differences between each party's support level in the two parts of Germany, markedly increased from 1990 to 1998, but then retracted somewhat in 2002 because of the decline of the PDS and the surge of the FDP. Without having adequate data to test the argument, a guess can be hazarded that many former voters of the extreme right or authoritarian non-voters rallied to the FDP in Eastern Germany prompted by Möllemann's one-man campaign. From 1998 to 2002, the FDP enjoyed greater gains in the east than in the west (+2.6 per cent compared to +0.6 per cent) and even greater gains than the CDU in the east, but not in the west (+2.2 per cent and +4.0 per cent).

Table 3 shows how the discrepancy between support for the social protectionist camp (SPD + Greens + PDS) and the opposition camp (CDU/CSU + FDP) grew and shrunk from 1994 to 2002. In the west, the social protectionist camp in 2002 gave back most of its 1998 gains. In fact,

TABLE 2

PARTY SYSTEM FRAGMENTATION AND VOLATILITY IN GERMANY 1969–2002

	Germany		West Germany		East Germany		Disparity between East and West German Parties[3]
	N Effective no. of Parties[1]	V Volatility of Voter Support[2]	N	V	N	V	
1969			2.50 (SPD, CDU, FDP, NPD)	11.4 (SPD, CDU, FDP, NPD, other)			
1972			2.39	11.4			
1976			2.36	7.4			
1980			2.54 (add Greens)	8.4 (add Greens)			
1983			2.55	16.7			
1987			2.88	11.4			
1990	3.13 (CDU, SPD, FDP, PDS, Greens, REPs, other)	15.8 (from West German 1987 party support levels)	2.95 (add REPs, PDS)	9.6 (add REPs, PDS)	3.75 (all parties)	n/a	29.8
1994	3.15	16.7	3.03	11.2	3.46	31.8	37.7
1998	3.31	16.1	3.06	13.0	4.06	24.1	47.6
2002	3.22	12.9	3.044	12.84	3.614	19.54	37.74

Notes: 1. Inversed value (1/x) of the sum of squared fractional support pi for all parties i in election t.
2. Sum of differences between electoral support for party i in election t-1 and election t.
3. Sum of differences between electoral support for party i in West and East Germany, includes CDU/CSU, SPD, FDP, PDS, Greens, and residual category 'other'.
4. The 2002 calculations of East and West German volatility do not include the state of Berlin because several electoral districts share East and West German populations.

had the election taken place in West Germany only, the conservative opposition camp would have won a legislative majority. But in East Germany, the region with the most intense and widespread interests in social protection, the social protectionist parties started with a large advantage in 1994 (55.6:42.0 per cent), dramatically increased that advantage in 1998 (60.8:30.6 per cent), and then gave back little in 2002 (60.1:35.4 per cent). These gross differences between the regions suggest that the intensifying battle over Germany's relative economic stagnation crystallises the divide between social protectionism and market liberalisation along regional lines between east and west.

Regional Alignments within Western Germany

The east–west divide is only a special case of a social protectionist versus market-liberal divide that also surfaces within West Germany, as is evidenced by levels and change rates of electoral support in the ten western states. First, let us establish trend patterns of support for the social protectionist camp (SPD + Greens + PDS, with the latter making a marginal, statistically irrelevant contribution to the overall strength of the camp in Western Germany) and for the more conservative market-liberal camp (line 1 in Table 4). A positive correlation of 1998 levels of each camp's support

TABLE 3

PERFORMANCE OF THE MAJOR PARTY CAMPS IN EAST AND WEST GERMANY
IN THE FEDERAL ELECTIONS 1994–2002 (% VALID VOTES)

	West Germany			East Germany		
	Social protectionist camp (SPD + Greens + PDS)	Conservative camp (CDU/CSU + FDP)	Net advantage of social protectio- nist camp	Social protectio- nist camp (SPD + Greens + PDS)	Conservative camp (CDU/ CSU + FDP)	Net advantage of social protec- tionist camp
Election 1994	46.4	49.8	–3.4	55.6	42.0	+13.6
Change 1994–98	+4.4	–5.8	+10.2	+5.2	–11.4	+16.6
Election 1998	50.8	44.0	+6.8	60.8	30.6	+30.2
Change 1998–2002	–2.3	+4.6	–6.9	–0.7	+4.8	–5.5
Election 2002[1]	48.5	48.6	–0.1	60.1	35.4	+24.7

Note: 1. The 2002 calculations of East and West German volatility do not include the state of Berlin because several electoral districts share East and West German populations.

TABLE 4

PARTY CAMPS AND POLITICAL ECONOMIC CONDITIONS IN
TEN WEST GERMAN STATES[1]

	Social Protectionist camp (SPD + Greens + PDS)	Conservative camp (CDU/CSU + FDP)
1. Is there convergence or divergence of partisan strongholds over time?		
1.1 1998 levels of electoral support as predictor of change in electoral support 1998–2002	+0.61	+0.75
2. Does sectoral structure influence the strength of partisan camps in 2002?		
2.1 Unemployment levels in 2001 as predictor of 2002 electoral support	+0.86	–0.82
2.2 Percentage of wage labour employed in manufacturing as predictor of 2002 electoral support	–0.65	+0.65
2.3 Percentage of wage labour employed in services as predictor of 2002 electoral support	+0.55	–0.57
3. Does sectoral structure influence change rates of partisan camps from 1998 to 2002?		
3.1 Unemployment levels in 2001 as predictor of electoral change 1998–2002	+0.41	–0.61
3.2 Percentage of wage labour employed in manufacturing as predictor of electoral change 1998–2002	–0.61	+0.73
3.3 Percentage of wage labour employed in services as predictor of electoral change 1998–2002	+0.56	–0.49

Note: 1. Bavaria, Baden-Württemberg, Bremen, Hamburg, Hesse, Lower Saxony, North Rhine-Westphalia, Rhineland-Palatinate, Saarland, Schleswig-Holstein; Berlin is excluded because of composition of eastern and western components.

with the camps' change rates from 1998 to 2002 indicates that each camp proved particularly resilient in its strongholds. This is exactly what the results show (r = +.61 for the social protectionist camp, r = +.75 for the conservative camp).

What are those regions of strength for each camp? If the realignment argument holds, then the social protectionist camp should thrive in economically weak regions with a high share of employees in non-profit and (quasi-)public social services. Federal election statistics allow us to determine the levels of manufacturing sector employment in each state (as a percentage of total employment) and the percentage of service sector employment (without transport and communication). The former is a good measure of the export-exposed component of the market-based German economy. The latter includes some market-oriented private and business sector bits of service employment, especially in finance and insurance, and thus identifies not only sectors without competitive exposure that predispose their employees to social protectionism. Nevertheless, the non-profit social service sectors (health, education, public administration) most likely account for the bulk of employment in the reported service sector figures. Lines 2.1 to 2.3 in Table 4 clearly show that levels of support for the social protectionist party camp benefit from higher service sector employment and unemployment, but suffer in an environment of more manufacturing employment. The results for the conservative camp are the mirror image of these findings. What is more important, level of unemployment and size of employment sectors also predict change rates of party camp support from 1998 to 2002 (lines 3.1. to 3.3). In other words, in 2002 the social protectionist camp lost relatively fewer votes or even gained a few votes in areas characterised by high unemployment, low levels of manufacturing employment and high service sector employment. Conversely, the conservative camp benefited most in regions of low unemployment, high manufacturing sector employment and low service sector employment.

Because of the small number of cases, a multivariate robustness test of the bivariate analysis is not possible. First, unemployment and occupational structure of German states are only moderately correlated (+.51). Hence both elements are likely to make an independent contribution to the observed pattern pitting more social protectionist against more market-liberal partisan alignments. Second, this pattern of correlations is not a result of the fact that the conservative camp made extraordinary gains (+10.3 per cent) in Bavaria, the home state of the conservative chancellor-candidate Stoiber. By dropping Bavaria, the statistical correlations are even stronger. Third, the pattern is not driven by conservative gains in southern Catholic states as opposed to social protectionist resilience in Protestant states. The conservative camp scores substantial gains in fairly industrial mostly Protestant states such as North Rhine-Westphalia (+3.4 per cent) or in mixed states such as Baden-Württemberg (+4.1 per cent), while scoring less impressively in the less industrial and highly Catholic state of Rhineland-Palatinate (+3.3 per cent). Among more Protestant states the fortunes of the two camps vary with levels of industrialisation.

It is probable that a more disaggregate analysis of the 299 districts would confirm the general alignment of high unemployment, service sector areas with the social protectionist parties and of low unemployment and manufacturing areas with the conservative, more market-liberal camp. Social protectionist parties held up best in major West or East German metropolitan service-sector areas, regardless of whether they are located in the north or south (for example, districts 84 or 86 in Berlin, district 94 in Cologne, district 222 in Munich), while the social democratic losses and the conservative gains were very substantial in northern and southern German manufacturing areas (for example, district 124 Gelsenkirchen or 268 Heilbronn) and in southern German agrarian and light industrial areas (extreme examples are districts 231 Zollernalb and 295 Rottal-Inn).

Occupation, Age and Gender: Individual-Level Evidence for a Realignment of the German Electorate

All aggregate results presented so far are vulnerable to the charge of an ecological fallacy. Individual-level vote choices are inferred from observed aggregate patterns of electoral behaviour. Thus, individual-level data must supplement the ecological analysis presented so far. One observable implication of electoral realignment is the social protectionist camp's declining share among blue-collar workers. Because of their affiliation with market-exposed industries, blue-collar workers are concerned about the continued economic viability of their employers. Except in the most profitable firms, such workers may, therefore, see benefits in lower payroll taxes rather than in higher social benefits. Conversely, the social protectionist camp should do particularly well among white-collar service sector employees, a large share of whom work in non-profit and (quasi-) public employment with only soft budget constraints and no risk of bankruptcy.

Indeed, this pattern is borne out by the data. Already from 1994 to 1998, when the SPD gained almost six per cent of the general electorate, the party could not increase its share among industrial workers. Instead, almost ten per cent of workers voted for minor parties in 1998, presumably mostly those of the extreme right. The Red–Green coalition was elected into office with a large transfer of white-collar votes from the conservative camp (accounting for over 1.6 million votes in an SPD vote total of 20.2 million).[16]

Interestingly, already in 1998 the blue-collar workers were no longer the most leftist occupational category, when measured in terms of the group's profile on a ten-point Left–Right self-placement scale. Social protectionist occupational categories with jobs outside the competitive market economy took the leftist leadership. Radical left scores of 1–3 prevailed among respondents still undergoing education (41 per cent), followed by highly educated civil servants and employees (35 per cent). Only 25 per cent of the entire population and 22 per cent of workers shared this leftist self-perception. Only the self-employed and professions (17 per cent), and inactive homemakers and pensioners (17 per cent) showed lower enthusiasm for radical leftist positions.[17]

Results for 2002 provide even more striking evidence for the emerging realignment. The SPD lost dramatically among workers (-7 per cent), while CDU/CSU (+8 per cent) and FDP (+3 per cent) showed their strongest gains in that occupational group.[18] The 'Alford Index', measuring the difference between the percentage of workers and non-workers supporting social democracy, fell for the first time to almost zero in 2002. That same year, 58 per cent of voters undergoing education voted for the social protectionist camp, 55 per cent of all civil servants and 54 per cent of white-collar employees. Among workers, only 52 per cent supported that camp, followed by 50 per cent among pensioners and 36 per cent among the self-employed. Among those with high education, the social protectionist camp had a 55 to 42 per cent advantage over the conservative camp, whereas among those with low education it came out ahead only by a whisker (49 to 48 per cent).

The pattern of differences across party camps is also striking with regard to gender. Among men, the social protectionist camp lost four per cent compared to 1998, reducing its share from 52 to 48 per cent, while that of the conservative opposition grew from 41 per cent to 48 per cent. In contrast, among women the social protectionist camp started in 1998 with the same share as among men (52 per cent), but actually added one per cent in 2002 thanks to the strong performance of the Greens (53 per cent).[19] For the first time a gender gap familiar to democracies like those of the United States and Scandinavia is showing up in Germany as well. Women are more dependent on the welfare state and vote in larger numbers for social protectionist parties.

So far, the results for the movement of workers, women and white-collar employees would also be consistent with a socio-cultural, rather than a political-economic explanation: Because of socio-cultural authoritarian leanings, workers and men progressively move to the conservative camp of CDU/CSU as well as the Möllemann wing of the FDP, often after a detour from the SPD via extreme rightist parties in 1998. In contrast, white-collar employees, and especially highly educated employees, as well as women increasingly support the more libertarian parties. This explanation may capture part of the true picture. After all, the FDP won most new voters in North Rhine-Westphalia, where its leader Möllemann ran a distinctively non-libertarian campaign, and in Eastern Germany, where affluent and more libertarian professionals are few and far between. Even with the limited data available now, there is at least one key fact that supports only a political-economic and not a socio-cultural interpretation of voter movements: the behaviour of pensioners. Traditionally, the CDU/CSU garnered the vote of over 50 per cent of retirees, but in 1998, after the pension reform, that share fell for the first time to only 45 per cent. In 2002, the CDU/CSU and the FDP camp could not increase their share of the pensioners' vote at all, whereas the social protectionist camp could slightly add to their previous support level in that age bracket. In contrast, the social protectionist camp sustained the greatest losses in the age bracket of the 25 to 34 year olds who are beginning to establish themselves economically and are most concerned about a future-oriented productivity-enhancing economic and social policy. In that bracket, the social protectionist camp lost six per cent (down to 52 per cent), whereas the conservative more market-liberal camp added 11 per cent (up to 44 per cent). The age-related voter movements fly in the face of a socio-cultural explanation. Older voters are distinctly more authoritarian and culturally intolerant than younger voters. Yet it is the old who increasingly flock to the social protectionist parties, whereas support levels among younger voters in that cohort are waning.[20]

The analysis has focused on camps rather than individual parties. However, in the social protectionist camp, there is one party, the Greens, that may progressively fit less in the pattern described for the aggregate camp whereas the SPD and the PDS embody the camp's ideal-typical incarnation. Contrary to the social protectionist image, the Greens' strong support is no longer primarily among social service sector employees, but increasingly among the self-employed and professions. Already in 1998 the self-employed over-proportionally supported the Greens.[21] Since then, this pattern has become more pronounced in state-level elections.[22] In the federal election of 2002, the Greens reached a whopping 13 per cent among the self-employed, up from nine per cent in 1998.[23] Only the FDP in the conservative camp managed a comparable over-representation among young, highly educated and self-employed voters. This shows that the Greens may be in the process of reorienting their policies beyond the social protectionist camp and embracing more market-liberal policies, combined with continuity in their strong libertarian profile.

CONCLUSION

This empirical analysis of trends towards realignment in German politics is preliminary and has obvious limitations. Detailed survey research that links voters' socio-demographic attributes to their issue opinions and perceptions of party positions over time is needed. Such analysis would have to focus particularly on vote switchers. Unfortunately, given small sample size in most national election studies (1,500 to 2,000 respondents), empirical research can rarely probe into the particular subgroups that are of vital interest to study the micro-dynamics of electoral change.

Another qualifier deserves repetition. While the electoral coalitions of the major parties may be gradually realigning around a more social protectionist and a more market-liberal camp, the politics of centripetalism will not disappear in Germany overnight. Politicians in the major parties fear this realignment and the internal conflicts and strains it is likely to precipitate in their parties. The CDU/CSU is far from embracing an unqualified market-liberal stance, given that it would hasten a momentous shake-up of its current electoral coalition. Pensioners would increasingly defect, although they constitute a growing proportion of the German electorate, and would need to be replaced by market-liberal, but predominantly socio-culturally libertarian younger urban voters. It is not easy to imagine how CDU/CSU politicians would accomplish this feat. Conversely, SPD politicians would have to concede employees in the market sector to more liberal parties and build coalitions around non-profit-sector employees combined with pensioners. For now, neither politicians in the major parties nor most voters support a profound realignment and politics of reform. In that sense, the snappy comment in the *Economist* about the September 2002 election is correct: '[I]t does not suggest that the German people have an appetite for radical reform. Mr. Schröder has no mandate for it. Nor would Mr. Stoiber, if he had won. That is the election's gloomiest lesson.'[24]

The analysis has emphasised popular demand as a constraint on politicians' strategies to offer public policy. Could the opposite not be true: that is, that supply-side factors constrain what voters can choose from? Is it not the case that politicians find themselves in a centripetal politics trap, amplified by the federal and bicameral fragmentation of the decision process, which makes it impossible to offer new alternatives? This hypothesis seems implausible. The entry of the Greens and PDS into the electoral market with heterodox policy menus demonstrates that offering new programmatic alternatives is not prohibitively difficult. This should apply particularly in a time of widely sensed economic malaise and political drift. Furthermore, the FDP offered a more market-liberal alternative, but found relatively few takers, although its failure to raise its electoral share may in part be attributable to Möllemann's one-man campaign that paralysed the momentum of the party's strategy.

The main obstacle to policy change may lie behind both demand-side popular preference distribution and supply-side partisan issue stances in the structure of the German welfare state and the co-operative political economy. As Esping-Anderson argued, the conservative welfare state, of which the German model is one important example, has tried to manage economic structural change towards post-industrialism by excluding citizens from labour markets, especially women and older wage earners, and by compensating them for their hardships. At the same time, conservative welfare states have discouraged fertility by making it difficult for families to combine labour market participation and child rearing.[25] Taken together, these policies have produced economic inflexibility and an impending demographic crisis in which the ratio of citizens active in labour markets to elderly dependants becomes increasingly unfavourable.

What will it take to change the mutual reinforcement between the current state of German party competition and the political-economic status quo? One option would be a Grand Coalition of SPD and CDU/CSU in which both parties agree to painful reforms without blaming them on the coalition partner. The politics of centripetalism could thus yield non-centripetal policies. Short and medium term beneficiaries of such reforms, however, would be more social protectionist opposition parties, such as the PDS in Eastern Germany and some new (right-wing?) party in the west. More likely than dramatic reform engineered soon by a coalition of the two parties most responsible for the current German political-economic paralysis is the gradual worsening of the political-economic paralysis reinforcing the continuation of electoral realignment. This process may eventually create an alliance around market liberalisation that includes not only the bulk of a reconstituted CDU/CSU and FDP, but also the Greens, if they continue to reposition themselves beyond the confines of the social protectionist camp. This alliance would become more likely if both Greens and FDP would continue to gain support among younger, educated voters leaning towards market-liberal and libertarian positions at the expense of the two largest parties in German politics. Both SPD and CDU are likely to sustain heavy losses before profound economic reform becomes possible. Both parties face powerful special interests opposing fundamental political-economic change. The labour unions in the SPD and the pensioners' lobby in the CDU/CSU are likely to fight against a major reorientation of their respective parties vigorously. Only the ambitions of political office-seekers, forced into reform by the imperatives of economic conditions, might counteract the special interest lobbyists. For this reason, much stronger competition from Greens and FDP, with messages unambiguously advocating liberalising political-economic reform, would force the major parties to compete with their invigorated challengers in a non-centripetal fashion. The German model will experience major reforms only if things become sufficiently bad so that enough voters and politicians see the cost of inaction as even greater than the costs of action. The emerging realignment in the party system would make a proactive response of the major party politicians more likely.

NOTES

1. On the alternatives of class/economic factor and sectoral interest alignments see J.A. Frieden and R. Rogowski, 'Internationalization, Institutions, and Political Change', in R.O. Keohane and H. Milner (eds.), *Internationalization and Domestic Politics* (Cambridge: Cambridge University Press 1996), pp.47–75.
2. I worked out this framework first in H. Kitschelt, *The Transformation of European Social Democracy* (Cambridge: Cambridge University Press 1994), and *The Radical Right in Western Europe* (Ann Arbor: Michigan University Press 1995).
3. For an analysis of post-industrial change and size of the welfare state, see T. Iversen, 'The Dynamics of Welfare State Expansion. Trade Openness, De-industrialization, and Partisan Politics', in P. Pierson (ed.), *The New Politics of the Welfare State* (Oxford: Oxford University Press 2001), pp.45–80.
4 . A recent survey among West Germans found that younger, male and higher educated citizens are more likely to accept a partial privatisation of social security, but only if that partial privatisation does not entail a net reduction of the combined public and private benefits. See T. Boeri, A. Börsch-Supan and G. Tabellini, 'Would You Like to Shrink the Welfare State? A Survey of European Citizens', *Economic Policy* (April 2001), pp.9–50. For the comparatively great resistance of Germans to change of the welfare state, see also E. Roller, ?Shrinking the Welfare State. Citizens' Attitudes Towards Cuts in Social Spending in the 1990s', *German Politics* 8/1 (1999), pp.21–39; R.H. Cox, 'The Social Construction of an Imperative. Why Welfare Reform Happened in Denmark and the Netherlands but not in Germany', *World Politics* 53/3 (2001), pp.463–98.
5. They are based on H. Kitschelt, 'Politische Konfliktlinien in westlichen Demokratien. Ethnisch-kulturelle und wirtschaftliche Verteilungskonflikte', in D. Loch and W. Heitmeyer (eds.), *Schattenseiten der Globalisierung* (Frankfurt/Main: Suhrkamp), pp.418–42.
6. For a detailed analysis of post-communist partisan alignments, see H. Kitschelt *et al.*, *Post-Communist Party Systems* (Cambridge: Cambridge University Press 1999).
7. I follow here Zaller's focus on voters with 'intermediate sophistication' as the targets of political communication, although I do not quite share his pessimism about the instability of underlying basic ideological values and orientations in the population. See J. Zaller, *The Nature and Origins of Mass Opinions* (Cambridge: Cambridge University Press 1992).
8. See H.G. Jaschke, 'Die rechtsextremen Parteien nach der Bundestagswahl 1998: Stehen sie sich selbst im Weg?' in O. Niedermayer *et al.* (eds.), *Die Parteien nach der Bundestagswahl 1998* (Opladen: Leske und Budrich 1999), pp.45–80.
9. My analysis builds here on H. Kitschelt, 'Partisan Competition and Welfare State Retrenchment. When Do Politicians Choose Unpopular Policies?' in P. Pierson (ed.), *The New Politics of the Welfare State* (Oxford: Oxford University Press 2001).
10. See K. van Kersbergen, 'Contemporary Christian Democracy and the Demise of the Politics of Mediation', in H. Kitschelt *et al.* (eds.), *Continuity and Change in Contemporary Capitalism* (Cambridge: Cambridge University Press 1999), pp.346–70.
11. For a discussion of the problem of union defection, see M. Schludi, 'The Politics of Pensions in European Social Insurance Countries', MPIfG Discussion Paper 01/11 (Köln: Max Planck Institut für Gesellschaftsforschung 2001).
12. For a detailed empirical analysis of the issue positions of different partisan electorates consistent with my framework, see R. Stöss, *Stabilität im Umbruch. Wahlbeständigkeit und Parteienwettbewerb im 'Superwahljahr' 1994* (Opladen: Westdeutscher Verlag 1997).

13. See the articles by Streeck and Hassel, and Leibfried and Obinger in this volume.
14. For empirical details, see R. Stöss, 'Gesellschaftliche Konflikte und Wettbewerbssituationen der Parteien vor der Bundestagswahl 1998', in D. Fuchs, E. Roller and B. Wessels (eds.), *Bürger und Demokratie in Ost und West. Studien zur politischen Kultur und zum politischen Prozeß* (Opladen: Westdeutscher Verlag 2002).
15. On strong German support for the existing welfare state, see Boeri *et al.*, 'Would You Like to Shrink the Welfare State?'
16. For a detailed analysis of voter movements from 1994 to 1998, see U. Feist and J. Hoffmann, 'Die Bundestagswahlanalyse 1998: Wahl des Wechsels', *Zeitschrift für Parlamentsfragen* 30/2 (1999), pp.215–51.
17. Feist and Hoffmann, 'Die Bundestagswahlanalyse', p.223.
18. These and following figures in this paragraph are from J. Graf and V. Neu, *Analyse der Bundestagswahl vom 22. September 2002*. Politikkompaß No. 91 (Sankt Augustin: Konrad Adenauer Stiftung 2002). The results are virtually identical with those reported in Forschungsgruppe Wahlen e.V., *Bundestagswahl 22. September 2002: Die Union gewinnt, die Regierung bleibt,* www.forschungsgruppewahlen.de
19. See Graf and Neu, *Analyse der Bundestagswahl,* p. 21.
20. For data in this paragraph see Graf and Neu, *Analyse der Bundestagswahl,* p.21.
21. See Feist and Hoffmann, 'Die Bundestagswahlanalyse 1998', p.242.
22. Data can be gleaned from the state election analyses reported in *Zeitschrift für Parlamentsfragen,* 1998–2001.
23. Graf and Neu, *Analyse der Bundestagswahl,* p.24.
24. *The Economist,* 28 Sept. 2002, p.46.
25. See G. Esping-Andersen, *Social Foundations of Postindustrial Economies* (Oxford: Oxford University Press 1999).

The Changing Role of
Political Protest Movements

DIETER RUCHT

Politics in the Federal Republic of Germany (FRG) has never been exclusively characterised by established elites and institutionalised collective actors such as political parties and interest groups.[1] Social and political movements have come into play as well. For the most part, they have challenged the status quo from the outside. In some cases, these movements conceived of themselves as forces besieging 'the system' as though it were a fortress. Quite a number of these confrontations have been highly significant and visible. They mobilised large numbers of people and triggered public debate. In other instances, however, lines of conflict have been blurred, marked by a complex constellation of multiple actors, shifting alliances, negotiations, and only partial agreements. While some interactions between the established and non-established forces have produced only noise and excitement, others have contributed to policy change, rearrangements within the polity, new power constellations, and changes in both the social movement sector and the attitudes of the wider population.

This article is concerned with the variable role of political protest movements in the FRG, paying special attention to two types of groups: left-libertarian movements, on the one hand, and right-wing radical and xenophobic movements, on the other. It seeks to answer four questions. How have German social movements challenged the political establishment over the past several decades? How have the challenged parties reacted, and which patterns of strategic interaction have emerged? What were the consequences of these interactions for both sides and for the wider public? And, finally, how can the changing pattern of interactions and their respective outcomes be explained?

In trying to answer these questions, a brief overview and some background information are provided to help clarify the context in which various kinds of protest movements have emerged and developed. Second, the protest activities of the different movements and their interactions with their opponents are described. Third, the article discusses the policy impact and wider consequences of these struggles and offers some explanations regarding the patterns of interaction and their consequences.

BACKGROUND AND OVERVIEW[2]

Different kinds of political protest movements have prevailed in different periods since the early 1950s. Broadly speaking, issues related to the consequences of war, the re-establishment of a West German military force and attempts to equip the latter with nuclear weapons triggered the most protest during the 1950s. Hence, this was by no means a quiet period, although it is generally associated with a conservative mood and an authoritarian heritage.[3] The first half of the 1960s was characterised by remarkably low mobilisation. By contrast, the New Left and the student protest movement proliferated in the second half of this decade. The Left–Right cleavage that had diminished in intensity towards the end of the 1950s seemed to resurge and threaten the country's political stability. During the Grand Coalition of the conservative and social-democratic parties from 1966 to 1969, the right-wing NPD party (Nationaldemokratische Partei Deutschlands) gained ground and, apart from its presence in several state parliaments, came close to the five per cent threshold necessary to enter the Bundestag. On the other hand – and more importantly – a so-called extra-parliamentary opposition gained momentum. This movement challenged what its supporters saw as the corporatist, elitist and bureaucratised power structure, and criticised what they considered capitalist and imperialist exploitation (including the military engagement of Western states in Third World countries) as well as the rigidity, hypocrisy and shallowness of bourgeois values and lifestyles – made even more repulsive in Germany by silence in the face of the legacies of the Nazi regime.

After a relatively short, but impressive revolt, this anti-capitalist and anti-authoritarian movement rapidly decayed. It dispersed into various fragments, chief among which were a radical and eventually terrorist strand, a cluster of communist sects that engaged in bitter internecine ideological struggles, reform-minded activists who joined the Social Democratic Party (SPD) and, most importantly, a considerable number of activists who inspired and fuelled the left-libertarian movements[4] – or, as many call them, new social movements.[5] These movements centre around issues of ecology and nuclear power, human rights, women's liberation, gay rights, development in poor countries, urban renewal, peace and disarmament, protection of asylum seekers and the like. A comparative study of four countries, covering the period from 1975–89, found that such movements contributed to nearly three-quarters of the overall number of unconventional[6] protest events in West Germany, while the corresponding proportion in France – the country at the other end of the spectrum – was only around 36 per cent.[7]

The early 1970s were marked by ambitious plans for political reform, including the governing coalition's attempts to modernise the state apparatus, strengthen citizen participation and 'normalise' relations with the East European Communist bloc and particularly with the German Democratic Republic (GDR). Except for the latter, these reforms largely failed. Moreover, the West German economy, like those of most other Western countries, exhibited shrinking growth rates and increasing unemployment. *Model Germany*,[8] as it was promoted by social-democratic Chancellor Helmut Schmidt, came under dual pressure from the left-libertarian movements on one side, and the ascendant neo-conservatives and neo-liberals on the other.

For a few more years, however, model Germany essentially remained in place. In particular, the corporatist system, though gradually weakening, survived until the late 1980s, despite the growing weight of conservative political forces. By the end of 1982, the CDU/CSU had replaced the social democrats in the federal government. Yet this did not bring about a sharp political and ideological turnaround like those that occurred with the neo-conservatives in the US and Great Britain. While the rhetoric of neo-liberalism gained ground in Germany, it was mitigated by the continuing commitment of even the conservative parties to support the welfare state. In addition, the Republic's federal structure, with the social democrats in government in some of the states, prevented a decisive shift towards neo-conservative policies.

More generally – and in spite of shifting majorities in governments at various levels – the state, along with the system of parties and interest groups, became more open, more fragmented and diversified, and in some respects more participatory and responsive to movement demands. This was a remarkable change compared to the 1970s, when movements were challenging the 'established system'. During the 1970s, the political parties and the corporatist configuration were perceived as closed and sclerotic – in spite of all the rhetoric of reform that characterised the early part of the decade. During the 1980s, however, the left-libertarians shifted towards a more pragmatic course. Confrontation with the established system was gradually replaced by bargaining and even co-operation.

German unification did not fundamentally alter the social movement sector in the western part of the country. The movements' protest activities definitely lost some of their impetus during and after the peaceful revolution, but they then regained strength thanks to a solid infrastructure and a considerable number of adherents. Hence, the overall constellation of the movement sector was fairly stable.

In the post-communist east, however, the change was dramatic. Until 1988/89, the state more or less controlled the sector of interest groups. The opposition forces were confined to niches. This situation was transformed after the fall of the regime. The citizens' movements that had contributed to the demise of the regime soon decayed. Yet a wide range of new interest groups and social movements emerged – partly building on pre-existing organisations, but largely being created from scratch, often with strong support from the west. Today, the set of interest groups, political parties and social movements in East Germany is similar to that of the west, although three important differences do exist. First, the Party of Democratic Socialism (PDS) only receives substantial electoral support in Eastern Germany and is a critical link to many East German movements and interest groups. Furthermore, left-libertarian movements enjoy less support in the east than the west. Finally, right-wing extremism is clearly stronger in the east than in the west, particularly when measured in terms of prejudice and acts of aggression against ethnic minorities.

POLITICAL PROTEST MOVEMENTS AND THEIR INTERPLAY WITH
ESTABLISHED POLITICS

When it comes to covering many protests over a lengthy period of time, protest event analysis is the appropriate research tool.[9] This method usually draws on a systematic coding of newspaper reports or – in rare cases – police records. The unit of coding is the individual protest event, however this is defined. Yet there is no direct technique for aggregating protests into social movements and, more specifically, into political protest movements. While such groups rely on collective and publicly visible protest as their primary resource for political intervention, they encompass many more activities than protest alone. For example, they collect information and other resources, settle internal conflicts, build alliances and negotiate with authorities. Thus, counting protest events registers only one facet of social movement activities, albeit a critical one. Another caveat results from the fact that the use of collective and publicly visible protest is not restricted to genuine protest movements. Political parties and well-established interest groups may also call for or participate in protest activities. In quite a number of cases, particularly when using newspaper sources, we have little or no information about the type and composition of the protest participants. It is therefore unclear whether, or to which extent, acts of protest can be attributed to social movements. However, based on a closer knowledge of various kinds of movements, as well as on more detailed analyses of protests in some areas and some periods, we can safely say that for a number of issue domains, most or almost all protests are organised by or involve active members of social movements. This is true, for example, for environmental, anti-nuclear power and civil rights protests. So, with some exceptions and further qualifications, we can use collective protest as a tracer to many social movements and, above all, political protest movements as our ultimate unit of analysis.

These key terms are defined as follows. *Social movement* means a mobilised network of groups and organisations which, based on a shared collective identity, seeks to realise or resist social change mainly, but not exclusively, by means of some sort of protest. A political protest movement is a type of social movement. Unlike sub-cultural groups and movements focusing on personal change, *political protest movements* (or, as a shorthand, protest movements) engage in political confrontation and thereby tend to identify a clear opponent. *Protest*, their key activity, is defined as a collective, public action by a non-state group or organisation which includes the formulation and expression of societal and/or political demands.[10] Protest events may be aggregated into protest campaigns or – as in our case – serve as a proxy for the key actions of wholesale protest movements. Yet it is important to keep the aforementioned reservations about the differences between coding units and units of analysis in mind. Not every protest we register in the context of the research presented below can be attributed to a social movement actor.

Mapping Protest Activities

A large database drawing on two nationwide daily newspapers (the *Süddeutsche Zeitung* and the *Frankfurter Rundschau*) allows us to identify the evolution and patterns of protest in West Germany from 1950 to 1997. It also includes protest in East Germany from 1989 onwards. Details on the sampling procedure and methodology of the so-called 'Prodat project', from which these data originate, have been presented elsewhere.[11]

One caveat, however, should be reiterated here. The newspapers, like any other sources that may be used for protest event analysis, are necessarily selective. Although their bias can be, and actually has been, assessed in both Prodat[12] and other research contexts,[13] we should not mistake the picture provided here for a non-biased sample of the total volume of protests that actually occur. Many protests, particularly those that are small and local, remain unnoticed by national newspapers. Consider, for example, that in recent years the local administration in Berlin has registered around 2,000 protests annually.[14] And this number is obviously an underestimation in that it only includes events that have been announced to the authorities in advance.

Nevertheless, the data from Prodat are valid insofar as they mirror the events that are actually known to both the wider public and to political decision-makers. These events, and not the great bulk of unreported activities, are the ones that potentially influence people's perceptions and minds and may, therefore, become politically relevant. Moreover, virtually all protests that are large and/or have significant consequences in terms of injuries, material damage, arrests and so forth are reported on by the newspapers we have investigated. But there is no doubt that a violent protest makes better news than, say, a similarly sized vigil and that therefore disruptive protests are over-reported relative to more moderate forms of action. Finally, while the selection of the protests reported by newspapers is biased due to the differential news values attached to these events, we have little reason to assume that the proportions and trends of the registered types of events are significantly distorted.

Volume of Protest

When considering the volume of protest over time, both the number of protests and the number of participants in these protests should be taken into account. These two indicators do not always run parallel. Figure 1 presents aggregate protests from 1950 to 1997. The 1950s and the first half of the 1960s had relatively few protests. Not surprisingly, the late 1960s, the prime era of the extra-parliamentary opposition, represent a significant peak. After a decline in the early 1970s, the level of protest rose again and, with some ups and downs, remained relatively high until 1997, the last year of observation. Contrary to the intuition of many observers, protest did not decline in the 1990s. With East Germany included, the prior peak of 1968 was exceeded several times during the 1990s.

When calculating the numbers of protests according to periods of federal governments (figures not displayed here), we find that the annual number of protests per year increased gradually from the first Adenauer government to the most recent Kohl government. The only exception to this stair-like pattern is the period of the Grand Coalition.

FIGURE 1

EVOLUTION OF PROTEST 1950–97, INCLUDING EAST GERMANY SINCE 1989

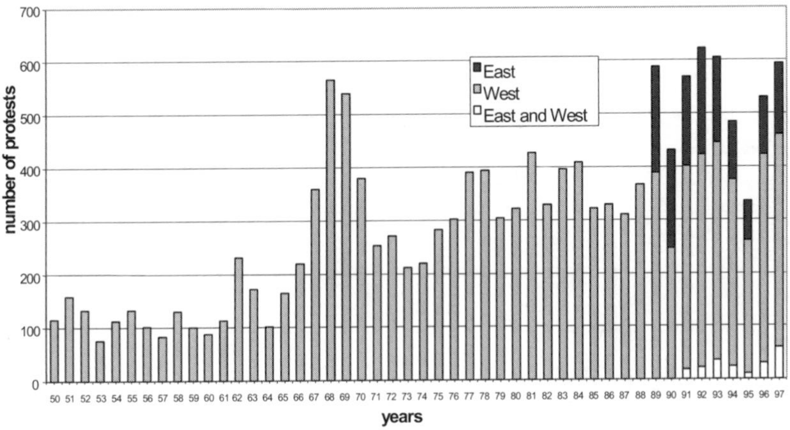

A different picture emerges when considering protest measured in numbers of participants (Figure 2). The 1950s were not a period of low mobilisation, as the numbers of protest events suggest. Nor did the Grand Coalition mark a peak period. In other words, the 1950s was a period of numerous but relatively small protests. After a phase of low mobilisation until the 1980s, the numbers of protesters suddenly rose and reached an unprecedented level in 1983. From more detailed analyses we know that this mobilisation was mainly an effect of the peace movement's opposition to the deployment of new nuclear missiles.[15] After a decline during the second half of the 1980s, mobilisation – in the west – increased again, with a significant exception in 1995. In East Germany, protest mobilisation was extremely high in 1989 and still remarkable in the next year, but then declined to a lower level than in the west, even when standardising for population size.

When considering governmental periods, it comes as a surprise that mobilisation in West Germany – measured as the average number of protest participants per year – was higher during the governments headed by Kohl than in all previous governments, including the Grand Coalition.

Themes of Protest

Aggregate numbers for recording protest are not very telling unless they are broken down according to issue-oriented activities (or related movements).

FIGURE 2

EVOLUTION OF NUMBERS OF PROTESTERS 1950–97,
INCLUDING EAST GERMANY SINCE 1989

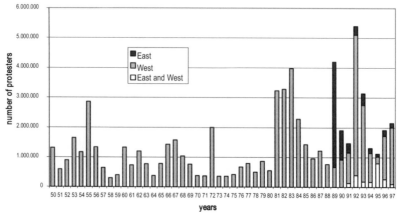

Table 1 displays the relative numbers of protests by domains and decades from the 1970s onwards (with separate figures for Eastern Germany for 1990–97). Women's protests are marginal. Peace, environmental, anti-nuclear and pro-ethnic minorities protests became more predominant over time, although the numbers vary widely. Among the various types of left-libertarian movements, the role of pro-democracy protests[16] was the most impressive in all three decades, as was that of peace protests in the 1980s. Labour protests – of which strikes are by far the most frequent kind of activity – made up a considerable and stable share of all protests.[17] Protests against ethnic minorities reached a high level in the east in the 1990s.

Again, the distribution of the numbers of protest participants may not mirror the number of protest events. As Table 2 shows, the role of women's protest was even more marginal in terms of participants than it was in terms of protest events. The peace movement attracted more than half of all protesters during the 1980s, but relatively few before and after this decade. Mobilisation for environmental protests remained stable, while that for anti-nuclear protests decreased until 1996 but then rose again, as we know from other and more recent data.[18] Interestingly, mobilisation against ethnic minorities was low in the west throughout the whole period (although the number of protest events was not!). Mobilisation in support of ethnic minorities in the west was very high in the 1990s.

TABLE 1

PROPORTION OF PROTEST EVENTS OF FIVE PROTEST DOMAINS,
GERMANY 1990–97 (%)

Kind of issue domain	1970–79 West	1980–89 West	1990–97 West	1990–97 East	1970–97 West Total
Women	2.6	1.7	1.2	0.9	1.8
Peace	6.6	18.2	8.5	6.3	11.6
Environment	2.0	8.6	5.1	3.2	5.5
Anti-nuclear	5.2	9.4	7.2	2.3	7.4
Pro democracy	30.8	17.9	20.2	12.1	22.6
Pro ethnic minorities	2.2	4.0	11.5	5.2	5.8
Contra ethnic minorities	0.6	1.0	7.0	20.1	2.7
Labour	17.8	17.3	18.1	17.2	17.7
Other domains	32.1	21.8	21.2	32.7	24.8
Total	100	100	100	100	100
N (events)	3,009	3,599	3,036	1,133	9,644

Note: Numbers for West Germany 1990–97 include Berlin.

TABLE 2

PROPORTION OF PARTICIPANTS IN FIVE PROTEST DOMAINS,
GERMANY 1970–97 (%)

Kind of movement	1970–79 West	1980–89 West	1990–97 West	1990–97 East	1970–97 West Total
Women	0.8	0.7	0.4	0.3	0.6
Peace	6.4	51.9	5.8	3.6	26.6
Environment	11.3	9.2	9.8	10.1	9.8
Anti-nuclear	9.1	6.6	2.8	0.2	5.6
Pro democracy	24.0	4.1	19.3	16.8	13.2
Pro ethnic minorities	0.4	1.1	23.3	3.7	9.6
Contra ethnic minorities	0.0	0.0	0.2	0.3	0.1
Labour	13.7	11.6	8.2	25.6	10.6
All other domains	34.4	14.9	30.3	39.4	24.1
Total	100	100	100	100	100
N (participants)	6,735,949	18,331,825	13,765,506	2,538,491	38,833,280

Note: Numbers for West-Germany 1990–97 include Berlin.

Forms of Action

Forms of protest vary widely, including collection of signatures, rallies, strikes, litigation, picketing, blockades and physical attacks on property and people. These various forms of protest can be grouped into four broad categories, of which only the confrontational and violent categories are presented here.

In the aggregate, the proportion of violent protest has gradually increased over the past several decades, reaching its highest levels in the 1990s (see Table 3). During these years, the proportion of protests that included some form of violence was, on average, 15.3 per cent in the west (and an amazing 30.2 per cent in the east), while it was at its lowest in the 1950s, with an average of 4.3 per cent.

Again, these summary data can be disaggregated by protest domains. Following the basic structure of the two preceding tables, Table 3 displays the proportions of both confrontational and violent protests for selected protest domains by decade and region. The most striking finding is the extraordinarily high proportion of violent events directed against ethnic minorities in the 1990s (more than 87 per cent in the west). We should note, however, that this high proportion is based on a relatively low number of events with few participants. Typically, violence against ethnic minorities includes small groups – such as youth gangs – that physically attack immigrants in public places or commit arson attacks on shelters for asylum seekers. In the category of pro-democracy protests, we also find a significant proportion of violent protests (26.8 per cent) during the 1990s. Considering that the number of pro-democracy protests is much higher than that of protests against ethnic minorities, we have to conclude that the increase of violence in protests as a whole from the 1980s to the 1990s cannot be attributed only to xenophobic groups. When considering numbers of protesters, it is important to note that in many cases, newspaper reports on xenophobic acts of violence do not provide figures simply because these events happen during the night and/or without spectators. But even taking the large number of missing values into account, it is unlikely that the actual numbers of participants in xenophobic events would surpass the number of participants in violent events that we have, based on the claims, attributed to pro-democracy protests.

The findings on violent events may appear disturbing to all of those interested in peaceful conflict resolution. However, two facts should be taken into account. First, due to the high sensitivity of media to such events in general and to right-wing violence against ethnic minorities in particular, we can expect these events to be over-reported. Moreover, there are no

TABLE 3

PROPORTION OF CONFRONTATIONAL AND VIOLENT PROTESTS BY SELECTED
DOMAINS, 1970–97 (%*)

Protest domain	Confrontational					Violent				
	70–79 West	80–89 West	90–97 West	90–97 East	70–97 West Total	70–79 West	80–89 West	90–97 West	90–97 East	70–97 West Total
Women	6.3	3.3	2.7	12.5	4.5	1.3	13.3	0.0	0.0	5.1
Peace	6.5	17.3	14.3	4.2	14.7	7.5	6.4	1.9	1.4	5.6
Environment	6.8	15.8	17.6	16.7	15.3	1.7	16.5	5.2	11.1	11.5
Anti-nuclear	15.3	26.8	33.2	23.1	26.2	2.5	11.2	17.3	15.4	11.2
Pro democracy	8.8	13.0	16.6	19.1	12.2	4.5	14.4	26.8	16.9	13.7
Pro ethnic minorities	6.1	11.4	15.9	6.9	13.6	4.5	6.4	2.0	10.3	3.4
Contra ethnic minorities	17.6	8.3	3.8	5.3	5.3	70.6	72.2	87.3	91.7	84.2
Labour	6.3	3.7	4.2	9.2	4.7	0.0	0.8	0.2	0.0	0.4
Other domains	17.2	27.9	13.7	20.8	19.8	5.3	10.4	8.7	25.4	7.9
All domains	11.1	16.7	13.7	13.6	14.0	4.3	9.8	15.3	30.2	9.8
N	334	599	414	153	1,347	129	353	464	341	946

Notes: Numbers for West Germany 1990–97 include Berlin.
* Out of all protests per period.

indications of a general spread of violent protest. The increase in the frequency of violent events is confined to radical right and xenophobic groups. Second, unlike the measurement of levels of violence, the measurement of trends is almost completely unbiased. We have no reason to assume that the selective attention of the media to violent protests changes significantly over time, particularly when looking at the aggregate numbers of violent protests. However, it is important to note that the rising proportion of violent events is not paralleled by increasing participation in such protests. Throughout the whole period, the proportion of people engaged in violent protests remained insignificant, with values far below one per cent.

Protests in Eastern and Western Germany

Not surprisingly, Eastern and Western Germany show significantly different patterns of protest. As already shown in Figure 1 above, 1989 and 1990 were marked by a huge wave of mass protest in East Germany. It was this mobilisation that eventually triggered the fall of the communist regime. When we leave aside this atypical situation, other patterns become apparent.

First, the frequency of protest in the east tended to exceed slightly that in the west when population size is taken into account. In terms of numbers of protesters controlled for population size, more participants were mobilised in the west compared to the east. Second, with regard to forms of protest, the differences become even more apparent. In the aggregate, the proportion of violent protests was significantly higher in the east (24.4 per cent) than in the west (8.7 per cent). On the other hand, confrontational protests, particularly various forms of civil disobedience, were relatively more frequent in the west than in the east. Third, regarding the themes of protest after the *Wende* period (the weeks and months of the collapse of the East German regime), we find that labour protests and protests against ethnic minorities made up a greater share in the east, while left-libertarian protests represented a significantly higher proportion in the west. Finally, established interest groups organised protests to a greater extent in the west than in the east. Especially in the early years after the *Wende*, informal groups prevailed in the east.

THE INTERPLAY BETWEEN PROTEST MOVEMENTS AND ESTABLISHED ACTORS

Particularly when disaggregated into smaller and/or more refined categories, the protest data displayed above show many details that deserve special attention. Leaving these aside, we can identify three major periods, each of which has a unique profile of prevalent issues and patterns of interaction between the protesters and their opponents – in particular, state authorities.

The Years of Rage

The prime era of the extra-parliamentary opposition and student revolts of the late 1960s was marked by sharp confrontations with the authorities. Although the reform-minded political parties absorbed a segment of the protestors, most continued to perceive the establishment as more or less closed, intransigent and immobile. While a few leftists shifted to terrorism, most left-libertarian movement activists tried to establish counter-institutions, sought to bring about radical reforms and focused on specific issue domains such as urban renewal. For a few years, it seemed that two markedly different and opposing political cultures would crystallise. No wonder that many of the protesters in the late 1970s referred to themselves as a 'second' or 'alternative' culture which seemed to have little in common with the 'first' or 'established' culture. The new libertarian left clearly set itself apart from the traditional and more moderate left – as represented by the mainstream social democrats and the labour unions – whom the new left perceived as part of the establishment camp. This constellation became particularly salient in the struggle over the civil use of nuclear power. Some trade unions – with the help of employers – responded to the activities of the anti-nuclear power movement in the second half of the 1970s by organising mass rallies in support of nuclear power. Bitter struggles also took place concerning urban restructuring and led to a wave of squatting in a number of large cities, most notably in Berlin in the early 1980s. These years of rage clearly demonstrate the fact that protest movements flourish and radicalise when the existing parties and patterns of interest mediation ignore the concerns they wanted placed on the political agenda.

Bridging the Gap: The Kohl Era until the Wende *(1982/83 to 1989)*

From 1980 onwards, this confrontational situation in Germany gradually waned, although this did not become fully visible because of ongoing conflicts over nuclear power and the highly salient confrontation over NATO's decision to station medium-range nuclear missiles in Europe. This conflict attracted the largest mass mobilisation of the period. In general, however, negotiations, bargaining and even co-operation gradually replaced fundamentally opposing worldviews and heated clashes. This was clear at the local level, where governments began to acknowledge not only the continuing presence but also the utility of left-libertarian groups which – in such areas as environmental protection, health care (for example, AIDS, drugs), services for deprived women and housing – were often more efficient and effective than state-run institutions. When, by 1980, state administrations began to offer support and subsidies to some movement groups, this triggered a debate among left-libertarian movements as to whether or not it was politically correct to accept the offer (the so-called *Staatsknete-Debatte*). A few years later, this was no longer an issue. On the contrary, many groups proactively requested state subsidies by highlighting their valuable contribution to the public good.

Strikingly, this greater openness on the part of governments and mainstream parties towards their (former) challengers was not restricted to their progressive streams but, to a lesser degree, could also be observed among the more conservative ranks. In part, the mutual rapprochement between left-libertarians and the political establishment was fully compatible with conservative thinking that promoted the principle of non-profit private initiatives over public intervention ('subsidiarity'), reduced state size and involvement with civic associations. Another powerful factor contributing to, and even symbolising, the building of a bridge between the challengers and the political establishment was the rise of the Green Party and its entrance into local, state and federal parliaments. All of these developments made left-libertarians – and particularly environmental groups, feminist groups and urban planners – relevant stakeholders in the system of interest mediation.

The dominant pattern of interaction between left-libertarian movements and the state continued to be conflict-ridden, but most conflicts became confined within institutional settings. For example, a close observer of the German women's movement referred to this phenomenon as the 'NGOization of Feminism' and its 'adaptation to the existing pillars of society and politics'.[19] Parallel to its moderation, the women's movement achieved some procedural and substantive concessions, despite the existence of a conservative hegemony in the realm of policy-making. For example, the proportion of women in political parties, parliaments and public administration slowly increased, although women continue to be significantly under-represented in positions of power. For the environmental movement as well, negotiation and bargaining have become routine. The highly symbolic clashes that characterised the 1970s have become less common. And where these do occur, they no longer provoke the same strong reaction as they did in the past.

Along with this more open attitude on the part of political parties and administrations, trade unions also became more receptive to left-libertarian demands. More nuanced choices replaced the juxtaposition of economic growth versus environmental protection. Marginal groups within the unions that had shown sympathy with the ecologists gradually gained strength. This trend was significantly accelerated by the Chernobyl nuclear accident in the spring of 1986. In the wake of this event, the social democrats and most trade unions agreed to phase out nuclear power. Moreover, the conservative federal government eventually installed a ministry for environmental protection.

During the second half of the 1980s, left-libertarian movements had stabilised and won partial successes – with the exception of the peace movements, which suffered a sharp decline. Even though the institutional configuration of the state had not changed much, state administrations had become more receptive to left-libertarian demands – although this is contingent upon the policy domain. This trend underlines Tarrow's observation of 'dynamic opportunities',[20] which are not simply given, but – at least in some cases – can be shaped by social movements. Overall, the

West German state had become more permeable to protest movements whose demands are not so much a matter of either/or alternatives (for example, war or peace; nuclear power yes/no) but rather of gradations, such as concerning emission standards and quotas for women. Hence, environmental and women's groups, in contrast to the peace and anti-nuclear groups, were engaged in ongoing interaction with the state. Their relations were characterised by co-operation and conflict, but little confrontation. This *modus vivendi* only became possible to the extent that both parties moderated their oppositional stances – a development that can be interpreted as an interactive learning process.

While the general disposition of political elites towards left-libertarian demands had become more friendly and supportive, the same cannot be said for attitudes towards the trade unions. With the rise of neo-conservative ideas and a stable conservative government in power, the unions were placed on the defensive. Nevertheless, with few exceptions, unions had remained relatively quiet, probably less because of political circumstances than because of rising unemployment and an eroding social basis for the mobilisation of labour.

In Search of a New Model: From the Collapse of East German Socialism to the Present

The few months surrounding the collapse of East German socialism marked the most spectacular and consequential events in German history since the establishment of two German states in 1949. In East Germany, interaction between protest movements and the state changed rapidly. It started with the open critique of the socialist regime by small oppositional groups, then shifted to mass mobilisation in the streets, followed by round table negotiations at various levels during a short power vacuum in late 1989/early 1990. Popular attention and elite activities then focused on the upcoming first free East German legislative elections of March 1990, while at the same time popular grassroots democracy movements waned.

With the legislative elections, the decision to unite the two Germanies, and the monetary union preceding unification, a totally new period began in the east. By contrast, Western Germany – including its social movements – experienced few structural changes. The only exception to this was the sudden rise – and continuing presence – of a highly aggressive radical right which, in turn, provoked a strong counter-mobilisation in defence of ethnic minorities. Demonstrators in support of the latter groups outnumbered by far the mobilisation against ethnic minorities (see Table 2).

Similar to the quick adoption of western party alternatives in Eastern Germany – with the exception of the communist successor Party of Democratic Socialism (PDS) – the eastern landscape of interest groups soon began to resemble its western counterpart. Most big players, including the trade unions, expanded to the east, either by absorbing the remnants of formerly state-controlled associations or by creating new affiliates from scratch. On the whole, however, eastern interest groups are weaker in terms of membership and resources than those in the west.

As for the left-libertarian cause, the presence of older leftist oppositional groups and of newly emerging citizens' movements calling for German unification initially restricted their space of articulation. But many of these groups withered away or were incorporated into parties, thus creating a space that could be filled by the newly emerging left-libertarian groups. Their themes, organisational forms and policy styles very much resemble their counterparts in the west. Although a sizeable cohort of left-libertarian movements emerged in the east during the 1990s, it cannot yet match that in the west in terms of scope, solidity and mobilisation capacity. This gap can be traced to the suppression of civic engagement in the east up until the fall of communism. Moreover, it is the result of the preponderance of bread-and-butter issues in the east due to the unfavourable economic situation. Union activity – and, more generally, mobilisation around social issues – therefore plays a greater role in the east when compared to the west.[21] Second, and more importantly, aggressive acts of right-wing extremism and xenophobia are significantly more frequent in the east than in the west when population size is taken into account,[22] even though the proportion of immigrants and asylum seekers is far lower in the east. Also, as shown above, counter-mobilisation against xenophobic and right-wing extremist groups tends to be weaker in the east than in the west.

Nevertheless, the differences between the movement sectors in Eastern and Western Germany have gradually become blurred. Probably more than the domestic configuration, the international situation has begun to shape the movement sector all over Germany. Above all, some groups perceive the accelerating process of globalisation – although by no means a recent phenomenon – as an economic threat.

Against the backdrop of such perceptions of threat, we are witnessing the rise of a new wave of movements that many refer to as the 'anti-globalisation movement'. While most of these groups are clearly on the left, and some even take a straight anti-capitalist stance, their 'libertarian' heritage is either weak or completely absent. Particularly to the extent that trade unions ally with these groups, they rather tend to support state intervention, most notably in the fields of economics, labour policy, taxes, property and the like. As argued elsewhere, this is neither a unified movement nor does it oppose globalisation in a general sense.[23] Rather, its common denominator is a struggle against a neo-liberal stream that promotes free trade on a global scale as the key remedy to the basic evils of this world, such as poverty, unemployment and lack of infrastructures. In these respects, there are thematic overlaps with the struggle of unions to protect wage labour from the vagaries of the market. Hence, compared to the situation in the 1970s, there is a real chance for creating an overarching alliance between the working class and anti-globalisation movements. In fact, the biggest German unions have joined Attac, the leading German umbrella organisation for anti-globalisation movements. Unlike unions with millions of members, however, Attac is an organisational dwarf with 12,000 members.

POLICY IMPACT AND STRUCTURAL TRANSFORMATIONS

The rationale of social movements is to profoundly change politics and society. So, in the context of this discussion, the question arises about the impact of protest movements in Germany during the last 25 years. Ideally, a number of dimensions should be considered, including the extent to which social movements are recognised as legitimate actors, influence the broader societal and political agenda, make procedural gains, realise their substantive (policy) demands, and influence the broader populace as well as their own constituencies. While it is impossible to discuss all of these dimensions for each of the types of movements that occurred in the period considered here, a more general picture can be sketched.

The Impact and Limitations of Movement Politics

It is clear that the two types of protest movement considered here did not completely fail in every one of these dimensions. Nor did they change society in as fundamental a sense as they would have wished.

The left-libertarian mainstream – but not its radical fringe – is now widely perceived as a legitimate political actor. Partly related to this, these movements have also strongly influenced the political agenda. In addition, they have been able to make some procedural and substantive gains, although these vary greatly within and across policy domains. As far as procedural impacts are concerned, some channels for citizen participation have been added or widened. Moreover, the Green Party, an outgrowth of the left-libertarian movements, has gained access to policy-making. The biggest institutional gain is probably the establishment of full-blown government departments in the areas of environmental protection, women's rights and, most recently, consumer interests. Other groups, including those focusing on peace and Third World issues, have made few, if any, inroads into established politics.

The greatest substantive policy impact of the left-libertarian movements has been in the areas of environmental policy, energy policy and women's rights. If one were to assess the fate of numerous concrete measures and projects – for example, construction of highways, airports, urban renewal and equal rights for women – the result would be mixed. Some of these measures and projects have been successfully prevented or pushed through by the movements. Yet in many other cases the movements failed. In still more cases, however, they have made a partial, though often minor impact – at least in the sense that things would have been worse from their perspective without the intervention of the movement.

Radical right-wing groups have experienced some subtle and even some explicit support from segments of the population, although mainstream political actors and the mass media do not accept them. In terms of agenda-setting, radical right-wing groups have been extremely successful. It is not without reason that they claim to have heightened public awareness of problems attributed to the influx of 'foreigners' and to have compelled the mainstream parties to put this issue on the policy agenda. Based on their agenda-setting role, they correctly claim to have indirectly forced the established parties' hands in instituting new legal restrictions to be imposed on asylum seekers, including that of a constitutional amendment. At the electoral level, however, radical right-wing parties have made few and fleeting inroads. In the odd instances where electoral support permitted them to enter local and state parliaments, these groups proved to be highly divisive and unstable. The legacy of a Nazi past (and of sectarian activism defining itself in terms of that Nazi past) has made it difficult for the German extreme right to overcome its divisions and present a 'modern' alternative akin to that offered by new radical right-wing parties in other European countries. Many right-wing extremists in Germany are still divided over the issue of the fascist past. While one fraction refers positively to the Third Reich – though often indirectly – others believe they must dissociate themselves from this heritage, not only in order to become more attractive to potential sympathisers, but also because the broader political context has completely changed.

Left-libertarian movements have probably had the most profound and enduring impact on the German polity over the last 25 years, especially in the realm of political culture. Following the student revolts of the 1960s, left-libertarians have helped to create a more active, more liberal, more democratic and more participatory political culture in Germany. It is difficult to isolate the causal impact of these movements on such developments when compared to other factors working in the same direction. But without the tenacious left-libertarian mobilisation it has experienced, Germany would most likely retain much more of the authoritarian heritage that characterised the Adenauer era. In addition, without left-libertarian counter-mobilisation against racism and xenophobia, Germany's right-wing radicalism would probably be more important and self-confident than it currently is.

Transformations of the Movement Sector

The composition of Germany's movement sector has changed in recent decades. Contrary to what many observers had expected, left-libertarian mobilisation has not declined. By and large, such movements have maintained their resources and infrastructures and even grown in some domains, such as environmental protection.[24] A closer look reveals a structural transformation of these movements. For example, informal groups and networks are increasingly in the foreground when it comes to protest. This has occurred to the detriment of the established and hierarchical groups that were dominant in the 1950s.

Another and probably more important change within the left-libertarian movements is their growing ideological and tactical pragmatism. Only a shrinking segment of movement supporters is bent on attacking a coherent 'system' of oppression, a belief confined to the segment of the so-called *autonome* and anti-imperialist groups. But even among the most radical strands, terrorism is no longer supported. Most left-libertarians aim at gradual – though not necessarily moderate – reform. The rise of the Green Party and its presence in parliaments and even governments have certainly fostered pragmatism and a policy-oriented style. Precisely because of this, the shrinking radical fringe will not support the Greens as a 'lesser evil'.

Finally, radical right-wing groups suffer from endemic volatility, internal divisiveness and organisational ineptitude. Nevertheless, the various organisations, informal groups and networks of the radical right have survived state repression and counter-mobilisation by leftist groups. It seems that the radical right has gradually – although mostly unintentionally – moved towards the loose and informal network structure that characterises many of the left-libertarian movements.

Towards a New Political Constellation?

For a long time, 'party state' and corporatism were the most appropriate labels used to characterise the political structures of the FRG. These structures have not disappeared, but they have lost some of their significance. Causally related to this transformation is the ongoing rise of movement organisations. Large formal and hierarchical structures continue to play a central role, but they are increasingly met with suspicion. What Germans call *Politikverdrossenheit* (frustration with politics) turns out to be essentially a critique of the major parties and interest groups. Political involvement is hardly decreasing, but it is being channelled less and less by large, formal organisations. Instead, more flexible, looser, more contingent forms of engagement have become attractive, particularly among the younger generations. This trend keeps movement politics alive and generates issues that are hard for parties and interest groups to adopt. There are also indicators that movement politics is attractive not only because it provides more room for individual needs and talents, but also because co-ordination of collective action around limited, specific issues is more effective.

As a corollary, we are witnessing the diffusion of movement structures and techniques of protest politics to such unlikely groups as the professions or even the police unions. Not all problems, however, will necessarily generate social movements. For example, the process of European integration that has – alleged or real – negative consequences for some members of society has not led to significant protest in Germany. Nor has the decline of small farms over the last decades provoked much resistance. Nevertheless, the extent to which protest politics has become attractive to diverse social groups is extraordinary. 'Movement politics have become an accepted way of doing politics and it provides an additional channel of political articulation linking the citizenry and the state – a channel that forms a complement rather than a substitute for the conventional politics in the arenas of party and interest group politics.'[25]

Related to this trend, we can observe that forms and symbols of protest tend to become 'modular' – detached from their original social and ideological context. As a result, we can observe right-wingers in the USA singing 'We Shall Overcome' when blocking the entrance to an abortion clinic. Likewise, we can see right-wingers with portraits of Che Guevara on their T-shirts when protesting against globalisation, the European Union and other 'evils' during their First of May parade on the outskirts of Berlin.

Finally, with the ascendance of neo-liberalism and the promotion of a technocratic social democracy divorced from its class roots, ecological modernisation, anti-globalisation and the like, we seem to be witnessing a rearrangement of ideological cleavages and corresponding alliances. Whatever the concrete outcome of these struggles over ideological and tangible hegemony, it seems plausible that our societies will deviate still further from the pattern that was dominant in the nineteenth century. Instead of stable cleavages marked by few and relatively simple world views, the political landscape of the future will be highly fragmented, allowing for more flexible alliances and arrangements.

CONCLUSION

During the last several decades, German politics has undergone profound changes. Political protest movements have been affected by these changes, but have also contributed to some of them. Most spectacular was the peaceful mass mobilisation in 1989/90 in East Germany that triggered the fall of the communist regime. Because this was a rather ephemeral and fleeting affair, it has been largely bracketed in this article, whose orientation was more towards structural changes and developments. Another significant development was the rise of right-wing extremism in unified Germany and the extraordinarily high level of hostility against immigrants, which, with some fluctuation, continues until today.

Most consequential, however, was a plethora of other protest groups with the left-libertarian movements at their centre. These have not only survived but, contrary to many perceptions, have continued to be active, particularly in the western part of Germany. These movements have had a remarkable impact in some policy areas, but little influence in others. Overall, they have contributed to the development of a more participatory democracy, more responsiveness on the part of the power holders, and to the crumbling of Model Germany. However, they have failed to reform the politico-administrative system from the ground up.

Whereas labour unions have suffered from attacks on the welfare state, right-wing extremism has profited from them by exploiting the anxieties of those who feel threatened by growing competition in the labour market, layoffs, cuts in welfare provisions and immigrants.[26] By contrast, these developments have only marginally affected left-libertarian movements.

With the rise of groups and movements against neo-liberalism and in favour of worldwide democracy and solidarity, parts of these movements may become even stronger, especially when creating alliances with the labour unions.

Overall, protest movements have been, and will most likely remain, critical in German politics. Compared to earlier movements from the 1950s to the 1970s, the subsequent movements have occupied a broader thematic range, relied on a more solid infrastructure, and have had a deeper impact on public debate and policy-making. This may also be the reason why protest politics is no longer restricted to outsiders, but has become an ingredient of what was previously the realm of 'conventional' politics.

NOTES

1. I am grateful to the editors of this volume, the participants in the preparatory workshop and to Gary Marks for their useful comments on an earlier version of this article.
2. This and the following section overlap to some extent with a forthcoming chapter. See D. Rucht, 'Interactions between Social Movements and States in a Comparative Perspective', in L.A. Banaszak, K. Beckwith and D. Rucht (eds.), *Women's Movements Facing the Reconfigured State* (Cambridge: Cambridge University Press, forthcoming 2003).
3. See R. Dahrendorf, *Gesellschaft und Demokratie in Deutschland* (Munich: Piper 1968); M. Greiffenhagen and S. Greiffenhagen, *Ein schwieriges Vaterland. Zur Politischen Kultur Deutschlands* (Frankfurt/Main: List 1981).
4. In analogy to a new type of political party characterised as left-libertarian, one can speak of left-libertarian movements. 'They are "Left" because they share with traditional socialism a mistrust of the marketplace, of private investment, and of the achievement of ethic, and a commitment to egalitarian distribution. They are "libertarian"' because they reject the authority of the private or public bureaucracies to regulate individual and collective conduct. They instead favour participatory democracy and the autonomy of groups and individuals to define their economic, political, and cultural institutions unencumbered by market or bureaucratic dictates.' H. Kitschelt, 'New Social Movements and the Decline of Party Organization', in R.J. Dalton and M. Kuechler (eds.), *Challenging the Political Order: New Social and Political Movements in Western Democracies* (Cambridge: Polity Press 1990), p.180; see also H. Kitschelt, 'Left-Libertarian Parties: Explaining Innovation in Competitive Party Systems', *World Politics* 40/2 (1988), pp.194–234.
5. See H. Kitschelt, 'New Social Movements in West Germany and the United States', *Political Power and Social Theory* 5 (1985), pp.273–324; K.-W. Brand, D. Büsser and D. Rucht, *Aufbruch in eine andere Gesellschaft. Neue soziale Bewegungen in der Bundesrepublik* (Frankfurt/M.: Campus 3rd rev. edn 1986); R. Roth, *Demokratie von unten. Neue soziale Bewegungen auf dem Wege zur politischen Institution* (Bonn: Bund 1994); R. Koopmans, *Democracy From Below: New Social Movements and the Political System in West Germany* (Boulder, CO: Westview Press 1995).
6. According to the authors, unconventional events 'cover all actions of a demonstrative, confrontational, or violent type'. H. Kriesi *et al.*, *New Social Movements in Western Europe: A Comparative Analysis* (Minneapolis: University of Minnesota Press 1995), p.19.
7. Kriesi *et al.*, *New Social Movements*, p.20.
8. A.S. Markovits (ed.), *The Political Economy of West Germany: Modell Deutschland* (New York: Praeger 1982); P. Katzenstein, *Policy and Politics in West Germany. The Growth of a*

Semi-sovereign State (Philadelphia: Temple University Press 1987) W. Streeck, *Social Institutions and Economic Performance. Studies of Industrial Relations in Advanced Capitalist Economies* (London: Sage 1992).

9. R. Koopmans and D. Rucht, 'Protest Event Analysis', in B. Klandermans and S. Staggenborg (eds.), *Methods in Social Movement Research* (Minneapolis/London: University of Minnesota Press), pp.231–59.

10. Obviously, all elements of this definition require further specification. For example, we operationalised 'collective' to mean a minimum of three participants. In 'non-state actors', we included all kinds of actors with the exception of governments and related public administrations (ranging from the local to the international), the judiciary, and parliaments (when acting on a unified basis or based on a majority decision).

11. D. Rucht and T. Ohlemacher, 'Protest Event Data: Collection, Uses and Perspectives', in R. Eyerman and M. Diani (eds.), *Issues in Contemporary Social Movement Research* (Beverly Hills: Sage 1992), pp.76–106; D. Rucht and F. Neidhardt, 'Methodological Issues in Collecting Protest Event Data: Units of Analysis, Sources and Sampling, Coding Problems', in D. Rucht, R. Koopmans and F. Neidhardt (eds.), *Acts of Dissent: New Developments in the Study of Protest* (Lanham, MD: Rowman & Littlefield 1999), pp.65–89.

12. P. Hocke, 'Determining the Selection Bias in Local and National Newspaper Reports on Protest Events', in Rucht *et al.* (eds.), *Acts of Dissent,* pp.131–63.

13. O. Fillieule, *Police Records and National Press in France. Issues in the Methodology of Data-Collections from Newspapers.* Working Paper of the Robert Schuman Centre. No. 96/25 (Florence: European University Institute 1996); J.D. McCarthy, C. McPhail and J. Smith, 'Images of Protest: Estimation Selection *Bias* in Media Coverage in Washington Demonstration, 1982, 1991', *The American Sociological Review* 61/3 (1996), pp.478–99.

14. To be more precise, the average number of outside 'public gatherings', of which most are indeed protests, was 2,167 per year from 1996 to 2001 (letter from the *Senatsstelle für Inneres*, Berlin, 13 June 2002).

15. See F. Neidhardt and D. Rucht, 'Protest und Protestgeschichte in der Bundesrepublik 1950–1994', in M. Kaase and G. Schmid (eds.), *Demokratie in der Bewährungsprobe. WZB-Jahrbuch 1999* (Berlin: Edition Sigma 1999), pp.129–64.

16. Pro-democracy protests is a shorthand for a broad range of themes related to human rights, citizen rights, citizen participation and the like. It includes specific issues such as free speech, freedom of religion, privacy, rights of prisoners, self-determination of peoples, anti-apartheid and critique of state repression. The protests subsumed under the label of pro-democracy cannot be attributed to a distinct social movement but rather to a set of campaigns that are largely independent from each other.

17. It is important to note that the coding procedure underrates labour protests. For example, strikes are often reported in newspapers in vague summary reports ('many strikes in the metal industry in northern Germany last week') and, in these instances, were not coded. According to our estimates, nearly half of the labour protests are missed in the dataset.

18. See D. Rucht, 'Bürgerschaftliches Engagement in sozialen Bewegungen und politischen Kampagnen', in Enquete-Kommission Zukunft des Bürgerschaftlichen Engagements, Deutscher Bundestag (ed.), *Bürgerschaftliches Engagement in Parteien und Bewegungen* (Opladen: Leske + Budrich 2003, forthcoming), pp.17–155.

19. S. Lang, 'The NGOization of Feminism', in J.W. Scott, C. Kaplan and D. Keates (eds.), *Transitions, Environments, Translations: Feminisms in International Politics* (New York and London: Routledge 1997), pp.101–20.

20. S. Tarrow, 'States and Opportunities: The Political Structuring of Social Movements', in D. McAdam, J.D. McCarthy and M.N. Zald (eds.), *Comparative Perspectives on Social Movements* (Cambridge: Cambridge University Press 1996), pp.41–61.

21. S. Burchhardt, *Problemlagen, Unzufriedenheit und Mobilisierung. Proteststrukturen in Ost- und Westdeutschland 1990–1994* (Marburg: Tectum 2001).

22. Neidhardt and Rucht, *Protest und Protestgeschichte*, p.157.

23. See D. Rucht, 'Social Movements Challenging Neo-liberal Globalization', in P. Ibarra (ed.),

     Social Movements and Democracy (New York: Palgrave, Macmillan 2003), 211–28.
24. D. Rucht and J. Roose, 'Neither Decline nor Sclerosis: The Organisational Structure of the German Environmental Movement', *West European Politics* 24/4 (2001), pp.55–81.
25. H. Kriesi, 'Movements of the Left, Movements of the Right: Putting the Mobilization of Two New Types of Social Movements into Political Context', in H. Kitschelt *et al.* (eds.), *Continuity and Change in Contemporary Capitalism* (Cambridge: Cambridge University Press 1999), p.421.
26. Ibid., p.406.

PART III

REORGANISATION OF STATE AND POLITICAL ECONOMY

The Disintegration of Organised Capitalism: German Corporate Governance in the 1990s

JÜRGEN BEYER and MARTIN HÖPNER

In comparative perspective, the consensus-oriented political system of Germany is not susceptible to radical policy shifts. Constancy and continuity are also key features of the German economic system, which in the past was regarded as a role model for other nations.[1] Institutional stability may be attributed to high coherence of the institutional configuration.[2] But today, in the face of an internationalised and thus more competitive world economy and the additional economic problems related to German unification, institutional stability is more often interpreted as a burden than as an advantage. In 1997, the expression *Reformstau* (reform jam) was voted 'word of the year', due to its frequent use in political debate. Reforms seemed to be impossible although most citizens perceived them as necessary. Nevertheless, there are fields of substantial change that do not fit the image of it being gradual at best in Germany. The sphere of corporate governance turned out to be highly dynamic in Germany, undergoing rapid changes towards market orientation in the 1990s after several decades of institutional stability. How was this possible?

Corporate governance in the 'organised' German economy was characterised by structures of company control that limited the influence of shareholders and distributed power among managers, employees, investors, regional authorities, suppliers, customers, creditors and co-operating companies; deep linkages between industrial and financial companies that could be used as a mechanism to achieve common goals; sheltered infrastructural sectors such as telecommunications, energy and transport, in which competition was limited to a minimum and state ownership and influence were high; and political regulation that promoted a dispersion of power between shareholders and other interests and protected the company network against invasion from outside.

German corporate governance remained stable throughout the post-war period, although impulses for change existed well before the 1990s.

However, they remained isolated and resulted in adjustments within the logic of the German corporate governance arrangement. In the 1990s, intensified institutional change departed from the logic of organised capitalism. We argue that the German variant of capitalism changed towards greater market orientation because of simultaneous and reciprocally reinforcing, complementary developments.[3] Thus, in our view, complementarity is not only a factor of stability, but it is also important in times of change.

Indications of change include the increasing shareholder orientation of companies; the strategic reorientation of the big banks from the *Hausbank* paradigm to investment banking that resulted in a loosening or abandoning of ties with industrial companies; the withdrawal of the state from infrastructural sectors via privatisation; and the break of continuity in German company regulation that supported and accelerated shareholder orientation and network dissolution.

We distinguish three phases. First, there were isolated and limited impulses for change up to the 1980s. In the second phase, from the mid-1980s to the mid-1990s, first indications of multiple and mutually reinforcing change appeared. The break with organised capitalism came in the second half of the 1990s. The most important events were the repositioning towards shareholder orientation of companies like Bayer, Hoechst, Daimler-Benz and VEBA, starting around 1995; the takeover battle between Krupp and Thyssen in 1997, when a hostile takeover attempt was supported by one of the three German big banks for the first time; the privatisation of Deutsche Telekom in 1996; and the KonTraG of 1998 that outlawed most forms of unequal voting rights. Changes started at the firm level but were soon translated into political change at the regime level, which then led to a reformulation of regulations.

This article is organised as follows. The first four sections discuss the disorganisation process in each of the spheres that characterised corporate governance in organised capitalism. The final section shows how the four spheres are linked with each other and how disorganisation processes in one sphere reinforced similar processes in others. The paper concludes with a brief discussion of the consequences for the German variant of capitalism, in particular for the willingness of companies to internalise public interest.

SHAREHOLDER VALUE

Social responsibility traditionally played a prominent role in the German ideal of entrepreneurship. Industrial leaders of the past like Werner von

Siemens, Ernst Abbe and Hugo Stinnes were admired both for their success in business and their public spirit.[4] The concept of the embedded firm influenced German business law and is deeply rooted in German society. It was so prominent that in the 1970s accountants began to discuss methods of 'social accounting'.

In the 1980s, academic discourse changed towards financial indicators. But it was not until the mid-1990s that some of the largest companies began to experiment with elements of a shareholder-oriented strategy. The starting point for the adoption of shareholder-oriented practices was different in each.[5] The management of the formerly state-owned VEBA (energy, now e.on) used elements of shareholder value strategy to change the bureaucratic spirit of the company; Jürgen Schrempp's proclamation of shareholder value principles enabled him to change the strategic orientation of Daimler-Benz (now Daimler-Chrysler) completely;[6] the management of highly diversified Bayer (chemicals and pharmaceuticals) increased the transparency of company reports to demonstrate that the disinvestments many analysts called for were not necessary; Jürgen Dormann, on the contrary, refocused and merged Hoechst (chemicals, now Aventis) in the name of shareholder value; and Gerhard Cromme introduced an aggressive takeover approach as an offensive strategy to overcome the technological backwardness of steel giant Krupp (now ThyssenKrupp).

In following years, more and more companies declared shareholder value to be a main factor guiding their operation. In the late 1990s a clear pattern evolved. Shareholder orientation was more pronounced not only in companies where ownership by institutional investors (investment and pension funds) was large, but also in companies affected by international product market competition or exposed to the takeover market. Causal relations like these make shareholder value appear to be pushed by external forces. But there are also indications that shareholder value is a strategy managers themselves may choose, regardless of external pressures.

Shareholder value strategies enjoy a high reputation among top managers. This has to do with the characteristics of the new managerial elite. While German managers once tended to have technical know-how but relatively little financial expertise compared to Anglo-American top management,[7] this difference no longer holds true. In the 1990s, a trend towards professionalisation, greater emphasis on economic and financial issues, recruitment from external labour markets and shorter in-house careers was observed. These changes influenced the perceptions and value orientations of managers, including their attitudes towards shareholder value.

Another reason why managers themselves may be interested in a shareholder-oriented company policy is that it legitimates higher pay. One side effect of a shareholder value policy is an increase in the variable part of managerial compensation, particularly in the form of stock options.[8] The reasoning involved is that managers will be more attentive to shareholder interests if their pay fluctuates in accordance with returns on equity. Managers usually receive stock options in addition to their fixed salaries. Shareholder value strategies thus tend to increase manager's salaries.

In the late 1990s, the fixed parts of managerial compensation increased rapidly as well. Among other things, this had to do with the decreasing bank monitoring (see below). In the past, bankers' board membership had significantly lowered managerial remuneration.[9] The impact of shareholder orientation on top management compensation demonstrates that managers themselves may have an interest in a reorientation of company policy. Not by accident, the shareholder value phenomenon appears at a time when the extent of internal control over management seems to be declining.

The orientation towards shareholder value in many companies reduced the commitment to take societal and collective aspects into account. Daimler-Benz, which used to be deeply involved in the German system of organised capitalism – shielded against unfriendly takeovers, on the one hand, and acting with national responsibility in the integration of bankrupt AEG,[10] on the other – has now merged with Chrysler to become a company with a global focus. Whereas its former CEO Edzard Reuter had refused to use a particular method to reduce taxes (*Schütt-aus-Hol-zurück-Verfahren*), arguing that companies of the size of Daimler-Benz should be socially responsible, his shareholder value-oriented successor Schrempp had no qualms about using this and other tax avoidance strategies. In 1995, he proudly declared that Daimler-Benz, although highly profitable, did not pay any taxes at all. Daimler-Benz/Daimler-Chrysler's tax status has not changed since then.

Another example is Siemens, which is engaged in electronics and electrical engineering. In the past Siemens provided secure life-long employment. Now, after the adoption of a shareholder value philosophy, it responds highly flexibly to weakening demand and has reduced employment drastically. The company has spun off several of its segments and discontinued cross-subsidisation of its business units.

Shareholder-oriented companies in general reduced employment costs considerably in the 1990s. Comparative analyses show, as expected, that the distribution of value-added changed significantly in favour of share owners. However, employees in shareholder value companies did not lose out in pay.

Labour cost reduction was achieved by a new orientation among the conflicting aims of company growth and profitability growth.[11] This increased unemployment and exacerbated the financial problems of the social security and pension system, as many companies reduced the number of employees via early retirement schemes. Especially important is the reduced willingness of companies following shareholder value principles to keep employment constant in times of economic crisis.

NETWORK DISSOLUTION

The cohesion and density of the German network of interlocking directorates and ownership ties decreased significantly in the late 1990s, thus drastically undermining opportunities for co-ordinating economic interests. In the past it was said that managers acting in the centre of this network were capable of controlling economic and political processes far beyond the boundaries of their own companies. The term *Deutschland AG* (Germany Inc.) was often used as a label for this special feature of the German economy. It implied that the managers involved pursued not only the economic interest of their own companies, but also considered general interests of the national economy.

Opportunities for co-ordinating company behaviour were rooted in a combination of structural components that made co-operation among potential competitors easier. An essential feature of this structure were high density networks within branches of industry. This factor was associated with several additional features favouring co-ordination: a high degree of ownership concentration, meaning that firms were mostly ruled by other firms (*Konzernierung*); high congruence between interlocking directorates and capital relationships, whereby personal ties exceeded the scope of the ownership network; and a frequent overlap between official business and employers' associations, on the one hand, and the 'multiple directors', the individuals most integrated into the network, on the other.[12] The core of this structure was made up of a centre integrating the largest German companies into a network denser and more closely knit than almost anywhere else in the Western world.[13]

Financial companies, particularly Deutsche Bank, Dresdner Bank, Allianz and Münchener Rück, were traditionally most involved in the network of capital-based relationships and had a dominant role within personal networks of interlocking directorships. Financial companies established a link between the economic activities of industrial companies and the state.[14] The financial companies acted in the 'shadow of hierarchy'[15] and were often pressurised by the state to use their funds to help firms in crisis and to prevent influence from outside the company network.

Deutschland AG was characterised by a connection between the economic strategies of the state, the banks and industrial companies. The latter profited from the internalisation of risks by the company network, could rely on their *Hausbanks* to prevent bankruptcies, and could concentrate on growth of sales as they were protected from hostile takeovers. Banks had freedom of action in industrial policy and company monitoring, initiating restructuring in several sectors, while the state could normally abstain from direct intervention and, in the case of company crises, helped build anti-crisis cartels. In such exceptional situations, finance companies were sometimes forced to make concessions to prevent bankruptcies. Extensive personal links existed between the state and large banks, especially with respect to foreign economic policy.[16] In the *Landesbanken,* like West LB and Bayerische LB, which were intensely engaged in regional industrial policy, regional authorities were directly involved as shareholders.

Because financial companies were at the centre of the company network, the issue of interlocking capital was closely linked to that of the power of banks. In the mid-1960s, discussion about the multiple supervisory board mandates held by bankers led to a legal limitation of the permitted number of mandates per person (*Lex Abs*).[17] Although this resulted in a restructuring of the network of interlocking directorates, it did not change the position of the main financial companies inside the network. Supervisory board mandates were passed to other representatives from the same banks.[18] The structure of the network remained the same until the 1990s.

Extensive restructuring of the corporate network started in the late 1980s and picked up speed in the mid-1990s. Until the mid-1980s, the extent of interlocking directorates between the 100 biggest German companies was stable; starting in 1984, it began to decline from 12 per cent of all possible interlocks to less than seven per cent by 1998.[19] Capital ties between financial and industrial companies also began to dissolve in the late 1990s. Between 1996 and 2000, the number of capital ties between the 100 biggest German companies declined from 169 to 80.[20] Deutsche Bank and Dresdner Bank moved from the centre to a more peripheral network position. Deutsche Bank's retreat from the monitoring of non-financial firms was especially noteworthy. In 1996, 29 of the supervisory board chairmen of the 100 biggest firms were representatives of Deutsche Bank. Only two years later, this number had declined to 17. In its corporate governance principles published in 2001, Deutsche Bank announced that it would resign from supervisory board chairs altogether.

Why do banks stop monitoring industrial companies even though supervisory board seats provide access to information and influence? The explanation lies in the reorientation of the big banks towards investment banking, which broke up formerly coherent banking strategies.[21] Investment banking conflicts with main bank activities because close relationships with domestic industrial companies interfere with reputation-building on international financial markets and impair the ability of a bank to acquire orders from foreign customers. One of the main fields of activity of investment banks is the arrangement of mergers and acquisitions, which includes hostile takeovers. Reputation-building in this field would be impossible if a potential supplier of such services defined the protection of its domestic relations with domestic industrial firms as a goal of its business activity. While credit banking and close relations with industrial companies can be combined, investment banking and organisational ties to non-financial companies cannot.

The reorientation towards investment banking was caused by a combination of push and pull factors.[22] The risk-reducing effect of ties with industrial companies diminished as internationalisation increased bankruptcy risks and altered their nature. A trend towards higher transparency additionally reduced the relative advantage of internal control. Moreover, retail banking, formerly the main source for capital mobilisation, became more costly. At the same time, investment banking became more attractive. Fields of activity for investment banks grew because of rising demand for consultancy services in mergers and acquisitions, privatisation and rising public debt making states sell more bonds.

A watershed event for the behaviour of German banks happened in 1997 when Deutsche Bank supported a hostile takeover attempt for the first time, even though it had a representative on the supervisory board of the takeover target.[23] The takeover battle between the steel companies Krupp and Thyssen was accompanied by a power struggle inside the management board of Deutsche Bank in which the investment bankers prevailed over the traditionalists. The battle transformed the strategy of German banks and made them dismantle ties with industrial companies to avoid conflicts of interest.

At the end of 1999, the Schröder government decided to support the dissolution of the ties between banks and industry and moved towards a more market-orientated corporate governance system by abolishing the capital gains tax on sales of stock. However, the initial impetus to weaken the ties between banks and industry had come from the market and was not political. In addition, existing ties changed their nature. In 2001, most managers in the centre of the network of interlocking directorates represented financially-oriented concepts, such as Paul Achleitner (Allianz), Rolf-E. Breuer (Deutsche Bank), Gerhard Cromme (Thyssen-Krupp), Heinrich von Pierer (Siemens) and Jürgen Schrempp (DaimlerChrysler), indicating an important change with regard to the economic and political function of the network.

Privatisation

Privatisation in Germany accelerated in the 1990s, extending even to those parts of the infrastructure where state ownership had once been regarded as indispensable. In interaction with complementary processes, privatisation was a catalyst for the alteration of the German corporate governance regime. Particularly important was the initial public offering of the privatised telephone monopoly Deutsche Telekom in late 1996. In an extensive advertising campaign the shares of Deutsche Telekom were presented as *Volksaktien* ('people's stock'). Generous special offers for those who subscribed early, and even a kind of investment insurance to protect small shareholders from major losses in the first years, were introduced by the German banks that acted as stock brokers.

The campaign was very successful. After one year Deutsche Telekom announced that it had sold 90 million more shares than anticipated, for a total of DM21 billion. Many investors purchased stock for the first time. In the following years the attitudes of the German population towards stock ownership changed fundamentally. From 1997 to 2001, the share of those owning stock or having invested in mutual funds rose from 8.9 per cent to 20 per cent.[24] Many firms followed the example of Deutsche Telekom. The number of initial public offerings at the German stock exchange increased continuously. In 1983, only 436 German companies had been listed, but by the end of the 1990s their number had risen to 933.[25] Obviously the German population had shed their notorious risk aversion of former times.

The extraordinary efforts made in the Telekom campaign had to do with the failure of the first German privatisation programme from 1959 to 1965, which was held to be partly responsible for the lack of confidence in stock ownership. The failure of the first privatisation programme played an important role in shaping the perceptions of subsequent governments.[26] Consequently, efforts to privatise state-owned firms remained marginal until the 1980s.

When the government of Helmut Kohl committed itself in 1983 to privatisation, it was reacting to ideological pressures from neo-liberal circles in the Christian Democratic Party and especially the Free Democrats.

The programme focused mainly on a reduction of state ownership in industrial companies. National monopolies in telecommunications, postal services and the railroads remained untouched. Furthermore, only in very few companies was state ownership eliminated altogether by the federal government (Salzgitter, VEBA, VIAG, Volkswagen).[27]

Due to its limited range, the privatisation programme of the mid-1980s was criticised as 'half-hearted'[28] or largely 'symbolic'.[29] Many observers had the impression that the only point on which the coalition was united was the need to sell parts of the 'family silver' in order to raise money for the state budget.[30] It is not surprising that the privatisation of state ownership at that time had only limited effects on the German stock exchange or the corporate governance system as a whole. At the end of the 1980s, further steps towards deregulation and privatisation seemed unlikely.[31] The symbolic policy had pacified the liberals, and political and societal opposition to privatisation appeared strong enough to inhibit further reforms.

However, the widely predicted deadlock in privatisation did not occur. In the late 1980s, the European Commission and the European Court of Justice enforced measures to enhance market integration and competition in telecommunication, postal services, air and rail transport, and energy and water supply (based on Art. 90 of the European Treaty), which had traditionally been shielded from competition and were confined within national boundaries. A number of directives were issued prohibiting member states from maintaining monopolies in various markets, especially telecommunications. The German government was forced to align itself with European legislation, and privatisation seemed the most viable option. In other industries such as energy and railroads, the European Commission did not pressurise member states to deregulate but intervened strategically to influence the decision-making of the Council of Ministers in favour of liberalisation.[32] The German government was thus required at the European level to take steps towards liberalisation that would have been impossible to achieve nationally.[33]

While European initiatives kept privatisation on the political agenda, it was German unification that put it on top of the priority list. All of a sudden more than 8,000 nationalised firms and holding companies with 4.1 million workers had to be converted into private sector firms in a market economy. The German government decided to sell off East German firms through a federal agency, the Treuhandanstalt. Vouchers or other forms of privatisation were not considered. Therefore, the direct effect of the denationalisation programme on German corporate governance remained small. As it turned out, the privatisation methods of the Treuhandanstalt produced gigantic losses instead of the expected profits,[34] which increased the need to reduce state deficits and indirectly paved the way for privatisation in the west.

In combination with European liberalisation, German unification ended hesitation regarding the denationalisation of the monopolistically organised sheltered sectors of telecommunications, postal services and the railroads. On the one hand, it would have been difficult to legitimate both deficit-making state monopolies in the west at a time of harsh privatisation in the east. On the other hand, given increasing public deficits, the German state was not able to finance the rebuilding of the telecommunication and railway systems of East Germany without external capital. In addition, the Maastricht Treaty, in effect since 1993, made deficit reduction a higher priority.

Previous discussions on the modernisation of the federally operated Post Office, the Deutsche Bundespost, accelerated and shifted radically towards the privatisation option in the 1990s. The Bundespost was divided into three parts, which were converted into incorporated companies (Deutsche Telekom AG, Deutsche Post AG and Deutsche Postbank AG). Prolonged discussions about how to reform the state-operated railroad, the Deutsche Bundesbahn (now Deutsche Bahn AG), also gained momentum after unification.[35] Deutsche Telekom, as mentioned above, went public in 1996, and state ownership was further reduced in several steps to the present level of 30.9 per cent.[36] Deutsche Post was listed on the stock exchange in 2000; 28.8 per cent of the stock is now privately owned and a second public offering is expected in the near future. Deutsche Postbank was sold completely to Deutsche Post in 1999, and Deutsche Bahn is preparing to go public in the next few years. These cases of privatisation, along with many others, such as Deutsche Lufthansa, the airports of Hamburg and Frankfurt, and even the Bundesdruckerei, the government printing office whose business includes the printing of bank notes, identity cards and passports, generated DM37.6 billion in revenue between 1994 and 2000 (see Figure 1).

Whereas European directives and rising deficits increased the pressure on the German state to privatise assets, political and social opposition against privatisation began to diminish in the 1990s. The liberal conception of safeguarding the accessibility, equality, continuity, security and affordability of services of general interest by regulation instead of state ownership gained dominance in the German political arena. Social democrats, formerly often in alliance with trade unions against the restructuring of the public sector, changed their position. In accordance with

FIGURE 1

CENTRAL GOVERNMENT REVENUES FROM PRIVATISATION, IN BILLION DM

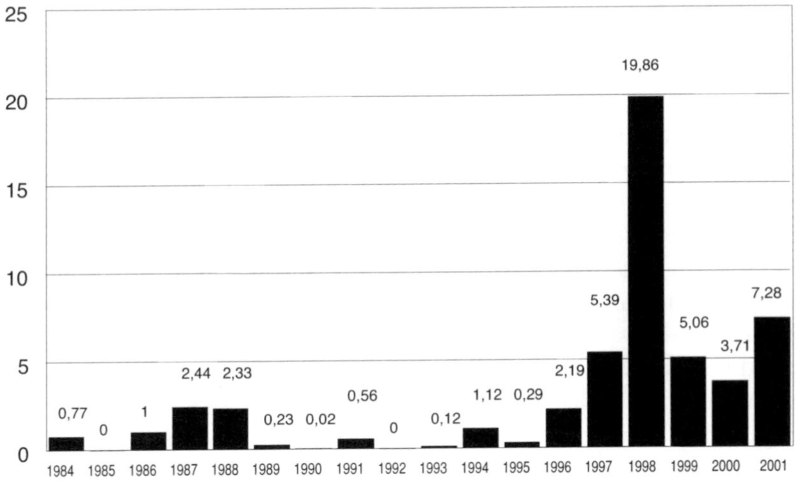

25 ─

19,86

20 ─

15 ─

10 ─

5,39   7,28

5,06

3,71

5 ─   2,44 2,33   2,19

0,56   1,12 0,29

0,77   1   0,23 0,02   0,12

0   0

0 ─

1984 1985 1986 1987 1988 1989 1990 1991 1992 1993 1994 1995 1996 1997 1998 1999 2000 2001

Source: German Ministry of Finance

a general European tendency away from interventionism and toward a regulatory state,[37] they summed up their changed ideas on the role of the state in the catchword of the 'activating state'.[38] The Red–Green coalition government of Chancellor Gerhard Schröder continued to follow the route of privatisation the Christian-democratic–liberal government had opened up. Unions such as the Eisenbahnergewerkschaft (German Railway Workers' Union) no longer opposed plans for privatisation in general and focused on the protection of the working conditions of employees. While the Länder occasionally opposed specific aspects of privatisation, they did not veto it the way the CSU government of Bavaria had prevented the privatisation of Deutsche Lufthansa in the 1980s.[39]

The effects of privatisation on capital markets, the banking sector and German corporate governance in general were not taken much into consideration in the political decision-making processes of the 1990s.[40] The mostly unintended effects of privatisation are nevertheless significant. The privatisation of Deutsche Telekom stimulated the development of the German capital market. Furthermore, many of the privatised companies are at the forefront in adopting shareholder value practices. In the previously sheltered sectors we can now observe tough competition, a global market orientation and a radical reduction in employment. Traditionally a counterpart to the internationally competitive export sectors, and as such an integral element of German organised capitalism, these sectors have changed almost beyond recognition.

POLITICAL REFORMS

The co-operative relationship between big German companies, with financial companies in the centre of a network of interlocking capital relations and directorates, was to a considerable extent a product of politics. In the era of post-war reconstruction, the state pressurised banks and insurance companies to give financial support to industrial companies, which led to financial companies holding large equity stakes.[41] Companies were highly taxed on profits from sales of share blocks, while profits on blocks they held on to were taxed favourably. Company monitoring was conducted by insiders, while the influence of the capital market was limited by corporate law and accounting regulations. Most notably, company law allowed unequal voting rights, thereby protecting companies from hostile takeovers by foreign companies. Co-determination law allowed employees and unions to participate in company policy. In sum, company law protected the dispersion of power, both among company network participants and groups of stakeholders.

German organised capitalism was never politically undisputed. Points of attack were the power of the banks and the co-operative links between corporations, criticised by both leftists and liberals. But attempts to limit the pivotal role of the banks inside the network remained marginal. Generally speaking, company regulation was remarkably stable in the post-war period, apart from the strengthening of employee rights by the Co-determination Act of 1976. This changed in the mid-1980s, when a series of reforms, which aimed to add a more active capital market to the German model without changing its fundamental corporate governance practices, were introduced in stock market and company regulation.[42] In 1986, a reorganisation of the stock exchange system was initiated, combined with a slight increase in the protection of minority shareholders.

However, the move towards a corporate governance system more strongly driven by capital markets did not start before 1996 and 1998, when the Corporate Sector Supervision and Transparency Act (KonTraG)[43] was negotiated and passed. The Liberal Party was the driving force behind the KonTraG whose main objective was to abolish most of the unequal voting rights and legalise share buybacks and stock option plans. With the KonTraG, Germany was one of the first in Europe to adopt a 'one share, one vote' rule. Another significant development in 1998 was the passage of a controversial law that allowed joint stock companies to adopt capital market oriented accounting standards (IAS or US-GAAP)[44] instead of the German HGB[45] rules, which deregulated accounting in Germany. A spectacular reform was introduced in 2001 when the capital gains tax on sales of share blocks was abolished. Further capital market-oriented reforms were the introduction of the corporate governance code of practice in 2001 and the takeover law to protect minority shareholders in friendly or hostile takeovers in 2002.

The KonTraG represented a departure from a long tradition. In the Stock Corporation Act of 1937, management was obliged to guide the company not only in the interest of owners, but also in the interest of employees and the company as a whole.[46] When the Federal Constitutional Court dismissed the suit of the employers against the Co-determination Act of 1976, it pointed out that managers have to protect interests that are not necessarily the interests of the owners.[47] This tradition was cut off abruptly by the KonTraG. The commentary on the KonTraG lacked any reference to the stakeholder view of the firm. It explained that the purpose of the law was to put the shareholder value front and centre and that there was no alternative to this.

How can this change in regulation and interpretation be explained? The agreement to create a Single European Market in 1986 led to a debate about Germany as an investment location. While it began as a discussion over German competitiveness on international product markets, it ended up including capital markets as well. The weak development of the German capital market was increasingly viewed as a competitive disadvantage, and the competitiveness of German companies on international capital markets was regarded as limited. Until the mid-1990s, the political goal of strengthening internal capital markets was pursued without relating it to issues of corporate governance. The debate intensified when international institutional investors demanded more investor-oriented corporate governance standards for European companies.

German companies began to compete for capital market orientation, which for decades had been considered practically irrelevant. As a consequence, the coherence of economic policy seemed to vanish. Suddenly interlocking directorates, insider-oriented accounting standards and limited minority shareholder protection were inconsistent with the political goals of an emerging 'competition state'.[48] The takeover wave in the USA illustrated the importance of share prices in competition between companies. In 1990, a tyre producer, Continental, became the first German target of a hostile takeover attempt. In this situation the CDU – encouraged by its coalition partner, the Liberals – changed towards a more sceptical view of German corporate governance. Various spectacular company crises – Klöckner, Bremer Vulkan, Metallgesellschaft, Schneider – added to the willingness to reform.

The move towards a more market-driven corporate governance system was made possible by a specific constellation of actors. The competition-limiting institutions of German organised capitalism were politically attacked from two different directions. The Left, including trade unions, criticised interlocking directorates and ownership networks because of the power they gave to banks.[47] Liberals, both politicians and mainstream economists, interpreted such institutions as welfare-reducing rent-seeking arrangements.[50] Coming from different ideological points of view, both sides agreed that banks should be barred from owning blocks of industrial shares.

When the KonTraG was debated in the Bundestag, it turned out that the *Deutschland AG* no longer had political supporters. Liberals complained that they unfortunately could not push the CDU towards more radical reforms. The SPD called the KonTraG a law to protect managers against shareholders and demanded a stronger shareholder orientation. The Greens argued that the capital market should be transformed into a market for corporate control, and even a speaker of the post-communist PDS complained that interlocking ownership eliminated competition.[51] In the late 1990s, there was no political party or movement in sight that would have been willing to veto the reforms – as long as the points of reference were capital ties, the power of banks, transparency, supervisory board organisation and the reduction of capital market restrictions. Even social democrats and trade unionists opted for more market-driven arrangements. In contrast to this, any attempt to restrict co-determination of employees would have immediately been blocked by trade unions, social democrats and the trade union wing of the CDU. In the discussion about a more market-driven corporate governance system, the CDU came closest to being the party of traditional organised capitalism, pointing out that the German system was not worse than the American system. In the debate on the takeover law in 2001, it was the CDU that wanted managements to have more powers in defending companies against hostile takeovers.[52]

Two possible paths existed to move away from interlocking capital and especially from industrial capital held by banks. The first, mostly demanded by the Left, was to make it illegal for financial companies to own more than five per cent of the shares of an industrial company. Liberals insisted that this was only possible in combination with lower taxes on profits from the sale of share blocks, which was the second possible path. Otherwise, they argued, a law against industrial ownership of banks would be an act of expropriation.[53] It was a surprise for all observers, including capital market participants, that the Schröder government opted for the total abolition of capital gains tax without linking this to a prohibition act. It was a 'Nixon goes to China' situation[54] that made this decision possible. Under the Kohl government, even a reduction of the tax was thought to be politically unfeasible.[55] Schröder and his finance minister used an opportunity to disentangle interlocking capital by strengthening forces that already existed, without having to fear the opposition of large companies.

THE DYNAMICS OF CHANGE

We have argued that the German variant of organised capitalism changed towards greater market orientation because of simultaneous and mutually reinforcing developments. Impulses for change in corporate governance already existed before the mid-1980s, but they remained isolated and resulted in adjustments within the logic of the old regime. The path of institutional reproduction was not left until the mid-1990s. From that time on, changes in privatisation policy, company regulation, shareholder orientation and corporate network density intensified. Initially, the parallel processes in the different fields were independent from each other. They had different external and internal causes. Privatisation was set in motion by the European Union, by increasing state deficits and a shift from state intervention to regulation, while the orientation of German companies towards shareholder value was related to competition in product and capital markets, growing importance of markets for corporate control, and the link between shareholder value practices and the compensation of managers. After a while simultaneous external and internal causes combined into an intensifying co-evolutionary process. In isolation each causal factor might not have made much of an impact. As in the past, discussions on the power of banks would have come to nothing or privatisation would have been mostly symbolic. However, simultaneous complementary influences led to a deep transformation of the German corporate governance regime. This began when the different processes started to stimulate each other. Interaction effects existed in several respects.

The interaction between privatisation and shareholder orientation was twofold. The sale of blocks of shares held by the state exposed companies like VEBA to the market for hostile takeovers, which forced them to become more share price-oriented. Additionally, the deregulation of infrastructural sectors led to increased competition and the need for restructuring. In this situation, managements used the shareholder value concept to enforce restructuring internally. VEBA, RWE, Viag and Deutsche Telekom rapidly adopted international accounting, stock option programmes, intensive investor relations and profitability targets for the business segments or the company as a whole.

Privatisation also had an impact on the strategic change of banks towards investment banking as investment banks received lucrative orders to organise privatisation. As banks changed their behaviour towards hostile takeovers, they added to the willingness of managers to become investor-oriented. There were also links between the reorientation of the banks, the sale of company stocks and the shareholder orientation of non-financial companies. As financial companies became more shareholder-oriented by themselves, they began to reorganise their investment portfolios to raise short-term profitability. In this way they passed on the pressure for more profitability to the non-financial companies. When financial companies sold their non-financial share blocks, the number of shares potentially available for hostile bidders rose.

These processes, in turn, changed the interests of the banks in company regulation. As banks did business in privatisation, their interest in more privatisation grew. Big financial corporations demanded a tax reduction on profits from sales of stock. Their changing behaviour stimulated regulatory reforms in yet another manner. As banks withdrew from company monitoring, most notably from the chair positions in supervisory boards, they needed the capital market to monitor companies. Non-financial companies also promoted regulatory reforms. Daimler-Benz in particular pushed the act that deregulated accounting,[56] having disgraced itself by publishing two completely different balance sheets in 1994, one saying the company had earned DM600 million under German HGB accounting, the other indicating a loss of nearly two billion DM under US-GAAP. Political reforms, of course, aimed at supporting shareholder orientation and company networks by removing unequal voting rights, higher transparency, facilitating share buybacks and stock options, and abandoning capital gains tax. In this way, growing market orientation in given spheres reinforced similar tendencies in others that in turn produced feedback for them. Complementarity between different fields of corporate governance enhanced the dynamics of change and made substantial change possible.

The disintegration of organised capitalism affects the ability and the obligation of the state to exercise influence over corporations. This is obvious in the case of the privatised companies in infrastructural sectors. The times when public authorities and state-owned companies guaranteed stable employment for a large part of the German workforce are definitely over. The privatised companies are no longer able and willing to take responsibility for the societal problem of unemployment.

The shareholder value trend in many of the largest industrial companies also affected the relationship between corporations and the state. In the past, managers of large companies often emphasised their responsibility for their employees, their region and society as a whole. Even if this was lip service in some cases, in others there are indications that companies did act with a degree of social or national responsibility. For good or bad, shareholder value-oriented companies no longer have any need or legitimacy to do this, and the state is no longer able to appeal to their responsibility. These are now obliged only to satisfy shareholder interests. The same holds true for the financial sector. As banks abandoned their interlocking directorates and ownership ties, they also got out of reach of the state, which could no longer use them as vehicles to influence companies in line with common goals, such as industrial policy. Today, there is no economic or political reason for banks to continue to provide for the co-ordination of the German economy. Banks now refuse to be guarantors of the public or national interest.

The disintegration of organised capitalism in the field of corporate governance seems irreversible. German company law supported and accelerated the trend towards a new corporate governance system and now makes a return to the former system unlikely. Regulatory decisions, such as on the prohibition of unequal voting rights, cannot be reversed easily. Furthermore, change did not happen on the periphery of the German economy. Those companies that once were at the centre of 'Deutschland AG' – the largest private banks and financial companies and the highly internationalised industrial firms – have adopted new strategies and will not return to their past strategies.

What impact does change in corporate governance have on other parts of the German institutional order? Changes in corporate governance have gone further than in other fields. As a result, we may be observing a process of hybridisation of the once highly coherent German institutional system. Market orientation in corporate governance increased while other institutions stayed intact or changed only marginally. We already have indications that shareholder value strategies of firms and more market-oriented forms of corporate governance do not necessarily jeopardise the existence of co-determination and sectoral collective agreements.[57] Simultaneously, the same trends will probably change the distribution of value added in favour of shareholders.[58] It thus remains to be seen if the co-evolutionary process we are now observing will end in a stable configuration. The substantial changes in corporate governance in the 1990s certainly made it clear that not all German institutions are as stable as many observers believe.

NOTES

1. B. Cattero (ed.), *Modell Deutschland – Modell Europa* (Opladen: Leske und Budrich 1998).
2. P.A. Hall and D. Soskice, 'An Introduction to Varieties of Capitalism', in P.A. Hall and D. Soskice (ed.), *Varieties of Capitalism. The Institutional Foundations of Comparative Advantage* (Oxford: Oxford University Press 2001), pp.1–70.
3. Our impression is that there is no obvious hierarchy among disorganising forces. It is not possible to identify one starting point (for example, privatisation) that leads to the disorganisation of all other spheres.
4. Werner von Siemens (1816–92), inventor and entrepreneur, founder of Siemens Corporation; Ernst Abbe (1840–1905), inventor and entrepreneur, founder of Carl-Zeiss-Stiftung; Hugo Stinnes (1870–1924), industrialist, founder of several companies, including Stinnes Corporation and RWE.
5. We define 'shareholder value orientation' as a company strategy that targets market capitalisation. Indications for shareholder orientation are profitability goals, transparency, investor relations activities, and stock options.
6. Afterwards it turned out that Schrempp's internationalisation strategy definitely had not maximised shareholder value, and one can doubt if his strategic choices, such as the merger with Chrysler, were really motivated by the intention to enhance the profits of shareholders.
7. O.H. Poensgen, 'Der Weg in den Vorstand. Die Charakteristiken der Vorstandsmitglieder der Aktiengesellschaften des Verarbeitenden Gewerbes', *Die Betriebswirtschaft* 42/1 (1982), pp.3–25.
8. B.R. Cheffins, 'The Metamorphosis of Germany Inc.', *American Journal of Comparative Law* 49/3 (2001), pp.493–539.
9. See M. Höpner, *Wer beherrscht die Unternehmen? Shareholder Value, Managerherrschaft und Mitbestimmung in Deutschland* (Frankfurt a.M.: Campus 2003).
10. Formerly conglomerate (predominantly electronics and electrical engineering). Before its bankruptcy and subsequent integration into Daimler-Benz, AEG was one of the largest German companies.
11. J. Beyer and A. Hassel, 'The Effects of Convergence: Internationalization and the Changing Distribution of Net Value Added in Large German Firms', *Economy and Society* 31/3 (2002), pp.309–32.
12. P. Windolf and J. Beyer, 'Co-operative Capitalism: Corporate Networks in Germany and Britain', *British Journal of Sociology* 47/2 (1996), pp.205–31.
13. In international comparison, similarly dense integrating centers are observed only in Austria and Switzerland. See F.N. Stokman and F.W. Wasseur, 'National Networks: A Structural Comparison' in F.N. Stokman, R. Ziegler and J. Scott (eds.), *Networks of Corporate Power* (Oxford and New York: Polity Press 1985), pp.20–44.
14. J. Zysman, *Governments, Markets, and Growth. Financial Systems and the Politics of Industrial Change* (Ithaca: Cornell University Press 1983).
15. R. Mayntz and F.W. Scharpf, 'Steuerung und Selbstorganisation in staatsnahen Sektoren', in R. Mayntz and F.W. Scharpf (eds.), *Gesellschaftliche Selbstregulierung und politische Steuerung* (Frankfurt a.M.: Campus 1995), pp.9–39.
16. K. Dyson, 'The State, Banks and Industry: The West German Case', in A. Cox (ed.), *State, Finance and Industry. A Comparative Analysis of Post-War Trends in Six Advanced Industrial Economies* (Brighton: Wheatsheaf 1986), pp.118–41.
17. Section 100 (2) of the Stock Corporation Act of 1965.
18. H. Albach and H.-P. Kless, 'Personelle Verflechtungen bei deutschen Industrieaktien-gesellschaften', *Zeitschrift für Betriebswirtschaft* 52/10 (1982), pp.959–77.
19. Höpner, *Unternehmen*.
20. Based on Monopolkommission, *Marktöffnung umfassend verwirklichen. Zwölftes*

Hauptgutachten der Monopolkommission (Baden-Baden: Nomos 1998); Monopol-kommission, *Netzwettbewerb durch Regulierung. Vierzehntes Hauptgutachten der Monopolkommission* (Baden-Baden: Nomos forthcoming).

21. C. Dziobek and J.R. Garrett, 'Convergence of Financial Systems and Regulatory Policy Challenges in Europe and in the United States', in S.W. Black and M. Moersch (eds.), *Competition and Convergence in Financial Markets* (Amsterdam: Elsevier 1998), pp.195–215.

22. J. Beyer, 'Deutschland AG a.D. – Deutsche Bank, Allianz und das Verflechtungszentrum großer deutscher Unternehmen', *MPIfG Working Paper 02-4*, Cologne 2002.

23. M. Höpner and G. Jackson, 'An Emerging Market for Corporate Control? The Mannesmann Takeover and German Corporate Governance', *MPIfG Discussion Paper 01-04*, Cologne 2001.

24. Of people 14 years and older. See Deutsches Aktieninstitut, *DAI Factbook 2001* (Frankfurt a.M.: DAI 2001).

25. T. Baums, H.-G. Vogel and M. Tacheva, 'Rechtstatsachen zur Beschlusskontrolle im Aktienrecht', *Zeitschrift für Wirtschaftsrecht* 38/00 (2000), pp.1649–55.

26. J. Esser, 'Germany: Symbolic Privatizations in a Social Market Economy', in V. Wright (ed.), *Industrial Privatization in Western Europe: Pressures, Problems and Paradoxes* (London: Pinter 1994), pp.105–21.

27. At Volkswagen and VIAG the Länder of Lower Saxony and Bavaria did not follow the federal example and retained their shares.

28. E. Grande, *Vom Monopol zum Wettbewerb? Die neokonservative Reform der Telekommunikation in Großbritannien und der Bundesrepublik Deutschland* (Wiesbaden: DUV 1989).

29. Esser, 'Germany'.

30. G.F. Schuppert, 'Die Privatisierungsdiskussion in der deutschen Staatsrechtslehre', in T. Ellwein *et al.* (eds.), *Jahrbuch zur Staats- und Verwaltungswissenschaft* (Baden-Baden: Nomos 1995), pp.325–48.

31. I. Vogelsang, 'Deregulation and Privatization in Germany', *Journal of Public Policy* 8/2 (1988), pp.195–212.

32. S.K. Schmidt, 'Only an Agenda Setter? The European Commission's Power over the Council of Ministers', *European Union Politics* 1/1 (2000), pp.37–61.

33. F.W. Scharpf, *Regieren in Europa: Effektiv und demokratisch?* (Frankfurt a.M.: Campus 1999); W. Streeck, 'The Internationalization of Industrial Relations in Europe: Prospects and Problems', *Politics and Society* 26/4 (1998), pp.429–59.

34. In early 1990, a potential revenue from privatisation of DM1,365 billion was estimated. This was changed by Treuhand's president Rohwedder to DM600 billion a few months later. In 1992, when the opening balance sheets were released, they indicated a value of DM81 billion and restructuring and closing costs of DM215 billion. See M. Cassell, *How Governments Privatize. The Politics of Divestment in the United States and Germany* (Washington: Georgetown University Press 2002), p.181.

35. D. Lehmkuhl, and W. Herr, 'Reform im Spannungsfeld von Dezentralisierung und Entstaatlichung: Die Neuordnung des Eisenbahnwesens in Deutschland', *Politische Vierteljahresschrift* 35/4 (1994), pp.631–57.

36. The state-owned bank, Kreditanstalt für Wiederaufbau, owns an additional 12.3 per cent.

37. G. Majone, 'The Rise of the Regulatory State in Europe', in W.C. Müller and V. Wright (eds.), *The State in Western Europe: Retreat or Redefinition?* (London: Frank Cass 1994), pp.77–101.

38. G. Schröder, 'Der aktivierende Staat aus der Sicht der Politik: Perspektiven für die Zukunftsfähigkeit von Wirtschaft und Politik', in F. Behrens *et al.* (eds.), *Den Staat neu denken* (Berlin: Edition Sigma 1995), pp.277–91.

39. Bavaria opposed the privatisation of Deutsche Lufthansa in the mid-1980s because the CSU government feared that it could undermine the close links between Lufthansa and the aircraft and aerospace industry located in Bavaria. See Esser, 'Germany', p.113.

40. By comparison, they had played much more of a role in the debate of the 1950 and 1960s.

41. See W. Abelshauser, *Wirtschaftsgeschichte der Bundesrepublik Deutschland 1945–1980* (Frankfurt a.M.: Suhrkamp 1983), pp.76–84.

42. J.W. Cioffi and S.S. Cohen, 'The State, Law and Corporate Governance', in S.S. Cohen and G. Boyd (eds.), *Corporate Governance and Globalization* (Cheltenham: Elgar 2000), pp.307–49; S. Lütz, 'From Managed to Market Capitalism? German Finance in Transition', *German Politics* 9/2 (2000), pp.149–71.

43. *Gesetz zur Kontrolle und Transparenz im Unternehmensbereich.*

44. International Accounting Standards (IAS) or General Accepted Accounting Principles (US-GAAP).

45. *Handelsgesetzbuch*, the German Commercial Code.

46. Section 70 (1) of the 1937 Stock Corporation Act obliged the to rule the company 'so wie das Wohl des Betriebes und seiner Gefolgschaft und der gemeine Nutzen von Volk und Reich es erfordern'.

47. 'Die eigenverantwortliche Nutzung des von den Anteilseignern zur Verfügung gestellten Kapitals ist dem Vertretungs- und Leitungsorgan übertragen, dem dabei die Wahrung von Interessen aufgegeben ist, die nicht notwendig die der Anteilseigner sein müssen.' See Bundesministerium für Arbeit und Sozialordnung, *Mitbestimmungsgesetz, Anmerkungen zum Mitbestimmungsurteil des Bundesverfassungsgerichts, Montan-Mitbestimmung, Betriebsverfassung* (Bonn: Bundesministerium 1983), p.301.

48. P.G. Cerny, 'Paradoxes of the Competition State: The Dynamics of Political Globalization', *Government and Opposition* 32/2 (1997), pp.251–74.

49. See H.M. Bury and T. Schmidt, *Das Bankenkartell. Die Verflechtung von Geld, Macht und Politik* (München: Knaur 1996).

50. M. Adams, 'Cross-holdings in Germany', *Journal of Institutional and Theoretical Economics* 155/1 (1999), pp.80–109; Monopolkommission, *Ordnungspolitische Leitlinien für ein funktionsfähiges Finanzsystem. Sondergutachten der Monopolkommission* (Baden-Baden: Nomos 1998).

51. See the statements by Lambsdorff (FDP), Bury (SPD), Wolf (Bündnis '90/Grüne) and Heuer (PDS) in the debate about the KonTraG. Plenarprotokoll Deutscher Bundestag 13/222, 5 March 1998.

52. See Bericht des Finanzausschusses, Drucksache 12/7477, 14 Nov. 2001; Schauerte (CDU) in the debate about the takeover law, Plenarprotokoll Deutscher Bundestag, 11 Oct. 2001.

53. See the statement of Lambsdorff (FDP) in the debate over the KonTraG.

54. See F. Ross, 'Beyond Left and Right: The New Partisan Politics of Welfare', *Governance* 13/2 (2000), pp.155–83.

55. See Monopolkommission, *Leitlinien*, p.118.

56. *Kapitalaufnahmeerleichterungsgesetz* (KapAEG).

57. See Höpner, *Unternehmen*.

58. See Beyer and Hassel, 'Effects'.

The State of the Welfare State: German Social Policy between Macroeconomic Retrenchment and Microeconomic Recalibration

STEPHAN LEIBFRIED and HERBERT OBINGER

From the start, Germany's welfare state served as a model, particularly in continental Europe, and substantially influenced social policy development. The issue at the heart of Bismarck's social reforms was the *Arbeiterfrage*.[1] The institutional response was mandatory as well as occupationally fragmented insurance that aimed at the preservation of a worker's status. The patterns of early welfare state-building in the 1880s shaped the trajectory of Germany's twentieth-century welfare state in its scope and size. Despite several general political turnarounds in the twentieth century, the welfare state survived upheavals by and large unscathed.

West Germany's post-war economic miracle laid the groundwork for continuous welfare state expansion, mostly pre-configured by the existing welfare state structures. Until the early 1970s, Germany was the biggest social spender in the Western world. In the aftermath of World War II, the welfare state was seen as an integral part of the social market economy (*soziale Marktwirtschaft*). In this way, in a divided nation, a balance was struck between socialism and unfettered capitalism. Schmidt has described this type of public policy pattern as 'policy of the middle way'. Learning from historical catastrophes – via the institutional checks and balances of the constitution (*Grundgesetz*) and the practice of broad social co-operation – paved the way for a system of social politics grounded on the compromise between Christian-democratic, social-democratic and liberal political forces. The coexistence of an advanced welfare state with a booming market economy became widely acknowledged as a model of the successful marriage of efficiency with equality.

However, the post-war equilibrium derailed after the 1973 and 1979 oil shocks. In the end, Germany's welfare state was no longer perceived as a model but rather as a problem. Declining economic growth, soaring unemployment, increasing public debt, ageing, transformation of the international political economy – and, particularly, German re-unification – placed the welfare state systematically under pressure.

This article deals with the extent to which the German welfare state has been reformed in the past two decades to cope with these challenges. Specifically, we are interested in continuity and change in social policy. Did the changes in the partisan complexion of government in 1982 and 1998 lead to major changes in social policy? It is argued that social policy over the last two decades corresponds to the paradigm of a 'new politics of the welfare state'. Recalibration of the German welfare state went hand in hand with an expenditure freeze and a shift to *einnahmenorientierte Ausgabenpolitik*, where benefit provision is driven by the availability of public revenues – and not vice versa, as in earlier times. Overall, welfare state patterns remained unchanged or shifted further towards consumption and away from social investments such as education and family services. The Schröder government's most recent legislation points to more substantial changes in labour market and pension policy which will take full effect only in the long run.

This article outlines the central characteristics of the German welfare state, discusses the challenges it faces as well as the problems originating from its architecture, and identifies the internal and external constraints on policy change. Next, it looks at welfare state development in Germany – in the aggregate and in comparison with 21 OECD democracies – between 1980 and 1997 (using OECD data) and between 1960 and 2000 (relying on national expenditure data compiled by the Federal Ministry of Social Affairs). In a change of perspective, it then describes some of the welfare state reforms pursued by the Kohl and Schröder governments. The article concludes with a discussion of whether these measures amount to a change of course in social policy.

THE GERMAN WELFARE STATE: STRUCTURAL MAKEUP, CHALLENGES AND REFORM CONSTRAINTS

Germany's welfare state is mostly classified as 'conservative', according to Esping-Andersen's welfare regime triad. The forces underpinning this type are strong Christian-democratic parties advocating Catholic social doctrines, such as the subsidiarity principle, the male breadwinner model, the rejection of class struggle in favour of corporatist conflict resolution, and a legacy of paternalist policies mirrored in occupationally fragmented and mandatory social insurance. Status preservation via earnings-related transfer payments and preservation of the male breadwinner model are central to this regime type.[2]

Indeed, Germany's welfare state is a bifurcated arrangement where compulsory social insurance outweighs means-tested programmes like social assistance. Despite Germany's federal structure, social policy legislation occurs mainly at the national level. The five pillars of social insurance now in existence (health, accident, age, unemployment – and, most recently, care) cover the vast majority of all employees and their families. Civil servants are not included in social insurance and are covered by special schemes,[3] while the self-employed insure themselves privately or are covered by special programmes. Social insurance is predominantly wage-centred. Entitlements are regularly tied to employment status, while the level of benefits is earnings-related. Co-insurance of spouses and dependent children, the inclusion of certain groups of self-employed persons and the integration of students into social insurance, however, have substantially extended the 'social insurance state' beyond workers. Social insurance is primarily funded through earmarked contributions, mostly paid in equal parts by employers and employees. Family-related benefits, educational allowances, housing benefits and several other programme categories – such as income support to victims of war and Nazi rule – are entirely tax-funded. Social assistance is administered and funded by the municipalities – their budgets, however, are determined by nationwide revenue-sharing – and provides a means-tested minimum income in the low wage sector as well. Assistance thus serves as an equivalent to (otherwise absent) minimum wage legislation.

This arrangement was an integral part of the German success story after World War II. But since the mid-1970s Germany's welfare state has been confronted with a series of new challenges:

• Rising and persistent mass unemployment began in the 1970s and accelerated further after German unification, a development which also amplified the pressure on the corporatist labour market (through a massive lack of territorial homogeneity). This created new demands on the welfare state and new pressures on its labour market foundations while public revenues declined.
• The proportion of elderly (aged 65 and above) exceeds the OECD average and will increase sharply in the next decades, while the rate of net reproduction has bottomed out and will not be compensated for by additional immigration. Changing age composition will expose pension and health insurance to profound fiscal stress.
• The occupational structure has changed, and new forms of employment have surfaced at the margins of the labour market. Also, family structure has changed significantly. Rising divorce rates, an increasing number of single-parent households and new, more flexible forms of employment (part-time work, temping work and so on) have fed an escalating

mismatch between a traditional (social insurance and labour market) regulatory regime and a new social reality.

- Income inequality has increased over time – although slightly, and a good deal less than in the USA, where it has squeezed the middle classes.[4] Over the course of several decades, the poverty risk has shifted demographically downwards from the elderly to families, children and the long-term unemployed.

- Since the 1980s, European integration has slowly transformed sovereign welfare states into semi-sovereign ones. In the 1990s, this became most visible in the health services and, outside the welfare state proper, in the general privatisation of public provisions (transforming the *Staat der Daseinsvorsorge*, that is, electricity, gas, water, telephone, postal service, city services, rail, air and other public transport) that used to underpin the welfare state.[5] A re-regulation of social welfare at the European level has been at best slow and halting, while national welfare states are exposed to increased competition as markets have integrated and become deregulated.

- Substantial immigration up until the early 1990s, especially by people of German descent (*Aussiedler*), created new demands while slowing down the demographic transition and dampening welfare state financing problems. Immigration and comparatively generous asylum policies have placed a strain on social assistance and pensions, decreasing political support for the welfare state.[6] In particular, immigrants of German descent from the former Soviet Union have enjoyed privileged access to old age benefits. Immigration has also increased the low-skilled labour supply, further stirring up native labour market problems.

On top of all this, these challenges have been amplified by the entrenched structures of the welfare state. Structural problems stemming from the makeup of Germany's welfare state were largely hidden in the 'Golden Age' and thus overlooked. As the employment-cum-marriage nexus of benefits and the fixation on contributions in welfare state financing were exposed to a rapidly changing social structure and a more competitive global economy, the structural weakness of the German model became quite visible:

- The German welfare state has a bias towards backward-looking compensatory monetary transfers. This predisposition impedes its transition to a social service state, which is characterised by a forward-looking slant towards family and human capital formation and preventive measures.

- Germany's welfare state has fallen into an employment trap. Rigid labour market regulation and high non-wage labour costs (due to contribution-based welfare state funding) stifle job creation, especially in the labour-intensive domestic service sector. In addition, decades of labour shedding via early retirement programmes have created a time bomb.
- A missing low wage sector goes hand in hand with a service economy gap. A lack of childcare facilities, among other things, has moved Germany towards a low-fertility equilibrium.[7]
- The institutional framework of social security builds on a so-called standard employment relationship (*Normalarbeitsverhältnis*), which leaves little room for flexible adjustment to changing occupational structures.
- The sheer size of Germany's welfare state affects other policy sectors. Judging by *net* social expenditure (that is if we take into account taxes levied on benefits plus tax expenditures), Germany has the most expensive welfare state in the world. Since total government outlays are near the OECD mean, Germany's comparatively high social spending crowds out many other public policies. In particular, there seems to be a trade-off between education and social policy.[8] Backward-looking public expenditure devoted to repairing damages – the compensatory machinery of routine welfare state politics – limits expenditure on public education and research, which are of utmost importance in a more competitive global economy. While the average annual growth of nominal social expenditure per capita was 3.5 per cent between 1992 and 1999, nominal education expenditure per capita increased by only 0.9 per cent. In real terms, this amounts to a decline in expenditure devoted to education and research in the 1990s. Moreover, since 1991, the number of those employed in education, science and research has declined by ten per cent.[9]

In addition, all of the challenges outlined above are addressed to a political system distinguished by a high degree of vertical and horizontal dispersion of power. Germany's semi-sovereign state tends to allow for only incremental policy change, if any.[10] Furthermore, critical historical events accompanied by a combination of internal and external forces have imposed massive constraints that further rein in the government's capacity to act:

- German reunification has strained fiscal policy, especially since from the start a major portion of the costs of unification were displaced onto the social insurance systems – that is, contributions and not general taxation.

- While German unification requires huge fiscal transfers, national fiscal policy outside social security is constrained by the Maastricht Treaty, which impedes further expansion of subsidies to social insurance. In addition, the EU adds another veto-prone supranational level to Germany's already thoroughly multi-levelled veto-ridden politics. This imposes unique restrictions and strains on a welfare-cum-public service state already enveloped in a highly fragmented, centrifugal corporatism.
- Reallocation of resources towards education and family services is difficult to achieve as the elderly increasingly shape the electorate. The ratio of those 65 and older to people aged 20 to 64 will increase from 28 per cent in the year 2000 to approximately 50 per cent in 2030.[11] Moreover, Länder jurisdiction over education and provision of day care hinders swift policy change and counteracts a reallocation of resources to forward-looking social investments.
- The institutional checks and balances of the Basic Law also restrict policy change. Specifically, conflicting rationales that underpin partisan competition and vertical power sharing may lead to a policy stalemate. Germany's party system makes welfare state retrenchment quite unlikely, since the two major *Sozialstaatsparteien* – CDU/CSU and SPD – are not counterbalanced by a strong market-liberal party, as is the case in the US or the UK.[12] Straying from the German pathway and moving towards a problem-solving mode is unlikely. State structures and inherited welfare state patterns are almost insurmountable obstacles for dramatic change, while, concurrently, partisan competition drives the growth of the welfare state.

How has Germany attempted to bridge the gulf between the multiple challenges to, and restrictions on, policy change imposed by its polity and by the institutional inertia of indigenous welfare state patterns? Has it achieved a sustainable new equilibrium?

THE MACRO-QUANTITATIVE EVIDENCE: TRENDS AND PATTERNS OF SOCIAL EXPENDITURE, 1980–2000

In the first place, how have gross social expenditures developed over the last two decades? We take stock of recent trends in social spending in a cross-sectional perspective by comparing Germany with 21 advanced OECD democracies. In addition, we provide some time-series evidence on the development between 1960 and 2000. The data come from the OECD social expenditure database and the recent *Sozialbericht* issued by the (former)

Ministry for Labour and Social Affairs. According to OECD data, total social spending in percentage of GDP increased from 25.4 per cent in 1980 to 27.8 per cent in 1997. In 1997, public social expenditure accounted for 95.7 per cent of total social spending, whereas private mandatory benefits totalled only 4.3 per cent. A similar picture emerges when we rely directly on national data sources. However, national data point to a higher expenditure/GDP ratio, since the German *Sozialbudget* also includes indirect benefits like tax relief, which amounted to 3.5 per cent of the GDP in 2000. According to data compiled by the (former) minister for labour and social affairs, social expenditures in percentage of GDP increased slightly, from 30.6 in 1980 to 31.9 per cent in 2000. At first glance, this does not suggest a retrenchment, corroborating Paul Pierson's thesis of welfare state resilience.[13]

To draw this conclusion from aggregate spending data may, however, be quite misleading. First, benefit cuts may have effects only in the (very) long run ('beyond the horizon'), a strategy pursued especially in reforming old age pensions. Second, when we compare two time-points, we neglect temporal fluctuation in social spending. Fluctuation may result from policy changes or exogenous shocks. Third, patterns of social expenditure may have changed.

Indeed, while total social expenditures show no linear upward trend over time, the patterns of social spending have changed to some extent. Total social expenditures declined during the 1980s, especially after the Kohl government took office in 1982 and continued the politics of austerity already initiated under social-democratic Chancellor Helmut Schmidt in the mid-1970s (see Figure 1). After unification, however, social spending increased steadily until the late 1990s. Driven by socioeconomic turmoil in the new Länder and by the wholesale transfer of the western welfare state to the former German Democratic Republic, social spending soared. As large-scale eastern unemployment was absorbed through welfare state means, spending skyrocketed to an extent never observed in a Western democracy. In 1992, social expenditures in East Germany peaked at 55.5 per cent of the GDP, topping Sweden by far.

Regarding patterns of social spending, the OECD Social Expenditure Data Base allows spending to be broken down into 13 components. As in other advanced OECD democracies, old age and health care account for the bulk of German expenditures. Spending here substantially exceeds the OECD average, while expenditures on poverty and social services lag slightly. A cross-national comparison of programme-related spending reveals that Germany neither occupies a top position nor lags notably in any of the 13 categories. Extreme values are found in nations traditionally grouped into the liberal, southern or social-democratic worlds of welfare

FIGURE 1

TOTAL SOCIAL EXPENDITURE AS PERCENTAGE OF GDP IN GERMANY,
1960–2000

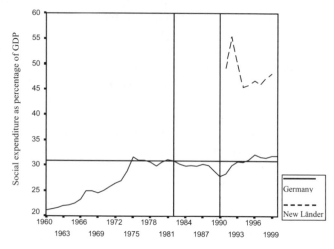

Note: The vertical lines denote the beginning of the Kohl government and of German
unification respectively. The horizontal line (bench)marks the level of total social
expenditure when Kohl first took office.

Source: Federal Ministry of Labour and Social Affairs, *Sozialbericht 2001*, Vol.2 (Bonn 2002),
p.12.

capitalism. A similar picture emerges when we compare replacement rates
of unemployment insurance and old age benefits.[14]

The dynamics of programme-related spending are such that insurance-
based programmes – with the exception of accident insurance – have
absorbed a steadily growing share of social expenditures since 1970. Today,
social insurance schemes, including unemployment insurance, account for
almost two-thirds of the *Sozialbudget*. Entirely tax-funded programmes –
like compensation to victims of war and Nazi rule and social security for
public sector employees – by contrast, lost a lot of ground, whereas family
and educational transfers remained roughly stable over time.

Table 1 shows the development of programme-related spending as a
percentage of GDP. The big items – like spending on old age and health –
grew further, whereas spending on families declined under the Kohl
government. Finally, since 1980, the end of full employment has led to
rapidly growing expenditure on employment programmes and
unemployment compensation. In the 1990s, these two types of programmes

accounted for almost ten per cent of the GDP in the eastern Länder. Overall, *ex post* compensation became increasingly important and came to significantly outweigh future-oriented *ex ante* investments in human capital, prevention and social services.

According to *Sozialbudget* data, social security contributions accounted for approximately 61 per cent of total revenue in 2000 (see Table 2). As reported in the *Sozialbericht*, total contribution payments increased from 12.4 per cent of the GDP in 1960 to 19.8 per cent in 2000. Relatively speaking,

TABLE 1

PROGRAMME-RELATED EXPENDITURE OF THE *SOZIALBUDGET* IN
PER CENT OF GDP, SEPARATED BY FUNCTION

	1960	1970	1980	1985	1991 (East)	1995 (East)	2000 (East)
Total social expenditure	21.1	25.1	30.6	30.0	28.4 (49.2)	31.2 (45.9)	31.9 (48.5)
Family and marriage	3.6	4.7	4.9	4.2	4.0 (7.0)	4.0 (5.1)	4.8 (6.0)
Health	5.8	7.3	10.0	9.8	9.9 (15.0)	11.1 (14.4)	10.9 (14.2)
Employment	0.6	0.8	1.6	2.0	2.7 (13.7)	3.1 (9.9)	3.1 (9.4)
Old age and survivors	9.2	10.3	11.9	12.0	10.7 (12.8)	11.6 (15.4)	11.9 (17.2)
Other contingencies (e.g. social assistance)	1.9	2.0	2.3	1.9	1.1 (0.7)	1.3 (1.2)	1.2 (1.6)

Note: East = former German Democratic Republic.

Source: Federal Ministry of Labour and Social Affairs, *Sozialbericht 2001*, Vol.2 (Bonn 2002), pp.27–30.

TABLE 2

FINANCING STRUCTURE OF THE *SOZIALBUDGET* AS % TOTAL REVENUES
AND OF GDP (BRACKETED)

	1960	1970	1980	1985	1990	1995	2000
Total contributions	54.3	57.3	61.1	63.6	66.3	63.9	60.7
– paid by insured persons	19.1	20.4	22.0	24.7	26.1	26.6	26.3
– paid by employers	35.2	36.9	39.1	39.0	40.2	37.2	34.4
Grants	43.4	40.9	37.5	34.9	32.0	34.7	37.7
Other revenues	2.3	1.9	1.4	1.5	1.7	1.5	1.6
Total	100.0	100.0	100.0	100.0	100.0	100.0	100.0
(% of GDP)	(22.8)	(26.6)	(31.9)	(31.1)	(29.5)	(31.8)	(32.7)

Source: Federal Ministry of Labour and Social Affairs, *Sozialbericht 2001*, Vol.2 (Bonn 2002), pp.39–42.

receipts from contributions were at an all-time high in the early 1990s. Since 1960, the share of contributions borne by the insured has increased markedly, whereas contributions paid by employers now make up a slightly smaller share of the *Sozialbudget* than they did 40 years ago (see Table 2). Also, the degree to which the state contributes to funding social programmes has diminished over time, although it increased slightly in the 1990s.

Our overview on aggregate spending and revenue points to three basic trends. First, social expenditure patterns reflect the basic structural attributes of the conservative welfare regime. Hence, they support the argument that Germany permanently subscribes to 'the policy of the middle way'. The dynamics of social spending suggest that the structural traits of German social policy have not changed fundamentally. This holds particularly true for funding patterns and for the increasing share of the *Sozialbudget* devoted to social insurance. The international comparison reveals that spending on social services in Germany is underdeveloped with regard to services to the elderly and near the OECD mean in family services. In addition, Germany's welfare state is clearly biased towards consumption at the expense of prospective investment in human capital and family policy. While spending on pensions and health is near the top OECD-wide, expenditures devoted to education and family cash benefits are grouped near the mean at best.

Second, spending data point neither to the radical dismantling of welfare state programmes in the two past decades, nor to a continuous rise in social expenditures. Recent social spending has mainly been driven by German unification. While social expenditure declined during the first years of the Kohl government, it exploded after unification as socioeconomic turmoil escalated.

Third, non-wage labour costs increased throughout the Kohl era, since social security contributions increased substantially. Total contribution rates as a percentage of gross earnings increased from 32.4 per cent in 1980 to an all-time high of 42.1 per cent in 1998. The welfare state burden was increasingly shifted to the insured themselves.

In sum, aggregate spending and revenue data suggest that no departure from the established social policy path has occurred in recent years. The problems of Germany's welfare state, which we outlined in the previous section, have apparently not been confronted. Let us now examine how this finding corresponds with a more detailed analysis of the social policy reforms enacted by the Kohl and Schröder governments. To study whether the ideological orientation of these two governments is mirrored in their policies, we will describe the measures taken by the Christian–Liberal government and the Red–Green coalition one by one.

GERMAN SOCIAL POLICY SINCE 1982

Kohl: 1982–98

In 1982, Kohl's new government promised key changes in economic and social policy. The state was to be cut back to its basic functions, and the concept of a social market economy was to be redefined in a more market-liberal way. The welfare state was to be contained, non-wage labour costs reduced, and the labour market deregulated. The institutional windows of opportunity for policy change stood wide open, since the Christian Democratic–Liberal government also had a majority in the Bundesrat from 1982 to 1991. Yet no consistent pattern of reform can be found. The government initially cut some benefits across the board, partially increasing contributions at the same time.[15] Survivors' benefits were means-tested for the first time, eligibility for unemployment benefits and invalidity pensions was made more stringent and social assistance benefits were decreased, while co-payments for prescriptions and medical services were increased. Pensioners were required to pay contributions to health insurance while recipients of sickness benefits (*Krankengeld*) had to contribute to pension and unemployment insurance. Expenditure containment continued with the 1992 Pension Reform legislated in 1989, and with the Health Care Reform of 1988. The latter was intended to limit the health care cost explosion, but it only succeeded in introducing a rather limited competition among health care providers.[16] Pension reform, however – legislated jointly by the Kohl government and its SPD opposition – cut deeper. Pension adjustment was now definitely tied to net rather than gross wages (although this had already been practised *de facto* since 1978, via delayed indexation), retirement age was increased, and pension credits for time spent in the university system were cut. In addition, a partial pension (*Teilrente*) was introduced to allow for gradual retirement.

Beginning in the mid-1980s, retrenchment was accompanied by selective welfare state expansion, focused at first on family policy. A parental allowance (*Erziehungsgeld*) was introduced, as were parental leave (*Erziehungsurlaub*) and child tax credits (*Kinderfreibetrag*). In addition, the child allowance (*Kindergeld*) was increased, and time invested in care for the young or the elderly was credited to some extent in the old age benefit formula.

Not much progress was made, however, in deregulating the labour market. Here, reform was limited to the *Beschäftigungsförderungsgesetz* (1985), but a reform of § 116 of the *Arbeitsförderungsgesetz* (concerning who should bear the indirect costs of strikes) was even opposed from within the Christian Democratic Party – specifically, by its trade union wing. Other attempts to increase flexibility – such as the *Arbeitszeitgesetz* allowing more work on Sundays – failed outright.[17] The path of least resistance was to expand generous early exit schemes. In the long run, however, labour shedding through early retirement turned out to be rather costly.

On the eve of German unification, the path to consolidation was securely established. The social expenditure/GDP ratio had declined throughout the 1980s, especially as the economy grew stronger towards the end of the decade (see Figure 1). Attempts to limit non-wage labour costs, however, were not successful, and contribution rates rose from 32.4 per cent of gross wages in 1982 to 35.6 per cent in 1990.

In the 1990s, social policy got stuck between the new social demands of unification and the attendant fiscal difficulties, which were further increased by the Maastricht criteria. Although the rapid construction of German 'Social Union' was an administrative masterpiece, other short-sighted and politically motivated decisions fed back massively and continuously on the welfare state. With unification, the West German status quo of social rights was extended *in toto* to the east, while extensive childcare in the east was discontinued rather than being spread westward. The hasty establishment of economic, monetary and social union shattered the balance between productivity and wages in the east. Unemployment escalated. These costs, along with the increase of eastern pensions to western levels, led to enormous increases in social spending (see Figure 1). Politicians claimed credit for higher pensions, but fiscal politics was dominated by blame avoidance. To a large extent, unification was financed through public debt and the social insurance system, pushing contribution rates still higher.[18] While unification amplified the pressures on social insurance, the general fiscal manoeuvrability of the state contracted. Moreover, the Kohl government lost its Bundesrat majority in 1991, endowing the SPD opposition with even more influence on federal policy-making.

Austerity plus selective expansion continued after unification. Consolidation mainly centred on asylum seekers, who where taken off social assistance and placed on a lower, second-class welfare track in 1993. Replacement rates for the unemployed were lowered, and social assistance benefit rates were not indexed for several years. Although fiscal scarcity constrained all public budgets, the welfare state also expanded when long-term care insurance was introduced in 1994. In an ageing society, care insurance socialised a growing private risk to a certain extent, with the Social Democrats consenting. As a consequence, Alber[19] sees Germany inadvertently making the transition from transfer to social service state (for the aged). Pressed by two rulings of the Federal Constitutional Court on respecting the subsistence minimum in the income tax system, family benefits were upgraded (child allowance and child tax credits). In the early 1990s, active labour market policy and wage subsidies expanded substantially in the eastern Länder. In addition, early retirement hugely cut the labour supply.

The Maastricht Treaty cast its shadow beginning in the mid-1990s. Its consolidation constraints on fiscal policy were also felt clearly in social policy, although not as massively as they were in Italy. Now the 'unification consensus' (*Vereinigungskonsens*) eroded and gave way to political confrontations between the government and the opposition. With the 'Programme for Economic Growth and Employment' of 1996, comprehensive retrenchment was implemented – meeting with strong resistance from Social Democrats and the unions, which abandoned Kohl's *Bündnis für Arbeit*. Sick pay (*Lohnfortzahlung im Krankheitsfall*) was reduced from 100 to 80 per cent, and cash sickness benefits were lowered. Pension credits for years spent in tertiary education were reduced (in several steps from an original 13 years) to three years, and the generous pension rights of German expatriates from the former USSR were cut extensively. The increase in the retirement age, which had already started with the pension reform of 1992, was accelerated.

The active component in labour market policy was also cut, and pressures on the unemployed to accept jobs were increased. Cuts in passive unemployment benefits were softened by some improvements for the long-term unemployed. In contrast to the 1980s, some progress was now made in deregulating the labour market and making it more flexible. Protection against dismissals was abolished in small-scale enterprises, and the options for fixed-term employment contracts were expanded. The Federal Labour Office (Bundesanstalt für Arbeit) lost its monopoly on employment services, triggered by EU legislation on freedom of services. A more market-liberal Working Time Act (*Arbeitszeitgesetz*) that had failed twice in parliament in the 1980s was finally passed in 1994.

In 1997, the Kohl government broke with the consensual pattern in pension policy that had characterised the Bonn Republic. The Pension Reform Act of 1999 was passed with only a coalition majority. In the act, a 'demographic component' was inserted into the pension formula; in benefit calculation, expenditures were to be restrained by taking average life expectancy into account. The numerous retrenchment measures enacted since the mid-1990s led to increased tensions between the government and the opposition and contributed to the success of the Social Democrats in the 1998 general election.

Schröder: 1998–2002

In its first term (1998–2002), the Schröder government's basic approach in social policy was to stick to its election campaign promises, that is, to undo some of the late retrenchment measures of the Kohl government (via a 'counter-reformation'). In contrast to Kohl, Schröder's Bundesrat window of opportunity (congruent majorities) was extremely small, closing as soon as the spring of 1999. Two quickly enacted laws came to characterise his efforts.[20]

First, in the *Gesetz zu Korrekturen in der Sozialversicherung und zur Sicherung der Arbeitnehmerrechte* (Law to Correct Social Insurance and Guarantee Employees' Rights) of 25 November 1998, Schröder's government suspended the pension-'dampening' demographic factor in the pension formula that the Kohl government had just introduced for 1999. In addition, all cuts in invalidity pensions were repealed. The law also extended the obligation to pay social insurance contributions to certain categories of the self-employed who were declared de facto employees ('pseudo self-employed'). Furthermore, it restored employment protection to companies engaging six to ten employees. Sick pay was restored to 100 per cent, and the sunset clause in the Law on Seconded Workers from other EU member states was dropped, making the legislation permanent.

The second major counter-Kohl reform was the *Gesetz zur Stärkung der Solidarität in der Gesetzlichen Krankenversicherung* (Law to Strengthen Solidarity in Health Insurance) of 10 December 1998, which lowered co-payments for prescription drugs. In addition, the chronically ill were relieved of co-payments for transportation, drugs and other treatment-related costs. The automatic rise of co-payments with increases in contribution rates was revoked.

Beyond these backtracking measures, the Red–Green coalition took some further steps toward social policy reform:

- On 3 March 1999, it legislated an ecological tax reform (*Ökologische Steuerreform*) that includes surcharges on energy. The revenues go to the pension insurance fund to cap the contribution rate and lower non-wage labour costs.
- Child allowances were increased in several steps, and income limits for parental allowances were raised slightly.
- A major pension reform was passed in 2001. The replacement rate of the standard public pension will decrease from 70 to 64 per cent in 2030. The gap is to be filled by a non-mandatory private pension, colloquially labelled *Riester-Rente* (after the minister of labour at the time). In addition, for the first time, a minimum pension was introduced in the German pension

system. Pensioners may receive means-tested supplements from the pension insurance offices that are calculated similarly to social assistance benefits. The *Riester-Rente* moves the German pension system slightly from a public pay-as-you-go system toward a privately funded system. The shift is limited in volume (amounting to four per cent of the total pension) and structure (it is not obligatory). The supplementary pension is strongly regulated to guarantee a high benefit level, and well subsidised to assure high take-up in a non-obligatory setting. Due to high subsidies, the *Riester-Rente* will not really save money – although, for the first time, it crosses the border to private provision. In the long run, the *Riester-Rente* may turn out to be a watershed, and thus a case of piecemeal engineering which precipitates systemic change. Some claim that the 2001 pension reform signals a departure from the objective to maintain living standards beyond retirement.[21]

- Labour market issues were not strongly addressed in the Schröder government's first term. But the issues had to be confronted when the low efficiency of the employment services provided by the Bundesanstalt für Arbeit became a subject of scandal in early 2002. Schröder seized upon this crisis and appointed a commission, named after its chairman, Peter Hartz, to draft labour market reform measures. In a single stroke, Schröder's move bypassed the SPD in parliament, the Federal Ministry of Labour and the Bundesanstalt für Arbeit.

At the beginning of its second term, the Red–Green coalition put the Hartz recommendations on the legislative agenda. These recommendations had to be renegotiated with the opposition, since major parts required the consent of the Bundesrat, which was dominated by the CDU/CSU and FDP. On 20 December 2002, several measures became law, including improved job services for the unemployed combined with tightening obligations for the unemployed to accept the jobs offered. Moreover, health insurance contribution rates and the budgets of doctors, dentists and hospitals were frozen for 2003; the upper monthly earnings limit (*Versicherungspflichtgrenze*) was raised from €3,375 to €3,825 to forestall exits into private insurance; pension contributions were raised from 19.1 to 19.5 per cent for 2003; and the social security contribution ceiling (*Beitragsbemessungsgrenze*) was increased by €600 per month in the west and €500 in the east.

Social insurance reforms in the first months after the 2002 election were exercises in cost containment. While efforts were made to confront the central weakness of continental welfare states and increase employment in the low-wage tertiary sector, contribution rates for pension and health insurance were increased or frozen (though for one year only) rather than lowered. At the end of 2002, another high level commission (again named after its chairman, the economist Bert Rürup) was appointed to develop a long-term and sustainable social security reform agenda within six months. Ad hoc 'government by commission' seems to be turning into a hallmark of German welfare state reform.

CONCLUSION

Has German politics cut the Gordian knot and moved towards a sustainable equilibrium in social policy? Some researchers have emphasised a 'conservative transformation' of the German welfare state. Some speak of a 'dual transformation': a stronger family orientation plus a re-commodification of welfare state clientele via the expanding role of the labour market.[22] These definitions single out some important social policy developments of the last two decades, but they do not adequately reflect the high overall stability of German social policy. Basically, the trend has been towards cost containment: the welfare state has, for the most part, been streamlined as 'social *insurance* state'. Cost containment has actually been quite substantial. Today's standard pension – which requires a work record of 45 years with average earnings – would, according to Alber, be 20 per cent higher had pension reform not taken place.

This, however, does not imply that the welfare state has essentially been dismantled. Rather, benefits have been scaled back to levels 'reached in the late-1960s before the Social-Liberal coalition reform government had come to office'.[23] Benefit levels, in other words, have returned to where they were in the Golden Age of the welfare state and have remained frozen at that level, while the real value of pensions has actually increased substantially over time.

A procedural shift in the nature of welfare state reform took place that characterises the last two decades. In the Golden Age, the notion of 'open-ended needs satisfaction' had been firmly established and drove the budgetary process. But common to both the Kohl and Schröder periods was a shift to 'contribution-defined spending' – the so-called *einnahmenorientierte Ausgabenpolitik*. Or, as the Business Advisory Board of the SPD put it: 'In principle, it is no longer the amount of benefits that determines the level of contributions, but the tolerable level of contributions which now controls the level of benefits.'[24]

While the numerous measures aimed at cost containment have made the German welfare state more viable, neither the Kohl nor the Schröder government has been able to overcome the fundamental structural weakness of Germany's welfare state. Although social service provision was expanded through long-term care insurance and the 1988 Health Care Reform, as Alber showed in 2000, day care for children is still weakly developed. For many years, no reform of social security has taken place that has been able to alleviate mass unemployment. Recent reforms of labour market policy may amount to a first step in overcoming the institutional rigidities constraining employment in the low-wage service sector.

The politics of German social policy over the last two decades thus fits neatly into Pierson's New Politics paradigm – the new logic of social policy-making in times of permanent austerity.[25] Benefit cutbacks entail concentrated costs in return for diffuse benefits. Politicians, aiming to hold on to their offices, refrain from welfare state retrenchment to avoid electoral punishment. The unpopular measures associated with austerity require new strategies of blame avoidance. This is particularly true in a political setting where two major *Sozialstaatsparteien* dominate and where sustaining the welfare state is always a central topic for electoral campaigns. Strategies that minimise the political costs of retrenchment are obfuscation, division, compensation or increasing the complexity of reform measures, thus diffusing accountability for unpopular retrenchment and reducing the visibility of painful cuts. This logic of austerity politics makes significant reform rather unlikely, unless the weight of the problem exceeds a critical threshold.

The aggregate spending data demonstrate that the German welfare state has not been dismantled. Moreover, there are several cases of cost-minimising political strategies. Retrenchment by stealth (or by obfuscation) has included measures such as changing the indexation rules for pensions or revising – as has happened repeatedly – the pension formula itself. Labour shedding via 'early exit' was also a short-term strategy employed consistently to hide labour market problems. Furthermore, there is some evidence that divisive strategies were pursued because some of the most significant benefit cuts focused on poorly organised groups at the margin of the labour market who lack the power to mobilise politically, a risk-shedding strategy most visible today in the struggle over the reform of the different tiers of national unemployment benefits in their relation to local social assistance. In the 1990s, the most painful benefit cuts were experienced by asylum seekers and immigrants of German descent from the former Soviet Union.

The evidence for compensation strategies is also strong. 'Symmetric retrenchment' across all major insurance schemes[26] and the rise of co-payments in health insurance were counterbalanced in 1994 by building a fifth pillar of social insurance, long-term care insurance. Moreover, family cash benefits were increased, although this was not reflected in aggregate social spending data. Compensation also occurred in social insurance and pension reform when the increase in the retirement age for women – the austere way to carry out an ECJ-enforced EU gender equality mandate (the 1990 Barber case)[27] – and the reform of survivors' benefits were coupled with crediting child-rearing periods in old age benefits. The 2001 reduction of the replacement rate for old age pensions was buffered by new state-subsidised private pensions (*Riester-Rente*), and in the early 1990s, the cut in unemployment benefits was accompanied by increased spending on active labour market policy.

Another example of compensation strategies is 'grandfather clauses' that protect current recipients from policy changes. Many of the enacted reforms will become effective in the (very) long run only, and thus are not immediately felt by the electorate. Some examples of this are massive cuts in education credits in the calculation of old age benefits, changes in the pension formula and increases in the retirement age that are scheduled to take place over a long transition period. Such measures shift the burden of the cuts onto future generations who are poorly organised today – or they at least push the cuts to the far end of the horizon for the generation that is presently active in the labour market. In addition, the younger generation has been negatively affected by cuts in public education and by higher social security contributions.

In line with the New Politics approach, there is only scant evidence that 'parties do matter'. Both the Kohl and the Schröder governments were able to influence social policy only at the margins and could not re-shape the welfare state according to their ideological orientation. The moderate welfare state retrenchment carried out under the CDU/CSU–FDP coalition and the reversal of cuts ('counter-reformation') enacted by the Schröder government in the late 1990s are cases in point. But the *Riester-Rente* and the recent liberalisation of low-wage employment sharply contradict the traditional policy objectives of the political Left. In comparison, the Kohl government could neither bring down non-wage labour costs, nor did it manage to cut the state back to its core functions as it had announced in 1982.

NOTES

1. F.-X. Kaufmann, 'Der deutsche Sozialstaat im internationalen Vergleich', in Bundesministerium für Arbeit und Sozialordnung and Bundesarchiv (eds.), *Geschichte der Sozialpolitik in Deutschland seit 1945*, Vol.1: *Grundlagen der Sozialpolitik* (Baden-Baden: Nomos 2001), pp.799–989, and now P. Manow, 'Social Protection, Capitalist Production: The Bismarckian Welfare State and the German Political Economy from the 1880s to the 1990s' (Habilitation thesis, Konstanz 2001). On the general direction of German politics, see M.G. Schmidt, 'The Policy of the Middle Way', *Journal of Public Policy* 7/2 (1987), pp.135–77. For a 1999 overview of the state of social policy see P. Manow and E. Seils,

'Adjusting Badly: The German Welfare State, Structural Change, and the Open Economy', in F.W. Scharpf and V. Schmidt (eds.), *Welfare and Work in the Open Economy* (Oxford: Oxford University Press 2000), pp.264–307.

2. G. Esping-Andersen, *The Three Worlds of Welfare Capitalism* (Cambridge: Polity Press 1990). For a first major synthesis of the challenges to the German welfare state, see F.-X. Kaufmann, *Herausforderungen des Sozialstaates* (Frankfurt a.M: Suhrkamp 1997). The challenges of European integration are synthesised in S. Leibfried and P. Pierson (eds.), *European Social Policy. Between Fragmentation and Integration* (Washington, DC: Brookings 1995); S. Leibfried and P. Pierson, 'Social Policy: Left to Courts and Markets?' in H. Wallace and W. Wallace (eds.), *Policy-Making in the EU* (Oxford: Oxford University Press, 4th edn. 2000), pp.267–91.

3. Since the civil servant historically served as a model for normal social policy development in Germany, the discrepancies to blue and white collar workers remain within bounds.

4. E. Rieger and S. Leibfried, *Limits to Globalization. Welfare States and the World Economy* (Cambridge: Polity 2003), p.160; see now E. Rieger, 'Die sozialpolitische Gegenreformation. Eine kritische Analyse der Wirtschafts- und Sozialpolitik seit 1998', *Aus Politik und Zeitgeschichte. Beilage zur Wochenzeitung Das Parlament*, B 46/47 (Nov. 2002), pp.3–12.

5. For a recent overview on European integration and health issues, see B. Schulte, 'Warenverkehrsfreiheit und Dienstleistungsfreiheit im gemeinsame Markt – Auswirkungen auf das Deutsche Gesundheitswesen. Part 1: Bestandsaufnahme', *Arbeit und Sozialpolitik* 7/8 (2001), pp.36–49; 'Part 2: Perspektiven', 1/2 (2002), pp.43–57; E. Mossialos *et al.*, *EU Law and the Social Character of Health Care* (Brussels: P.I.E. Lang 2002), especially Chapters 1 ('A European Social Model?'), 7 ('EU Competition Law and Health Care Systems') and 9 ('The Way Forward'), and M. McKee, E. Mossialos and R. Baeten (eds.), *The Impact of EU Law on Health Care Systems* (Brussels: P.I.E. Lang 2002, in press). For a good overview of the integration-induced or -supported developments in public provision in the context of the welfare state proper and on their infectious outcomes, see the account by two European public law experts, G. Haverkate and S. Huster, *Europäisches Sozialrecht. Eine Einführung* (Baden-Baden: Nomos 1999), pp.285–367 (this part was written by G. Haverkate).

6. J. Alber, 'Recent Developments of the German Welfare State: Basic Continuity or Paradigm Shift?', *ZeS-Working paper 6/2001* (Centre for Social Policy Research, University of Bremen 2001), p.13.

7. On this and the previous bullet, see F.W. Scharpf, 'The Viability of Advanced Welfare States in the International Economy: Vulnerabilities and Options', *Journal of European Public Policy* 7/2 (2000), pp.190–228, and G. Esping-Andersen, *Social Foundations of Postindustrial Economies* (Oxford: Oxford University Press 1999).

8. On net social expenditure, see W. Adema, 'Revisiting Real Social Spending Across Countries: A Brief Note', *OECD Economic Studies* 30 (2000), pp.191–7; and on the crowding out of education see M.G. Schmidt, 'Warum Mittelmaß? Deutschlands Bildungsausgaben im internationalen Vergleich', *Politische Vierteljahresschrift* 43/1 (2002), pp.3–19.

9. Data are taken from the Federal Ministry of Education and Research, *Grund- und Strukturdaten 2000/2001. Gesamtübersichten* (Bonn 2001), pp.21–2, and *Zahlenbarometer 2000/2001. Ein bildungs- und forschungsstatistischer Überblick* (Bonn 2001), p.22. The extremely negative results of the OECD-PISA study for Germany should be interpreted in this light. For a comparative approach see J. Allmendinger and S. Leibfried, 'Education and Social Policy. The Four Worlds of Competence Production', *Journal of European Social Policy* 13/1 (2003), pp.63–81.

10. P. Katzenstein, *Policy and Politics in West Germany: The Growth of a Semi-sovereign State* (Philadelphia: Temple University Press 1987); M.G. Schmidt, 'Germany. The Grand Coalition State', in J.M. Colomer (ed.), *Political Institutions in Europe* (London: Routledge 1986), pp.62–98.

11. D. Döring, *Die Zukunft der Alterssicherung* (Frankfurt a.M.: Suhrkamp 2002), p.46.

12. On general policy stalemate see G. Lehmbruch, *Parteienwettbewerb im Bundesstaat* (Opladen: Westdeutscher Verlag 1998), and on the particularity of two major welfare state parties see H. Kitschelt, 'Partisan Competition and Retrenchment', in P. Pierson (ed.), *The*

New Politics of the Welfare State (Oxford: Oxford University Press 2001), pp.265–302, esp. p.294.

13. P. Pierson, *Dismantling the Welfare State? Reagan, Thatcher, and the Politics of Retrenchment* (Cambridge: Cambridge University Press 1994); P. Pierson (ed.), *The New Politics of the Welfare State* (Oxford: Oxford University Press 2001).

14. On comparative general spending patterns see also F.G. Castles, 'Developing New Measures of Welfare State Change and Reform', *European Journal of Political Research* 41 (2002), pp.613–41. On comparing replacement rates see J. Alber, 'Der deutsche Sozialstaat im Licht international vergleichender Daten', *Leviathan* 26/2 (1998), pp.199–227, esp. pp.205–8.

15. For a general overview on the Kohl era see R. Zohlnhöfer, *Die Wirtschaftspolitik der Ära Kohl* (Opladen: Leske + Budrich 2001). For specific coverage of social policy developments see J. Alber, 'Recent Developments', p.22; A. Schmid, 'Sozialpolitische Kürzungsmaß- nahmen in Deutschland und Großbritannien seit Anfang der 80er Jahre' (Diplomarbeit, Universität Konstanz, 1997).

16. The *Gesundheitsstrukturgesetz* of 1992 achieved greater savings. See S. Jochem, 'Reformpolitik im deutschen Sozialversicherungsstaat', in M.G. Schmidt (ed.), *Wohlfahrtsstaatliche Politik* (Opladen: Leske + Budrich 2001), pp.193–226, esp. p.204.

17. On the family policy focus see M.G. Schmidt, 'Sozialstaatliche Politik in der Ära Kohl', in G. Wever (ed.), *Bilanz der Ära Kohl, Christlich-liberale Politik in Deutschland 1982–1998* (Opladen: Leske + Budrich 1998), pp.59–87; M. Seeleib-Kaiser, 'A Dual Transformation of the German Welfare State?', *West European Politics* 25/4 (2002), pp.25–48. On labour market policy see Zohlnhöfer, *Die Wirtschaftspolitik der Ära Kohl*, pp.120–41.

18. While M.G. Schmidt, 'Sozialstaatliche Politik in der Ära Kohl', stresses the administrative masterpiece, the general financing patterns are outlined in R. Czada, 'Der Kampf um die Finanzierung der deutschen Einheit', in G. Lehmbruch (ed.), *Einigung und Zerfall. Deutschland und Europa nach dem Ende des Ost-West-Konflikts* (Opladen: Leske + Budrich 1995), pp.73–102; Zohlnhöfer, *Die Wirtschaftspolitik der Ära Kohl*, pp.265, 270.

19. J. Alber, 'Der deutsche Sozialstaat in der Ära Kohl. Diagnosen und Daten', in S. Leibfried and U. Wagschal (eds.), *Der deutsche Sozialstaat. Bilanzen-Reformen-Perspektiven* (Frankfurt a.M.: Campus 2000), pp.235–75, esp. p.256.

20. See German Council of Economic Advisors (Sachverständigenrat zur Begutachtung der gesamtwirtschaftlichen Entwicklung), *Jahresgutachten 1999/2000* (Stuttgart: Kohlhammer 1999), pp.112–17.

21. W. Schmähl, 'The 2001 Pension Reform in Germany. A Paradigm Shift and its Effects', *Working Paper 11/2002* (Centre for Social Policy Research, University of Bremen 2002); Seeleib-Kaiser, 'A Dual Transformation', pp.30–32. Note that to actually prevent poverty systematically, the *Riester-Rente* would have to become obligatory. Since 2001, this is now a permanent issue of pension reform.

22. On the conservative transformation, see J. Borchert, *Die konservative Transformation des Wohlfahrtsstaates, Großbritannien, Kanada, die USA und Deutschland im Vergleich* (Frankfurt a.M.: Campus 1995). On the dual transformation see Seeleib-Kaiser, 'A Dual Transformation'.

23. J. Alber, 'Recent Developments of the German Welfare State', p.24.

24. W. Herz, 'Die Ohnmacht der Manager. Der SPD-nahe Managerkreis kommt mit seinen Reform-Vorschlägen im Wahlkampf nicht durch', *Die Zeit* 36, 29 Aug. 2002, p.27. Note that the first major institutional shift in this direction was packaged in welfare state expansion, that is, it was part and parcel of the introduction of long-term care insurance in 1994. From there, it spread out to the pension area. On *einnahmenorientierte Ausgabenpolitik* in general see Alber, 'Recent Developments', p.24; Schmähl, 'Pension Reform in Germany', p.44.

25. Pierson, *Dismantling the Welfare State?*, p.13; Pierson (ed.), *The New Politics of the Welfare State*.

26. Alber, 'Recent Developments of the German Welfare State, p.22.

27. Gender equality norms could have also been satisfied by adjusting the standard pension entry age for men downward to that of women. This option remained dormant as it did not fit in with the austerity of the time.

The Politics of Citizenship in the New Republic

MICHAEL MINKENBERG

For a long time, the German politics of citizenship was characterised by a defensive approach maintaining that 'Germany is not a country of immigration'. This was supposed to render unnecessary all efforts to change the rules of the games of citizenship and nationality fundamentally. At the same time, a policy network was created to deal with the reality of immigration and its consequences. Recently, under the Schröder government, there was a radical departure from this regime, beginning with the passage of the new citizenship law, effective on 1 January 2000; this continues, despite the annulment of the new immigration law of 2002 by the Constitutional Court. Many observers argue that this shift in the politics of citizenship reflects two major developments. First, it marks Germany's long-overdue 'catching up' with its Western European neighbours, that is, the modernisation of its politics of citizenship by combining a residence-based nationality code (*ius soli*) in addition to the origin-based current code (*ius sanguinis*) with a well-regulated immigration policy. Together, these codes offer official acknowledgement that Germany has become a country of immigration. Second, it reflects the need of the new Germany to abandon its time-honoured 'equilibrium strategy', that is, the labour-exclusionary strategy consistent with the German model which ignored, among other things, the long-term need to increase immigration to meet labour market needs.

In this article, Germany's handling of the unexpected and unfamiliar phenomenon of mass immigration is used to reconsider the claim that the new politics of citizenship and immigration constitutes a break with the past and an adequate adjustment to the present. It does so by examining the differences between the old and new politics of citizenship with regard to their demographic and socio-structural underpinnings, the related interest formulations and policy-making processes, and their cultural connotations. The article disputes that it is justified to see recent changes in German immigration policy (1) as a full 'catching up' with the policies of other Western countries and (2) as an adequate response to the country's long-term needs for immigrants to maintain the viability of its labour markets and its social insurance systems. The principal argument is that although German unification has, in fact, opened the door for a new politics of nationhood and citizenship, many changes were under way well before the fall of the wall, and a true break with the past has yet to occur.

THE OLD POLITICS OF CITIZENSHIP: PRINCIPLE AND PRAGMATISM IN THE BONN REPUBLIC

In 1977, a joint commission of the federal and state governments formulated some principles for the politics of citizenship. The first principle was simple: 'The Federal Republic of Germany is not a country of immigration.'[1] Despite this statement, the rest of the report stressed the continuing need for foreign workers in the Federal Republic, and recommended a full social integration of foreign workers and their families already living in West Germany. At the same time, the report advocated a permanent freeze of foreign workers and underlined that the readiness and ability of foreign workers and their families to return to their home countries should be reinforced. These contradictions reflect a peculiar feature of *Modell Deutschland* when compared to the rest of Western Europe. Like its neighbours, the Bonn Republic experienced mass immigration after World War II. Indeed, between 1954 and 1999, Germany became one of the largest immigrant-receiving countries in the world; the net balance of nine million immigrants during this period accounts for more than ten per cent of today's population.[2] Yet, unlike other European countries, since 1977 successive governments have proclaimed that, contrary to the facts, Germany was not an immigration country. This led one observer to remark: 'The discrepancy between de facto immigration and its political denial is the single most enduring puzzle in the German immigration debate.'[3] Another described Germany as an 'undeclared immigration country'.[4] For more than 20 years, a fundamental tension existed between stated principles, which denied the reality of immigration, and political practice, which pragmatically dealt with the facts.

This puzzle can be traced to the political economy of the German model and to its 'cultural embeddedness'.[5] As a variant of the Christian-democratic welfare state, the German model was built on a historical compromise between liberalism and capitalism, between social democracy and Christian democracy, and between capital and labour.[6] Among its main features was centripetal political competition in the electoral and legislative arena, which led to policy-making that accommodated political parties, large interest associations and private business. As a result, any changes tended to be incremental and positive. This led to a policy network with three major 'nodes': the political parties, co-operative federalism and 'para-public institutions'.[7] The policy network that controlled immigration and citizenship included the Labour Ministry, the Federal Employment Office and business interests. Consequently, 'in contrast to Britain, France, and Sweden, West Germans did not view recruitment as a political issue to be organised by an office in charge of immigration. Instead, the issue was defined exclusively in terms of labour market management and was thus given to the Federal Employment Office'.[8] In other words, immigration was handled in a technical and non-political fashion. As a result, in Germany, as in other conservative welfare states, immigrants without citizenship had no political rights but were immediately granted social citizenship rights (such as means-tested entitlements for housing, child benefits, unemployment insurance). This approach is problematic because the rapid social incorporation can trigger a so-called 'social welfare chauvinism' among segments of the native working class.[9] While such resentment is not a permanent fixture of ethnic relations in Germany and elsewhere, it has been mobilised in times of a politicisation of immigration and citizenship (see below).

The sources of immigration to Germany have been threefold: ethnic German immigrants, that is, re-settlers from the GDR (*Übersiedler*) and from Eastern Europe (*Aussiedler*), according to the nationality code of Article 116 of the Basic Law; labour migrants under the regime of various laws and regulations; and asylum seekers according to Article 16 of the Basic Law.[10] The phases of immigration can be roughly categorised according to the shifts between exclusionary and inclusionary criteria applied or publicly advocated.

First, between the end of World War II and the early 1960s, the Federal Republic absorbed and successfully integrated some 12 million Germans from outside its borders. More than eight million had fled the Red Army in the east or were expelled by Eastern European governments from the eastern territories of the German *Reich* and beyond. More than three million Germans left the German Democratic Republic (GDR), initially across the 'green border' and then, after it was closed in 1952, through the 'loophole' of Berlin until the Socialist Unity Party of Germany (SED) put an end to this exodus by erecting the Berlin Wall in August 1961. In later years, the bulk of Germans migrating to the Bonn Republic were re-settlers (*Aussiedler*) from Eastern Europe. Between 1988 and 1993, when a maximum quota of

220,000 admissions per year was introduced, 1.4 million arrived in the Federal Republic, almost as many as between 1950 and 1988, when 1.65 million people immigrated.[11] Based on the ethno-cultural idea of the German nation and the corresponding regulation of nationality, this policy was totally inclusionary since these migrants did not have the legal status of 'foreigners'.[12]

Second, the economic recovery of West German industry in the 1950s resulted in a growing demand for labour that could not be met solely by Germans, especially after the closing of the GDR borders. This led to the establishment of the so-called guest worker rotation system, under which foreign workers were supposed to stay for a limited time (originally, one to three years) and then return to their home countries. Until 1965, when the first Law on Foreigners (*Ausländergesetz*) was introduced, the legal base for their residence in Germany was the 1938 Foreigner's Police Ordinance (*Ausländerpolizeiverordnung*).[13] This system treated immigrants as 'raw labour' and was based on exclusionary criteria. It failed because it was against the long-term interests of both the workers and their employers.[14]

A drastic shift took place in 1973. Among the sparks for change was a series of wildcat strikes that broke out in the summer of 1973 among non-unionised immigrant workers and spread from Cologne to other parts of the Bonn Republic. The strikes triggered concerns among German officials about the social partnership system and led to restrictions on the recruitment of foreign labour. In November, the government, reacting to the changing international economic context, imposed a total ban on new recruitment from outside the European Community. The ban, which affected mainly Yugoslavia and Turkey, the main non-EC suppliers of foreign labour,[15] met the unions' demands that German workers be preferred in times of crisis. Immigration to Germany decreased for only the next few years; thereafter, it rose sharply and changed in character. Since migrants now ran the risk of losing their work permits if they left Germany for more than three months, many of them chose to settle. More importantly, they were joined by their families, who could move to Germany under international agreements.

Both the new sensitivity after 1968 to the vulnerable status of migrants in German society and the strikes of 1973 led to a growing concern about the social problems of foreign labour. The liberal views of the mass public were reinforced by an increasingly organised foreigner lobby (including churches and unions), and a consensus emerged among the political elite that Germany had a special responsibility towards foreign workers.[16] As a result, while the government was restricting the admission of new foreign workers, it was also making efforts to improve the legal status of long-term foreign residents and to enhance their social integration. By the end of the 1970s, this had led to a new policy, partially inclusive and partially exclusive, which endured to the end of the 1980s. As a result, at unification, there were five million foreigners (non-Germans according to article 116 of the Basic Law) living in the Federal Republic and West Berlin, making up eight per cent of the population. Most of this population was confined to an ethnic sub-stratum of low paying, low skill jobs that were no longer acceptable for West Germans.[17]

At the same time, political and economic problems in other countries created a growing number of asylum seekers, especially after the relaxation of relations between West Germany and its eastern neighbours in the 1970s in the wake of *Ostpolitik*. Asylum seekers could count on admission to the country and individual review of their cases under Article 16 of the Basic Law, which granted a general right to asylum beyond the obligations of the 1951 Geneva convention. Between 1953 and 1978, the number of applications averaged 7,000 per year. In the late 1970s and 1980s, this number rose to more than 100,000 per year.[18] Between 1952 and 1993, 2.1 million asylum seekers entered the Federal Republic, of whom 186,000 were given political refugee status (8.9 per cent of all applications during this period).

By 1999, immigration to Germany had reached a magnitude that was comparable only to that of the USA. Since 14 per cent of the population was born outside the country, the repeated claim that Germany was 'not a country of immigration' could be treated only as a *Lebenslüge* (a false myth) of the Federal Republic.[19] Its persistence could be seen as a feature of symbolic politics in the face of globalisation and loss of national control: 'For a time, symbolic politics may help governments to neutralise citizen demands for economic protection that the nation-state can, and will, no longer satisfy.'[20]

TOWARDS A NEW POLITICS OF CITIZENSHIP: POLITICISATION AND POLARISATION

The new approach to immigration and citizenship under the Schröder government, with its reform of the nationality code in 1999 that introduced the notion of *ius soli* and its (failed) attempt to introduce an immigration law in 2002, was widely characterised as a 'paradigm shift' in both legal and national traditions.[21] It is usually attributed to the domestic and international changes stemming from the end of the Cold War and German unification.[22] However, the impact of unification should not be overestimated because significant changes in the politics of citizenship had already occurred during the 1980s, in particular its politicisation and new incorporation strategies. Moreover, it took another ten years before the discrepancy between the discourse of denial and the pragmatism of practice was reduced.

The 1980s witnessed the break-up of the consensus between the major political parties not to use immigration as an issue in the political and electoral arena. This shift in political discourse occurred in the context of changing cleavage structures and party competition in many Western democracies. New parties and movements on the Left and Right emerged along a new value-based cleavage.[23] At one end of this new cleavage, new social movements and left-libertarian or Green parties challenged the elite consensus on many issues, including immigration; at the other end, radical right-wing parties and movements tried to mobilise authoritarian and xenophobic segments of the public. This new radical right cut across the established party spectrum; in its ideological and social respects, it was the polar opposite of new social movements and related parties or party sections. It was in the context of these changes that the immigration issue gained new significance and a mobilising function. In other words: 'In Germany, as in all West European countries, immigration has moved from "low politics" to "high politics", as immigration came to be a highly politicised issue during the 1980s.'[24]

Here, two developments deserve particular attention.[25] On the political Left, both among social democrats (SPD) and the Greens, a push to reform the politics of citizenship in a fundamental way had already been initiated. The Greens did not argue in terms of labour market requirements, but in terms of their ideal of a multicultural society and the particular responsibilities imposed by the German past in securing an open German society. These ideals led them to press for an extended interpretation of the asylum law, and for rigorous efforts to integrate migrants into German society while respecting their cultural differences. The Kühn memorandum of 1979 had proposed to include a *ius soli* notion in the nationality code and recommended active policies of anti-discrimination in schools, social services, housing and the workplace (Kühn was a former minister-president of North Rhine-Westphalia and the first federal ombudsman for foreigners' affairs). From these beginnings, the SPD began to adopt policy positions that represented a break with the past and called for an acceptance of immigration as a reality. In the summer of 1989, Oscar Lafontaine, leading in the polls over Chancellor Helmut Kohl, openly questioned the appropriateness of the German nationality code and called for an immigration policy similar to that of other Western countries.

On the other end of the political spectrum, the governing political Right, the Christian democrats (CDU/CSU), pursued the opposite strategy. It was motivated by the need to fight the left-wing opposition parties and to reduce the electoral chances of the new radical right-wing party Die Republikaner (REP). The REP, which had entered the scene in 1983, seemed on the rise since the Bavarian state elections in 1986. In his first speech after being elected chancellor, Helmut Kohl declared *Ausländerpolitik*, or the policy dealing with foreigners, as one of the four pillars of his government. With only 50,000 to 100,000 asylum seekers per year between 1980 and 1987 and a stable share (seven per cent) of non-German residents between 1975 and 1990, there was hardly an immigration crisis. Yet, in the election campaign of 1986/87, prominent CDU and CSU politicians, among them Federal Minister of Interior Affairs Friedrich Zimmermann (CSU), dramatised the issue of immigration, asylum and foreigners and helped raise fears among Germans of being swamped by aliens and their cultures.[26] This debate was seasoned with statistics on rising numbers of illegal aliens, exploding costs of immigration and asylum, and a dramatic increase of crime and violence as a result of foreigners in the country. All of this fuelled the anxieties of Germans several years before the breakthrough of the REP, the fall of the wall and a new wave of east–west migration.[27]

Beyond the rhetoric, the practical politics of citizenship continued to be embedded in the traditional incremental approach. The last effort to employ the slogan that Germany was not a country of immigration took place in 1988, when Minister of the Interior Zimmermann proposed a new law on foreigners. It was blocked by a coalition of actors from the broadening immigration policy network (parties, churches, unions, entrepreneurial associations and charity organisations), and ended Zimmermann's political career. The new law proposed by Zimmermann's successor, Wolfgang Schäuble (CDU), reflected greater pragmatism. Largely unnoticed by the public, which was preoccupied with the politics of unification, it was passed in 1990. It contained, for the first time, legal claims to citizenship 'as a rule' (*Regelanspruch*) for those migrants who had lived in Germany for at least 15 years and facilitated naturalisation procedures for young foreigners.[28]

THE IMPACT OF GERMAN UNIFICATION: LEGACIES AND A NEW 'SUBCULTURE OF RESISTANCE'

German unification in 1989/90 ended the need to stress an ethno-cultural as opposed to a territorial notion of Germans and to embrace the pan-German logic of the nationality code. However, unification was followed by a peak in immigration and a new type of mass migration, via the asylum regulations (see next section). Unification had two especially important effects on citizenship and immigration. First, it solved the 'German question' by re-establishing congruence between nation and nation-state. Second, it changed the new geopolitical position of Germany, giving it direct borders with low wage Central and Eastern European countries. These borders created a strong push-and-pull for migration to Germany.

Table 1 summarises the figures of immigration to Germany before and after unification. It shows a sharp rise in immigrants after 1989, especially among asylum seekers. The jump in the number of German re-settlers from 1987 to 1988 can be attributed to the domestic political changes in Central and Eastern Europe – the easing of their emigration controls under Gorbachev's politics of *perestroika* that took effect in 1987. Both developments, the rise in the number of asylum seekers and the rise in the number of German re-settlers, were regulated in the 1993 law, which prohibited the entry of asylum seekers from any neighbouring country considered by Germany to have sufficient civil liberties to forfeit asylum claims of its citizens in Germany and capped German re-settlers at 100,000 per year. Today, Germany still has the largest number of asylum seekers among the 15 member states of the EU (in 1998: Germany: 98,644, UK: 58,000, the Netherlands: 45,217, France: 22,375, Belgium: 21,965).[29] However, considering population size, Germany, with 1.2 asylum seekers per 1,000 inhabitants, no longer exceeds other EU countries (UK: 0.98; the Netherlands: 2.9; France: 0.38; Belgium: 2.15).[30]

The second impact of unification came from the addition of the new Länder and their particular 'legacies' or continuities.[31] For most of Central

TABLE 1

IMMIGRATION TO GERMANY BEFORE AND AFTER UNIFICATION

In 1000	1985	1986	1987	1988	1989	1990	1991	1992	1993	1994
German re-settlers	40	43	79	203	377	397	222	231	219	223
GDR refugees[1]	25	26	19	40	344	395	170	110	90	80
Asylum seekers	74	100	57	103	121	193	256	438	323	127
Foreigner pop. (%)[2]	7.2	7.4	6.9	7.3	7.2	8.3	7.2	7.9	8.2	8.7

Notes: 1 GDR refugees since 1991 are counted as internal migrants from East to West.
    2 Percentage of foreigner population dropped from 1990 to 1991 because the statistical basis changed from West German population to population of unified Germany.

Source: German Federal Statistical Office and OECD-SOPEMI, in H. Kurthen and M. Minkenberg, 'Germany in Transition: Immigration, Racism and the Extreme Right', *Nations and Nationalism* 1/2 (1995), p.180.

and Eastern Europe, including the GDR in times of transition, six key legacies have been identified: the cultural legacy (a history of backwardness, victimisation, and intolerance); the social legacy (the absence of an established successor elite); the political legacy (weak party systems with shallow roots in society); the national legacy (the interrupted process of nation-building); the institutional legacy (the survival of Leninist institutions); and the administrative and economic legacy (centralised states and command economies).[32] For the new Länder, most of these legacies have been resolved in the course of unification, particularly in the realm of institutions. However, while preserving the West German social order, the wholesale institutional transfer from west to east has overloaded the welfare state and created new quandaries in the labour market, where there is record (and stable) unemployment and regional impoverishment.[33] These developments provide the context for the push by parties and unions to safeguard high wages and to protect the labour market from Eastern Europeans. In addition, the successes of institutional transfers hid problems of adjustment in various sectors, some of which persisted in the years following unification. These were vividly demonstrated by the helpless manoeuvres of local authorities and police during the xenophobic riots in Hoyerswerda in 1991 and Rostock in 1992.[34]

These riots point to perhaps the most important legacy in the east, the cultural continuities in the new Länder and their effects on the realities of immigration and multiculturalism in unified Germany.[35] One of the cultural legacies stems from the official regime ideology and national identity. Before 1989, the East German leadership supported a symbolic framework centred on the principles of anti-fascism, democracy and socialism, while also fostering traditions of German working class culture, such as egalitarianism and social justice. In practice, however, this ideology coexisted with rather authoritarian structures in economy and polity and an underdeveloped civil society. The anti-fascist and internationalist foundations of the GDR's regime ideology turned out to be half-hearted attempts with counterproductive consequences.[36] Thus, a right-wing extremist youth culture developed in conscious demarcation from the SED regime during the 1980s.[37] Moreover, the SED regime nurtured an East German xenophobia by the second-class treatment of foreigners in the GDR, who numbered 191,000 in 1989 (or 1.2 per cent of the population). Most were contract workers and students from 'socialist brother countries' such as Vietnam, Mozambique, Cuba and Poland, who lived in complete segregation from the host society. The lack of real experience (or even contact) with these foreigners – except at the workplace – enabled stereotyped images of foreigners to thrive.

The conditions of the institutional transfer discussed above, together with the social consequences of unification, led to a rapid growth of East German anti-foreigner resentment that now exceeds levels in West Germany. Survey responses, collected in the spring of 1998, indicate significant east–west differences in radical right-wing attitudes (see Table 2). More East Germans appear to be authoritarian and xenophobic than West Germans. Among East and West Germans, 'welfare chauvinism', that is, the refusal to share the nation's wealth with 'foreigners' (measured by questions regarding the priority of jobs and social benefits for Germans) is widespread; however, the share of East Germans harbouring these views exceeds that of West Germans.

This difference is mirrored in East Germans' attitudes towards social spending cuts in the mid-1990s. The most preferred item for spending cuts in the new Länder were benefits for foreign asylum seekers: 53 per cent of the East Germans, but only 13 per cent of the West Germans would consider these benefits a prime area for budget cutting.[38] These rather widespread resentments, a component of a new 'subculture of resistance' to change in the politics of citizenship and immigration, are a severe obstacle to any immigration policy attempting to tackle the demographic realities and the economic needs in Germany (see also next section and Table 4).

Against this backdrop, the 'asylum crisis' of 1992/93 and the change in the asylum policy point at the particular interaction of political interest articulation, electoral competition and policy change in the context of new cleavage patterns and a new resistance to immigration after unification.[39] Between 1991 and 1993, the discourse on the 'abuse' of asylum and the alleged crime rate of foreigners, violent right-wing extremist mobilisation and activities, the electoral rise of new radical right-wing parties such as the Republikaner and the German People's Union (DVU), as well as the reaction by the established parties resulted in a distinct policy change. In order to fight the radical right at the polls and to contain the violence, the right to asylum was severely limited by a constitutional amendment with support by the oppositional SPD. In addition, the Bonn government pursued tough law and order policies. Leading CDU/CSU politicians continued this hard-line approach when the party found itself in opposition after the federal elections of 1998 and the Schröder government introduced its reforms. In Hesse, CDU leader Roland Koch engineered a signature campaign against the new nationality code, and his counterpart in North Rhine-Westphalia, Jürgen Rüttgers, campaigned against the 'green card' for computer experts from India with the slogan 'Kinder statt Inder' ('children instead of Indians').[40]

TABLE 2

DIMENSIONS OF RIGHT-WING RADICAL ATTITUDES IN
UNIFIED GERMANY (%), 1998

	Germany	West	East
Average	13	12	17
In ideological components			
Authoritarianism	11	10	16
Nationalism	13	13	13
Xenophobia	15	14	20
Welfare chauvinism	26	23	39
Pro-Naziism	6	6	5
Anti-Semitism	6	6	5

Source: R. Stöss, Rechtsextremismus im vereinten Deutschland (Bonn: Friedrich Ebert Stiftung, 3rd edn. 2000), p.29.

The drastic policy change in 1992/93, in conjunction with conservative politicians' continued efforts to incorporate parts of the radical right-wing agenda, blocked the electoral rise of right-wing radical parties (despite some further electoral successes in state elections in the late 1990s).[41] Nevertheless, the policy change – and the accompanying governmental strategy of repression towards the non-party sector of the radical right – did not succeed in fighting xenophobic violence and the proliferation of Nazi groups. In fact, some argue that the failure of radical right-wing parties to absorb and organise the right-wing scenes contributed to the spread of right-wing violence.[42] During the 1990s, the number of violent right-wing extremists grew continuously, reaching a record level of 10,000 in 2000.[43] Since the early 1990s, this scene's centre of gravity has been in the east, with 40 to 50 per cent of all Nazis and skinheads in the new Länder (where only a fifth of the German population lives). This trend was accompanied by an increase of right-wing violence in the east during the second half of the 1990s. Over recent years, right-wing violent acts, in proportion to population size, have consistently been more frequent in the five new Länder than in the old.[44] In general, party organisations were rather discredited in the east from the beginning, while movement-type activities and sub-cultural milieus of the extreme right flourished. This leads to a dilemma: where right-wing radical parties are stronger and 'integrate' small but significant voter blocs, violence against foreigners is less pronounced, and vice versa.[45]

POST-UNIFICATION POLITICS OF CITIZENSHIP: A RECOGNITION OF
REALITY?

The debate and policies of the 1990s continued the incremental approach
towards immigration of the previous decade. In 1993, a new law was passed
introducing an unlimited legal right to citizenship (*Rechtsanspruch*). The
law had little impact on naturalisation, as can be seen in Table 3, which lists
annual naturalisation rates in selected Western European nations as a
percentage of the entire residential population without a national passport.
The Netherlands is at the high end, and Luxembourg at the low end.
Throughout the 1990s, Germany ranked in the lower range of the list, with
an average of 1.1 per cent of foreigners naturalised each year. Given that in
Germany foreigners accounted for 8.9 per cent of the population in 1998
and the naturalisation rate in that year was 1.4 per cent, the overall
naturalisation rate was 0.13 per cent of the total resident population,
including German citizens. This is a comparatively low figure and in stark
contrast to France, Sweden and Switzerland, where the overall
naturalisation rate is about twice as high.

Obviously, the slight improvement of the naturalisation process in the
1993 law did not produce any jump in the figures. However, the new law on
foreigners had other, more severe implications. These derived from the fact

TABLE 3

NATURALISATION RATES IN SELECTED EUROPEAN COUNTRIES, 1990–2000 (%)

	1990	1991	1992	1993	1994	1995	1996	1997	1998	1999	2000	Ø Rate per foreign resident population	Rate per resident population[2]
NL	2.0	4.2	4.9	5.7	6.3	9.4	11.4	8.8	8.7	9.4	7.6	7.1	0.16
SW	3.7	5.7	5.9	8.5	6.9	6.0	4.8	5.5	8.9	7.6	8.9	6.6	0.26
F	2.5	2.7	2.7	2.8	3.7	2.7	3.3	3.5	3.8	4.5	4.7	3.3	0.28
GB	3.2	3.4	2.4	2.3	2.2	2.0	2.2	1.9	2.6	2.5	3.7	2.6	0.14
I	1.1	0.9	0.9	1.3	1.3	1.5	1.4	1.9	2.0	2.3	n.d.	1.5	0.12
CH	0.8	0.8	0.9	1.0	1.1	1.3	1.4	1.4	1.4	1.5	2.0	1.3	0.28
D[1]	0.4	0.5	0.6	0.7	0.9	1.0	1.2	1.1	1.4	2.0	2.5	1.1	0.13
LUX	0.7	0.5	0.6	0.6	0.7	0.8	0.7	0.7	0.6	0.5	0.5	0.6	0.15

Notes: 1 Naturalisation of ethnic German re-settlers not included.
2 Rate calculated on the basis of each country's census data on resident population in the
1990s, same year foreigner population and same year naturalisation rate per foreign
resident population.

Sources: Humboldt-Universität zu Berlin, Migration und Bevölkerung 4/2002 (May 2002), p.2;
Fischer Weltalmanach 2000 (Frankfurt/M.: Fischer Verlag, 1999), selected country
chapters.

that the new law was part of a deal struck between the governing parties CDU/CSU and FDP, and the opposition (except the Greens) to improve the nationalisation and integration procedures of migrants. The deal was in response to the 'asylum crisis' of 1992/93 caused by the growing number of migrants claiming asylum, on the one hand, and growing unrest in the population, on the other (see above). That unrest was centred in East German municipalities, which were required to host asylum seekers by the national quota system; many of these seekers were met with open hostility and even xenophobic violence. The immediate result of the change in the asylum law was a drastic decline in asylum applications: In 1992, 440,000 people claimed asylum in the Federal Republic, in 1998 and 1999 the number was less than 100,000 per year.

In the face of the changing demographics of the new Germany, the continuing discrepancies between a rigid asylum policy and an ethno-cultural admission policy favouring ethnic German re-settlers from Eastern Europe, and the absence of a coherent immigration policy, the new Red–Green coalition government in late 1998 pronounced nothing less than a turnaround in the politics of citizenship. In his government declaration on 10 November 1998, Chancellor Schröder announced a modernisation of the nationality code, which would provide full citizenship to all long-time residents and children born in Germany. The project met stiff resistance from the CDU/CSU opposition and some CDU/CSU-governed Länder, which objected to the possibility of dual citizenship. A signature campaign titled 'Yes to integration – no to dual citizenship', initiated by the Bavarian minister-president, Edmund Stoiber, and the CDU-candidate for minister-president in Hesse, Roland Koch, who was swept into office on this issue in the Land elections in early 1999, forced the governing coalition to revise the bill to require young adults between 18 and 23 years to choose between German or their (non-German) parents' nationality.[46]

Ironically, both German conservatives and Turkish immigrants raised the issue of dual citizenship. Turkish migrants in Germany considered their Turkish citizenship as more than just a link to their state, that is, a matter of identity that could not be traded in for, but was compatible with a German passport.[47] German conservatives considered dual citizenship a threat to both the loyalty of immigrants to the German state and to the identity and integrity of German nationhood. Their opposition to dual citizenship rested on two beliefs: Turks wanting to become Germans needed to assimilate in order to fit into the German culture, and dual citizenship undermined this assimilation.[48] This position overlooked the fact that there is already a significant immigrant population that holds two passports; 44.6 per cent of the total number of naturalised migrants in 2000 have dual citizenship.[49] The debate also rested on contestable assumptions about the effects of dual citizenship. Rather than undermining integration, as feared by the conservatives, some argue that dual citizenship may, in fact, facilitate integration by functioning as a 'politics of recognition' which fosters tolerance toward different life styles of transnational social spaces.[50]

Despite its compromise with the opposition on the issue of dual citizenship, the Schröder government carried out other reforms of the politics of immigration. Since Germany's occupational and higher education systems have not adjusted fast enough to the changing demands of an information technology (IT) and services-based post-industrial economy, Chancellor Schröder took the computer fair in Hanover in February 2000 as an opportunity to announce the introduction of long-term migration visas ('green cards') for computer experts. This triggered a new debate on immigration. Unlike previous debates, it did not focus on the admission of those who already wanted to migrate, but on how to recruit especially skilled labour migrants in order to ensure Germany's international economic competitiveness. The ensuing controversy was remarkable in that the traditional polarisation was inverted. The opposition parties CDU/CSU and FDP, the business associations and the unions demanded a fully developed concept of immigration (with the CDU/CSU asking for a further tightening of the asylum law). The Greens insisted on their earlier concepts of immigration and integration which stressed full-scale social and political incorporation. The SPD shied away from the debate and even criticised it as dangerous, because it not only required more preparation than was possible in one legislative term, but also had to be embedded in an EU-wide concept.[51] In the meantime, the federal minister of the interior introduced an immigration law to parliament that was passed in both chambers in March 2002, but was annulled by the Constitutional Court in December 2002 on procedural grounds.[52] Since then, a renegotiation of the law has been under way.

With the immigration law of 2002, the Schröder government finally abandoned the doctrine that Germany was not a country of immigration by acknowledging the need for specially qualified labour migrants, especially engineers, computer experts, mathematicians and experts in science and research. Permanent residence permits were to be given to those immigrants who had spent five years with a temporary resident permit, had demonstrated proof of their financial security, and had been employed legally. A quota was never set, but the immigration commission proposal suggested around 20,000 plus families.[53] Interestingly, the CDU's guidelines for a concept of an immigration law, while less precise, envisions a similar system of recruitment and residence permits, based on a system of points according to level and type of qualification. In fact, a content analysis of policy positions by all political parties with seats in the Bundestag and other actors in the broadened immigration policy network, such as the churches, trade unions and employer associations, demonstrates that all key actors now confront the issue of immigration and its regulation and no one repeats the old maxim of Germany not being a country of immigration.[54] The CDU and CSU, however, add a slight qualification that Germany cannot be a 'classical country of immigration' – a characterisation of the country which is up for interpretation. Moreover, the convergence between the major parties did not prevent the strict rejection by the opposition of the government bill when it was introduced into parliament: with the coming of the federal elections in September 2002, party strategy prevailed over the substantial agreements.

THE NEW POLITICS OF CITIZENSHIP BETWEEN RESISTANCE AND REALITY

Another more pronounced polarisation occurs between demographic experts, the governing coalition and parts of the opposition – all of whom agree on the need for immigration to help fill the long-term labour market gaps – and the German mass public. According to a survey conducted while the political parties discussed the new immigration law, the overwhelming majority (98 per cent) wanted a regulation of immigration to Germany; however, 68 per cent of the respondents rejected an increase of the number of immigrants, and 47 per cent favoured a law that would have reduced immigration to Germany.[55] These survey responses reflect a persistent trend in the 1990s according to which large majorities in East and West Germany favour the restriction of immigration to Germany for all groups: labour migrants from EU countries (which have the right to immigrate under the EU treaties), labour migrants from non-EU countries, asylum seekers and German re-settlers from Eastern Europe (see Table 4). Only minorities support the extreme position of prohibiting immigration of these groups altogether and, generally, a drop in the principled rejection to immigration can be observed between 1996 and 2000. However, whereas East and West Germans hardly differ with regard to German re-settlers and asylum seekers, significantly more East Germans than West Germans oppose any labour migrant immigration to Germany. For example, in 1996, about half of the East Germans favoured a complete prohibition of labour migrants

TABLE 4

ATTITUDES TOWARDS IMMIGRATION OF DIFFERENT MIGRANT GROUPS
TO GERMANY (%)

	West				East			
	1991	1992	1996	2000	1991	1992	1996	2000
Labour migrants from EU countries								
Allow immigration without constraints	34	35	33	32	13	13	11	13
Restrict immigration	56	56	55	62	62	63	51	66
Prohibit immigration completely	10	9	12	7	25	24	38	21
Labour migrants from non-EU countries								
Allow immigration without constraints	11	10	8	8	6	4	4	4
Restrict immigration	61	62	59	72	56	59	46	57
Prohibit immigration completely	28	28	33	20	39	36	49	40
Asylum seekers								
Allow immigration without constraints	13	12	13	10	16	14	12	9
Restrict immigration	65	65	66	74	69	67	67	71
Prohibit immigration completely	22	23	22	16	15	19	21	21
German re-settlers from Eastern Europe								
Allow immigration without constraints	22	19	15	14	15	16	13	11
Restrict immigration	68	71	74	76	73	73	69	74
Prohibit immigration completely	10	10	12	11	12	11	18	15

Source: ALLBUS 1991, 1992, 1996, 2000, in Statistisches Bundesamt (ed.), *Datenreport 2002* (Bonn 2002), p.561.

from non-EU countries – a clear sign of widespread anxieties about the labour market situation, especially in the new Länder, and an expression of 'welfare chauvinism' (see also Table 2).

These numbers fly in the face of projections that argue for higher rates of immigration than made possible by the new law, provided the objective is to maintain a labour market equilibrium and rescue the German social security system by bringing in more contributors to slow the move towards ever higher ratios of beneficiaries to contributors ('dependency ratio'). A calculation of the immigration scenarios, based on actual trends in the ageing of the residential population and the flow of migrants to Germany, reveals a steady decline of the German population available to supply labour markets and to shore up social security systems. Hence, there is a growing need for immigrants to fill the gap, even when taking into account the effects of the new nationality code and its principle of *ius soli*. Table 5 depicts a 'middle migration scenario' with regard to assumptions about fertility and immigration, as opposed to a 'low level' and a 'high level' scenario. It already incorporates a variant that takes the effects of the new law on foreigners and nationality code into account (right-hand column). As is evident from the figures, Germany is undergoing a dramatic demographic

TABLE 5

GROWTH OF FOREIGN POPULATION IN GERMANY UNTIL 2030

	Medium migration scenario	Memo: ius sanguinis
Germans		
1998	74,717,000	74,717,000
2015	72,269,000	71,403,000
2030	67,835,000	66,185,000
Foreigners		
1998	7,320,000	7,320,000
2015	8,802,000	9,676,000
2030	9,788,000	11,416,000
Total		
1998	82,037,000	82,037,000
2015	81,071,000	81,071,000
2030	77,623,000	77,623,000
% foreigners of total population		
1998	8.9	8.9
2015	10.9	11.9
2030	12.6	14.7

Source: R. Münz and R. Ulrich, 'Migration und zukünftige Bevölkerungsentwicklung in Deutschland', in K.J. Bade and R. Münz (eds.), *Migrationsreport 2000* (Bonn: Bundeszentrale für politische Bildung 2000), p.51.

decline that cannot be stopped even by the recruitment of more than 100,000 immigrants every year. In fact, the United Nations Population Division issued a report in 2000, which calculated that Germany needed an average annual net number of 480,000 migrants to maintain the size of its working-age population for the period 2000–2050.[56] The dim prospects for the labour market are even more dramatic when taking into account the politics surrounding migration in the electoral arena. Opening up the borders for high-skill migrants would be accompanied by a significant influx of people with no specific skills. In the short run, this would exacerbate Germany's problems of unemployment as well as requiring the provision of major resources for social policy programmes and institutions targeted towards this new population. In the long run, these migrants could then help alleviate the dramatic labour market disequilibrium that will result from the retirement of the baby boomers.

Politically, however, the technocratic strategy is not feasible. As noted above, East Germans are fiercely opposed to more immigration. Moreover, the increasing share of retirees in the entire German electorate makes it difficult for parties to advocate more immigration. Not only are elderly people particularly intolerant to cultural diversity, they also tend to have economic time horizons sufficiently short to block expenditures in human capital benefiting future generations, but requiring cutbacks in the consumption and social benefits of current retirees. Elsewhere in this volume Leibfried and Obinger report the logic of the conservative welfare state to stifle expenditures in schools and other human capital investments for the young, but to boost programmes benefiting the elderly. The politics of immigration constitutes another element of this pattern.

The entire debate about the new immigration law and the demographic prospects of Germany must, however, be seen in light of the fact that many of the issues discussed in public are already settled by the European Union. Due to various treaties and rulings of the European Court of Justice, citizens of EU member states not only have *de facto* unlimited rights to work-related immigration and settlement ('free movement of labour') but, according to Article 8 of the Maastricht Treaty of 1992, are entitled to a citizenship of the Union ('free movement of persons'). This supranational form of citizenship provides basic political rights such as the right to vote and stand for elections in local and European Parliament elections. Since the late 1980s, around 1.4 million foreigners in Germany are resident aliens from other EU member states and thus EU citizens.[57] Hence, the debate about immigration and dual citizenship in Germany is only about immigrants from outside the EU. Among these, two large groups have taken a central place in the debate, Turkish immigrants and immigrants from Central and Eastern Europe.

With the accession of several Eastern European countries to the EU, millions of today's potential immigrants to Germany will turn into EU citizens and be exempt from the restrictions in any new immigration law. This prospect, especially the fear of a considerable labour migration to Germany after the EU enlargement, has prompted the German government to negotiate a seven-year transition period during which immigration from new EU member states is restricted. Moreover, the Amsterdam Treaty, committing the EU to harmonise its asylum policy by 2004, has also provoked fears in Germany that the EU will undermine the principles of the national asylum policy. Hence, one observer concluded: 'Ironically, the Berlin Republic has therefore indirectly tempered Germany's support for a harmonised EU asylum and immigration policy, with its enthusiasm in principle set off against an ambivalence over the compromises that this will inevitably involve.'[58]

CONCLUSION

The legacies of the Bonn Republic's policy of migrant labour recruitment and liberal asylum law and the Berlin Republic's international location between Western Europe and post-communist Eastern Europe made questions of immigration, citizenship and multiculturalism highly salient in the 1990s. Whereas Model Germany presumed a culturally homogenous German population, supplemented by the flexible tool of temporary guest workers, the new Germany must confront the continuing presence of – and need for – immigrants and thus an increasingly heterogeneous culture. The passing of the new citizenship law in 1999 and the attempt to introduce the first German immigration law in 2002 were responses to these realities and represent a departure from the traditional German politics of citizenship.

However, the effects of this new politics of citizenship – and its significance – are constrained by both the dynamism of the labour market and the institutional and cultural consequences of German unification. The labour market and demographic developments require substantially more immigrants than the first (and failed) immigration law of 2002 was to allow. Although EU enlargement may contribute to a substantial migration to Germany under the principle of 'free movement of persons', the German government has already blocked this prospect for a number of years. Moreover, the 'green card' initiative cannot be considered a success. Although intended as an effective tool to attract some 20,000 IT experts, less than half of these have arrived so far.

Most importantly, the new politics of citizenship is countered by a 'subculture of resistance' to immigration. The institutional transfer from west to east resulted in record unemployment and regional impoverishment. Hence, a pronounced 'welfare chauvinism' has spread especially in the eastern part of Germany. Widespread public anxiety and resentment against more immigrants, together with reluctant unions and populist politics by some leading politicians of the CDU/CSU, stand in the way of effective and adequate changes in the politics of citizenship, forcing any political actor to continue an incremental approach. It seems that just like the past rhetoric of Germany 'not being an immigration country', the much celebrated 'paradigm shift' is an expression of symbolic politics rather than a reflection of truly substantial and effective changes.

NOTES

1. An excerpt of this report is reprinted in P.J. Katzenstein, *Policy and Politics in West Germany. The Growth of a Semisovereign State* (Philadelphia, PA: Temple University Press 1987), pp.239f.

2. R. Münz and R.E. Ulrich, 'Migration und zukünftige Bevölkerungsentwicklung in Deutschland', in K.J. Bade and R. Münz (eds.), *Migrationsreport 2000* (Bonn: Bundeszentrale für politische Bildung 2000), p.23.

3. C. Joppke, *Immigration and the Nation-State. The United States, Germany, and Great Britain* (Oxford: Oxford University Press 1999), p.62.

4. D. Thränhardt, 'Die Bundesrepublik Deutschland – ein unerklärtes Einwanderungsland', *Aus Politik und Zeitgeschichte* B24 (1988), pp.3–13; see also S. Green, 'Immigration, Asylum and Citizenship in Germany', *West European Politics* 24/4 (Oct. 2001), pp.82f.

5. See C. Crouch and W. Streeck, 'Introduction: The Future of Capitalist Diversity', in idem (eds.), *Political Economy of Modern Capitalism. Mapping Convergence and Diversity* (London: Sage 1997), p.4.

6. See W. Streeck, 'German Capitalism: Does It Exist? Can It Survive?', in Crouch and Streeck (eds.), *Political Economy of Modern Capitalism*, p.34. See also G. Esping-Andersen, *The Three Worlds of Welfare Capitalism* (Princeton, NJ: Princeton University Press 1990); K. van Kersbergen, *Social Capitalism. A Study of Christian Democracy and the Welfare State* (Boston, MA: Routledge 1995).

7. See Katzenstein, *Policy and Politics in West Germany*, pp.58–60.

8. Ibid., p.220.

9. H. Kitschelt, *The Radical Right in Western Europe* (Ann Arbor, MI: University of Michigan Press 1995), chap. 8. For the different strategies of the French and German states to incorporate immigrants and their effects, see also R. Kastoryano, *Negotiating Identities. States and Immigrants in France and Germany* (Princeton, NJ: Princeton University Press 2002).

10. For the following, see H. Kurthen and M. Minkenberg, 'Germany in Transition: Immigration, Racism and the Extreme Right', *Nations and Nationalism* 1/2 (1995), pp.176–81.

11. See K.J. Bade and M. Bommes, 'Migration und politische Kultur im "Nicht-Einwanderungsland"', in Bade and Münz (eds.), *Migrationsreport 2000*, p.181; Münz and Ulrich, 'Migration und zukünftige Bevölkerungsentwicklung in Deutschland', in ibid., p.26.

12. See R. Brubaker, *Citizenship and Nationhood in France and Germany* (Cambridge: Cambridge University Press 1992); D. Gosewinkel, *Einbürgern und Ausschließen. Die Nationalisierung der Staatsangehörigkeit vom Deutschen Bund zur Bundesrepublik Deutschland* (Göttingen: Vandenhoeck & Ruprecht 2001).

13. See B. Santel and A. Weber, 'Migrations- und Ausländerrecht in Deutschland', in Bade and Münz (eds.), *Migrationsreport 2000*, p.111.

14. For the following, see Katzenstein, *Policy and Politics in West Germany*, pp.216–19.

15. Labour migration from EC countries to West Germany could not be prohibited due to the agreements of the EC on free movement of labour.

16. See Joppke, *Immigration and the Nation State*, pp.76f.

17. See H. Gillmeister, H. Kurthen and J. Fijalkowski, *Ausländerbeschäftigung in der Krise?* (Berlin: Edition Sigma 1989).

18. See S. Green, 'Immigration, Asylum and Citizenship in Germany', pp.89f.

19. See Bade and Bommes, 'Migration und politische Kultur', p.168.

20. Crouch and Streeck, 'Introduction: The Future of Modern Capitalism', p.11.

21. See Santel and Weber, 'Migrations und Ausländerrecht in Deutschland', p.127; K. Hailbronner, 'Reform des Zuwanderungsrechts. Konsens und Dissens in der Ausländerpolitik', *Aus Politik und Zeitgeschichte* B43/2001, p.7; G.L. Braun, 'Paradigmenwechsel in der Zuwanderungspolitik', *Zeitschrift für Ausländerrecht* 21 (2001), pp.191–4.

22. See e.g. Green, 'Immigration, Asylum and Citizenship in Germany', pp.83f. See also Joppke, *Immigration and the Nation State*, p.95.

23. See M. Minkenberg, 'The New Right in Comparative Perspective: The USA and Germany', Western Societies Occasional l Paper #43 (Ithaca, NY: Cornell University Press 1993); idem, *Die neue radikale Rechte im Vergleich. USA, Frankreich, Deutschland* (Opladen/Wiesbaden: Westdeutscher Verlag 1998); Kitschelt, *The Radical Right in Western Europe*.

24. T. Faist, 'How to Define a Foreigner? The Symbolic Politics of Immigration in German

Partisan Discourse, 1978–1992', in M. Baldwin-Edwards and M.A. Schain (eds.), *The Politics of Immigration in Western Europe* (London: Frank Cass 1994), p.51.

25. For following, see Faist, 'How to Define a Foreigner? ', pp.55–67.

26. See D. Thränhardt, 'Einwanderungs und Integrationspolitik in Deutschland und den Niederlanden', *Leviathan* 30/2 (June 2002), pp.224–7.

27. See K. Bade, *Ausländer, Aussiedler, Asyl. Eine Bestandsaufnahme.* (Munich: Beck 1994), pp.99–103.

28. See Bade and Bommes, 'Migration und politische Kultur', p.179.

29. R. Koslowski, *Migrants and Citizens. Demographic Change in the European State System* (Ithaca: Cornell University Press 2000), p.163.

30. Rates are based on 1997 census data for the countries mentioned, see *Der Fischer Weltalmanach* (Frankfurt/Main: Fischer Taschenbuch Verlag 1999).

31. See K. Jowitt, 'The Leninist Legacy', in idem (ed.), *The New World Disorder: The Leninist Distinction* (Berkeley: University of California Press 1992), pp.284–305.

32. B. Crawford and A. Lijphart, 'Old Legacies, New Institutions. Explaining Political and Economic Trajectories in Post-Communist Regimes', in idem (eds.), *Liberalisation and Leninist Legacies. Comparative Perspectives on Democratic Transitions* (Berkeley: University of California Press 1997), p.11f.

33. See the contributions by H. Wiesenthal, and W. Streeck and A. Hassel to this volume.

34. See J. Schmidt, *Politische Brandstiftung. Warum 1992 in Rostock das Asylbewerberheim in Flammen aufging* (Berlin: edition ost 2002).

35. See M. Minkenberg, 'German Unification and the Continuity of Discontinuities: Cultural Change and the Far Right in East and West', *German Politics* 3/2 (Aug. 1994), pp.169–92; see also Bade, *Ausländer, Aussiedler, Asyl*, pp.175–206.

36. See for example B. Wittich, 'Die dritte Schuld. Antifaschismus, Stalinismus und Rechtsextremismus', in K.H. Heinemann and W. Schubarth (eds.), *Der antifaschistische Staat entläßt seine Kinder. Jugend und Rechtsextremismus in Ostdeutschland* (Köln: Papyrossa 1992), pp.29–37; A. Grunenberg, *Antifaschismus – ein deutscher Mythos* (Reinbeck bei Hamburg: Rowohlt 1993).

37. See B. Wagner, 'Rechtsradikalismus in Ostdeutschland', *Osteuropa* 52/3 (March 2002), pp.305–19.

38. See E. Roller, 'Shrinking the Welfare State: Citizens' Attitudes towards Cuts in Social Spending in Germany', *German Politics* 8/1 (April 1999), p.27.

39. For the following see M. Minkenberg, 'The New Radical Right in the Political Process: Interaction Effects in France and Germany', in M. Schain *et al.* (eds.), *Shadows over Europe: The Development and Impact of the Extreme Right in Western Europe* (New York: Palgrave 2002), pp.245–68; see also the contributions by H. Kitschelt and D. Rucht to this volume.

40. See M. Minkenberg, 'The Radical Right in Public Office: Agenda-Setting and Policy Effects', *West European Politics* 24/4 (Oct. 2001), pp.1–21.

41. See M. Minkenberg, 'What's Left of the Right? The New Right and *Superwahljahr* 1994 in Perspective', in D. Conradt *et al.* (eds.), *Germany's New Politics. Parties and Issues in the 1990s* (Providence, RI: Berghahn Books 1995), pp.255–71; idem, 'Im Osten was Neues: Die radikale Rechte im Wahljahr 1998', in G. Pickel, D. Walz and W. Brunner (eds.), *Deutschland nach den Wahlen. Befunde zur Bundestagswahl 1998 und zur Zukunft des deutschen Parteiensystems* (Opladen: Leske und Budrich 2000), pp.313–33.

42. See for example R. Koopmans, 'Dynamics of Repression and Mobilization. The German Extreme Right in the 1990s', *Mobilization* 2 (1997), pp.149–64.

43. See Bundesministerium des Innern, *Verfassungsschutzbericht 2000* (Bonn: Bundesministerium des Innern 2001).

44. See R. Stöss, *Rechtsextremismus im vereinten Deutschland* (Bonn: Friedrich Ebert Stiftung, 3rd edn. 2000), pp.149–67.

45. This relationship also seems to hold in a cross-national perspective. See Minkenberg, *Die neue radikale Rechte im Vergleich*, pp.307–9; idem, 'The Contemporary Radical Right in Western Europe: Ideological and Structural Variants between Party Formation and Movement Mobilization', *Comparative European Politics* 1/2 (2003), pp.149–70.

46. See Santel and Weber, 'Migrations- und Ausländerrecht', pp.125–7.

47. See R. Kastoryano, 'Türken mit deutschem Pass. Sociological and Political Perspectives on Dual Nationality in Germany', in R. Hansen and P. Weil (eds.), *Dual Nationality, Social Rights and Federal Citizenship in the US and Europe* (New York: Berghahn Books 2003, forthcoming).
48. See K. Stankiewicz, 'Changing Immigration and Integration Politics in Germany. Does the Demise of Ethnic-priority Policies Imply a Transformation of Nationhood Traditions?', paper at the 2002 ISA Annual convention in New Orleans (24 March 2002).
49. Die Beauftragte der Bundesregierung für Ausländerfragen (ed.), *Daten und Fakten zur Ausländersituation* (Bonn 2002), p.34.
50. See T. Faist, 'Doppelte Staatsbürgerschaft als überlappende Mitgliedschaft', *Politische Vierteljahresschrift* 42/2 (June 2001), pp.247–65.
51. See Bade and Bommes, 'Migration und politische Kultur', p.193.
52. See R. Leicht, 'Sieg der Rituale', *Die Zeit* (23 Dec. 2002), p.8.
53. See K. Hailbronner, 'Reform des Zuwanderungsrechts. Konsens und Dissens in der Ausländerpolitik', *Aus Politik und Zeitgeschichte* B43 (2001), pp.8f. See also www.bundesauslaenderbeauftragte.de/aktuell/zuwanderung.htm (22 March 2002).
54. Stankiewicz, 'Changing Immigration and Integration Politics in Germany'.
55. R. Köcher, 'Die Bevölkerung fordert ein Einwanderungsgesetz', *Frankfurter Allgemeine Zeitung* (20 Dec. 2000), p.5.
56. United Nations Population Division, *Replacement Migration: Is It a Solution to Declining and Ageing Population?* (New York 2000), see www.un.org/esa/population/publications/migration/migration.htm (11 Jan. 2003).
57. Koslowski, *Migrants and Citizens*, p.116.
58. Green, 'Immigration, Asylum and Citizenship in Germany', p.100.

Abstracts

From Stability to Stagnation: Germany at the Beginning of the Twenty-First Century, *by Herbert Kitschelt and Wolfgang Streeck*

Basic institutions and political power configurations that contributed to Germany's post-war social and economic success turned from assets into liabilities in the 1990s and beyond. This introduction highlights the emergence and interaction of the critical components of the German political economy. It provides evidence for its declining performance and details a set of causes for it. Collective actors and institutional bargaining modes make it difficult to adapt to new challenges. Nevertheless, the deepening crisis may trigger change initiated by office-seeking party politicians and political-economic actors engaged in local problem-solving which sidesteps rigid mechanisms of national co-ordination.

German Unification and 'Model Germany': An Adventure in Institutional Conservatism, *by Helmut Wiesenthal*

Germany today appears to be anything but the fortunate country it was on the eve of unification. The extension of model Germany to Eastern Germany has contributed to the predicament it has encountered in the emerging international political economic setting. The chosen mode of unification and its consequences have impaired the sustainability of the once cherished socio-economic order. Unification has made institutional reform both more urgent and more difficult. If major reform cannot be achieved without an external shock, a redistribution of political jurisdictions in favour of the Länder level could perhaps prove a feasible path to better performance.

Germany and European Integration: A Shifting of Tectonic Plates, by Charlie Jeffery and William E. Paterson

This article explores the interaction of German domestic politics with the European integration process. It argues that institutions of European integration were a stabilising force for the West German state. But West German engagement with Europe went further. As a persistent *demandeur* for European-level solutions, West Germany also provided many of the institutional templates adopted for Europe. An unusual level of congruence of institutional forms at German and European levels emerged, embedding not just stability but advantage for German actors. German–EU congruence has been challenged since 1990 by domestic resource tensions and the developing momentum of both integration and enlargement. Aspects of the EU are now seen as disadvantageous to Germany, challenging the instinctive preferences of German actors for Europeanisation.

New Ways of Life or Old Rigidities? Changes in Social Structures and Life Courses and their Political Impact, by Karl Ulrich Mayer and Steffen Hillmert

Like other advanced societies, Germany has experienced marked developments in its social structures during the last decades. But Germany has also been a rather special case due to historical events and institutional characteristics. This distinctiveness is now being called into question. This study traces the major changes in social structure during the last four decades. In particular, it looks at developments in population, family, education, labour markets, class structures and life-course patterns. The final section addresses the question of how these changes might have affected interest formation, political cleavages and policies.

The Crumbling Pillars of Social Partnership, by Wolfgang Streeck and Anke Hassel

Social partnership, once an asset in the 'German model', has turned into a liability. Fissures between trade unions, employers and the state first appeared in the 1980s but were papered over by government-sponsored early retirement of redundant workers. Unification for a short while reinvigorated corporatist co-operation but then produced a deep recession amidst growing budget deficits. Under Kohl, an 'Alliance for Employment' failed, which contributed to the change of government in 1998. During most of his first term Schröder felt too weak to confront union resistance to institutional and economic reform. Tripartism, however, was no longer viable, due among other things to increased fragmentation of the social base and weakening of the organisational capacities of both business associations and trade unions. After the Red–Green coalition was almost unseated in 2002, it finally gave up hope for consensual reform. From late 2002 it took a series of unilateral reform measures without and against the unions, deliberately pushing them out of the centre of power. It remains to be seen, however, whether state unilateralism will be more effective than tripartism under German conditions of divided government and permanent elections.

Political-Economic Context and Partisan Strategies in the German Federal Elections, 1990–2002, *by Herbert Kitschelt*

With the intensifying crisis of the German political-economic model, federal elections signal the beginning of a polarising realignment that rallies beneficiaries of the status quo, particularly white collar employees in non-profit sectors, individuals with weak human capital endowments, and the elderly living off public pensions, to the more social-protectionist social democrats and, to a declining extent, the Greens. In contrast, voters situated in the market-exposed sector and with strong professional skills to compete in that sector opt for liberals and Christian democrats, who begin to sharpen their market-liberal profile. In 1998 and 2002, the social-protectionist camp prevailed, but its opponents may win in the future if economic conditions worsen and the governing parties fail to deliver reform.

The Changing Role of Political Protest Movements, *by Dieter Rucht*

Protest movements have contributed to shaping the history of Germany during the last decades. This article focuses on two types of groups: left-libertarian movements on the one hand, and right-wing radical and xenophobic movements on the other. First, the article analyses the frequency of and participation in protest activities and the rising significance of violent protest. Second, it discusses the changing patterns of interaction between protest movements and state authorities. Third, it assesses both the transformations that the movement sector has undergone and the impact and limitations of movement politics. In the latter regard, the chapter highlights the agenda-setting role of radical right-wing groups, particularly since the 1990s. More important, however, is the role of the left-libertarian movements. They have contributed to a transformation of the political culture in Germany that has made it more participatory and more responsive on the part of the power holders.

The Disintegration of Organised Capitalism: German Corporate Governance in the 1990s, *by Jürgen Beyer and Martin Höppner*

Corporate governance in Germany changed rapidly in the 1990s, after several decades of institutional continuity. Indications of change are the increasing shareholder orientation of companies; the strategic reorientation of the big banks from the *Hausbank* paradigm to investment banking; the withdrawal of the state from infrastructural sectors via privatisation; and a break of continuity in company regulation. Impulses for change towards greater market orientation existed before the 1990s, but they remained isolated and resulted in adjustments within the logic of the German variant of organised capitalism. The article argues argues that the simultaneity of reciprocally reinforcing developments changed the situation in the 1990s, leading to an irreversible transformation of the German corporate governance regime.

The State of the Welfare State: German Social Policy between Macroeconomic Retrenchment and Microeconomic Recalibration, *by Stephan Leibfried and Herbert Obinger*

Germany's welfare state has been exposed to severe challenges since the mid-1970s. This article takes stock of the state of German social policy. It sketches the development and patterns of social expenditure since the 1980s and provides an overview of the social policy reforms enacted by the Kohl and Schröder governments. No comprehensive short or medium term recalibration of the German welfare state has taken place that is likely to overcome its structural problems; but the various reforms may, in the long run, bring about a substantial policy shift. In the social policy reforms carried out over the last two decades, there was both retrenchment and expansion. Overall, however, benefit provision has become fully dependent on the state of the budget, rather than being led by demand.

The Politics of Citizenship in the New Republic, *by Michael Minkenberg*

The legacies of the Bonn Republic's active policy of migrant labour recruitment and its liberal asylum law, together with the Berlin Republic's international location between Western Europe and post-communist Eastern Europe, made questions of immigration, citizenship and multiculturalism highly salient in the 1990s. Whereas 'model Germany' presumed a culturally homogenous German population, supplemented by a flexible contingent of temporary 'guest workers', the new Germany must confront the presence of and need for immigrants, and thus for an increasingly heterogeneous culture. Although the passing of the new citizenship law in 1999 and the attempt to introduce the first German immigration law in 2002 respond to these realities and represent a paradigm shift, they do so more symbolically than substantially. Their effects and significance are constrained by both the dynamism of the labour market and the institutional and cultural ramifications of German unification.

Notes on Contributors

Jürgen Beyer is a sociologist and a researcher at the Max Planck Institute for the Study of Societies in Cologne. His main fields of research include varieties of capitalism, corporate governance and economic reform in post-socialist countries. Recent publications include 'Please Invest in Our Country' (*Communist and Post-Communist Studies*, 2002) and 'The Effects of Convergence' (*Economy and Society*, 2002, with Anke Hassel). (beyer@mpi-fg-koeln.mpg.de)

Anke Hassel is senior researcher at the Max Planck Institute for the Study of Societies in Cologne, specialising in labour relations and comparative politics. She has been a visiting scholar at the London School of Economics, St. Johns College at Cambridge and the Social Science Centre in Berlin. Her latest publications have appeared in the *Journal of Management Studies*, *Economy and Society*, *The European* and the *British Journal of Industrial Relations*. (hassel@mpi-fg-koeln.mpg.de)

Steffen Hillmert is a research scientist at the Max Planck Institute for Human Development, Centre for Sociology and the Study of the Life Course, Berlin. He received his Ph.D. in sociology in 2000 and has worked on various issues of education, training, occupational careers and research methods. Recent publications include *Ausbildungssysteme und Arbeitsmarkt* (2001) and articles in *Work, Employment and Society* and *European Sociological Review*. (hillmert@mpib-berlin.mpg.de)

Martin Höpner is a political scientist and a researcher at the Max Planck Institute for the Study of Societies in Cologne. His research interests are comparative political economy, corporate governance and industrial relations. One of his latest publications is *Wer beherrscht die Unternehmen? Shareholder Value, Managerherrschaft und Mitbestimmung in Deutschland* (2003). (mh@mpi-fg-koeln.mpg.de)

Charlie Jeffery is Deputy Director and Professor of German Politics at the Institute for German Studies, University of Birmingham. He also directs the research programme on Devolution and Constitutional Change for the UK Economic and Social Research Council. He writes on German federalism, German EU policy and comparative regional government in Europe. (jefferca@hhs.bham.ac.uk)

Herbert Kitschelt is Professor of Political Science at Duke University. He works on the dynamics of political parties and party systems in established and in new democracies. He also publishes on the interface between democratic party competition and social and economic policy reform. (h3738@duke.edu)

Stephan Leibfried is Professor of Social Policy at the University of Bremen. He co-directs the Centre for Social Policy Research and the new National Research Centre on the Transformation of the State. His major publications are in the field of welfare state development and internationalisation: *European Social Policy* (1995); *Time and Poverty in Western Welfare States* (1999, 2001); *Limits to Globalization: Welfare States and the World Economy* (2003). (stlf@zes.uni-bremen.de)

Karl Ulrich Mayer is Director at the Max Planck Institute for Human Development, Centre for Sociology and the Study of the Life Course, and Professor of Sociology at Yale University. He directed the German Life History Study and co-directed the Berlin Aging Study. Recent publications include *The Berlin Aging Study* (1999, co-ed.), *Die Beste aller welten? Marktliberalismus versus Wohlfahrstaat* (2001) and *Das Bildungswesen der Bundesrepublik Deutschland* (2003, co-ed.). (mayer@mpib-berlin. mpg.de).

Michael Minkenberg is Professor of Political Science at Europa-Universität Viadrina, Frankfurt (Oder), Germany. He writes on comparative politics, especially the radical right, and religion and politics. His publications include *Die neue radikale Rechte im Vergleich. USA, Frankreich, Deutschland* (1998) and *Politik und Religion* (2002, co-ed.). (mminken@euv-frankfurt-o.de)

Herbert Obinger is Assistant Professor at the Centre for Social Policy Research of the University of Bremen. His research interests are in social policy and comparative political economy. His articles have appeared in the

Journal of Public Policy, *West European Politics*, and the *Journal of European Public Policy*. (hobinger@zes.uni-bremen.de)

William E. Paterson is Director of the Institute for German Studies at the University of Birmingham. He has published 23 books and currently co-edits the *Journal of Common Market Studies*. His most recent work on Germany includes *Developments in German Politics 3* (2003). (w.e.paterson@bham.ac.uk)

Dieter Rucht is Professor of Sociology at the Social Science Research Centre Berlin. His research interests include modernisation processes in a comparative perspective, political participation, social movements and political protest. He recently co-authored *Shaping Abortion Discourse: Democracy and the Public Sphere in Germany and the United States* (2002). (rucht@wz-berlin.de)

Wolfgang Streeck is Director at the Max Planck Institute for the Study of Societies in Cologne. He was Professor of Sociology and Industrial Relations at the University of Wisconsion-Madison from 1988 to 1995. (streeck@mpi-fg-koeln.mpg.de)

Helmut Wiesenthal is Professor of Political Science at Humboldt University in Berlin. Research interests are industrial relations and social policy reform in Germany, 'green' politics and institutional change in post-communist societies. Recent publications include *The Grand Experiment* (1997, with Andreas Pickel) and *Successful Transitions* (2001, co-ed.). (hw@sowi.hu-berlin.de)

Index